STUDY GUIDE TO ACCOMPANY
CALHOUN/LIGHT/KELLER

Sociology

SIXTH EDITION

Craig Calhoun
Donald Light
Suzanne Keller

Prepared by
Theodore C. Wagenaar
Miami University, Ohio

McGraw-Hill, Inc.

New York   St. Louis   San Francisco   Auckland   Bogotá   Caracas
Lisbon   London   Madrid   Mexico City   Milan   Montreal   New Delhi
San Juan   Singapore   Sydney   Tokyo   Toronto

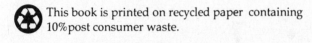 This book is printed on recycled paper containing
10% post consumer waste.

Study Guide to Accompany Calhoun/Light/Keller: **SOCIOLOGY,** Sixth Edition

234567890 MAL MAL 90987654

ISBN 0-07-067669-0

The editor was Phillip A. Butcher;
the production supervisor was Friederich W. Schulte.
Malloy Lithographing, Inc. was printer and binder.

CONTENTS

TO THE STUDENT

Your life experiences have prepared you well for the study of sociology. By observing and interacting with the environment around you and by reading about the environment, you have already gained some sense of how people typically behave and how societies are organized. This common-sense knowledge is the starting point for a course in sociology. Studying sociology may show you that some of your information about society is incomplete, and perhaps inaccurate. It can provide you with the basic knowledge for understanding the social world that you have experienced. And you can learn new things from sociology about the social world--things that you have had no previous reason to consider.

Sociology begins with a social world that is familiar to you through common sense, and expands this knowledge in two ways. First, sociology provides a new language, a set of technical concepts, that will help you better describe and understand the social world. (All scholarly and scientific disciplines have their own vocabularies. Imagine a course in chemistry where you did not have to learn that "water" is more accurately described as H_2O!) Sociological concepts may be unfamiliar to you at first, and it may take time and effort before you can recall them easily. But once you learn these concepts, you should be able to see the social world in a new light.

Second, sociology asks you to look at life in society from a detached, objective point of view. Usually we put ourselves at the very center of the social world, understanding society in terms of how it affects our personal lives. For example, most people are interested in the social organization of economic life only as it affects them directly: Will I get a job? Can I afford to buy a new car? In the sociological study of economic life, you can learn how the world of work is organized, why some kinds of people get the "good" jobs, and why certain people can afford to drive new cars. Once you learn about society from this detached perspective, you may better understand why your place in society is different from that of others.

This Study Guide, which accompanies the textbook *Sociology*, Sixth Edition, by Craig Calhoun, Donald Light, Jr., and Suzanne Keller is one tool for you to use in learning the sociological way of looking at the world. Each chapter in the textbook has a corresponding chapter in the Study Guide. The Study Guide is not, however, a substitute for careful reading and studying of the textbook itself. You should use the Study Guide as a tool for reviewing the textbook, for applying your new sociological knowledge, and for checking to find out how well you have mastered the language of sociology.

Each chapter in the Study Guide has six sections:

Objectives: This section provides a list of major points introduced in the textbook chapter. Each major point is followed by concepts or ideas that you can learn by carefully reading and studying the textbook. You should read through these objectives *before* you begin to read the textbook, as they will give a preview of the organization of the chapter and a good idea of the kind of material you will find there. After you have studied the chapter, you may use these objectives as a checklist to see which ideas are still unclear to you and will require further review.

Chapter Summary: The Chapter Summary contains major questions raised in the textbook chapter. Each question is answered in a few short paragraphs. The summaries in this Guide are longer and more detailed than those in the textbook, although they parallel the organization found there. The Study Guide summaries cannot replace a thorough reading of the textbook. Many of the ideas and concepts will be difficult to understand unless you have already studied the discussions and examples in the textbook. You will find it best to review each summary *after* you have read the chapter in the textbook. If parts of the summary are unclear, go back to the textbook and reread the appropriate sections.

Review of Concepts: Gaining the sociological perspective depends on learning technical concepts, and this section of the Guide can help you make sure that you know these essential conceptual tools. You will find an alphabetized list of concepts, followed by a scrambled list of definitions. You are asked to match each concept to its definition. Correct answers are provided at the end of the section. You may find it easier to remember these definitions if you think of an illustration of each concept from your personal experiences.

Review Questions: These multiple-choice questions test your knowledge of the material, and they offer a good way to review for examinations. You are asked to pick the one best answer from the list; correct answers appear at the end of the section. If you miss a question, read the explanation for the correct answer and then go back and review the indicated pages in the textbook. Remember: if you sneak a peek at the answers, you are only cheating yourself.

Exercises: This section encourages you to *apply* your sociological knowledge in short, written exercises. Each presents some practical or theoretical problem to be solved by the application of sociological concepts and ideas. These exercises can only be effective if you have thoroughly read and studied the textbook and successfully completed the reviews in the two preceding sections of the Guide. Your instructor may or may not assign these exercises as written assignments to be handed in. Even if written answers are not assigned, you may find it interesting and helpful to read through the exercises and jot down tentative answers. If you "draw a blank" for one particular question, perhaps your sociological knowledge of the material in the textbook is not as good as you thought it was.

I hope that this Study Guide will help to give you a better grasp of the material in Calhoun, Light, and Keller's *Sociology*, Sixth Edition, and that it will make your sociological journey a pleasant and enriching one.

I wish to thank my many students in sociology, who have helped me define my orientation to teaching. My editor, Phillip A. Butcher, and the rest of the McGraw-Hill staff have been supportive in my efforts to produce an effective Study Guide. Special thanks to Wyn Martello for her typing skills, to Amy Williamson for her proofreading skills, and to Karen Feinberg for her copy editing skills.

Theodore C. Wagenaar

Chapter 1

THE SOCIOLOGICAL PERSPECTIVE

OBJECTIVES

After reading Chapter 1, you should understand the following main points and be able to answer the objectives.

1. The sociological perspective enables us to see the impact of social forces in the larger social structure on individual attitudes and behaviors.
   1.1 Define sociology.
   1.2 Show how the sociological perspective goes beyond the psychological perspective.
   1.3 Explain why sociologists emphasize social contexts.
   1.4 Define and illustrate the sociological imagination.
   1.5 Define and give an example of a social fact.

2. Sociologists employ five key concepts to examine social reality.
   2.1 Define concept.
   2.2 Describe why social structure is a key concept.
   2.3 Describe why social action is a key concept.
   2.4 Describe why functional integration is a key concept.
   2.5 Describe why power is a key concept.
   2.6 Describe why culture is a key concept.
   2.7 Describe what is meant by critical thinking.

3. Sociologists employ the scientific method to explain social reality.
   3.1 Describe the role of abstraction in the scientific method.
   3.2 Describe the role of analysis in the scientific method.
   3.3 Describe the role of data in the scientific method.
   3.4 Describe the role of theories in the scientific method.
   3.5 Show how science goes beyond common sense.
   3.6 Differentiate sociology from psychology, economics, political science, and anthropology.

4. The sociological perspective originated in Europe in the late eighteenth and early nineteenth centuries.
   4.1 Describe life in Europe before the eighteenth century.
   4.2 Describe how sociology emerged during the American and French Revolutions.
   4.3 Define rational-choice theory.
   4.4 Synopsize the views of Adam Smith and Jeremy Bentham and show how they contributed to the development of sociology.

1

4.5 Illustrate how rational-choice theory is still influential in several areas of sociology.

4.6 Synopsize the views of Marx and show how they contributed to the development of sociology.

4.7 Define capitalists, proletariat, and class consciousness.

4.8 Synopsize the views of Durkheim and show how they contributed to the development of sociology.

4.9 Differentiate social solidarity from mechanical solidarity and organic solidarity.

4.10 Define anomie.

4.11 Synopsize the views of Weber and show how they contributed to the development of sociology.

4.12 Define *Verstehen*.

4.13 Define status groups.

4.14 Show how phenomenology and symbolic interactionism contributed to the development of sociology.

4.15 Compare and contrast the three major perspectives: structural-functionalism, conflict theory, and symbolic interactionism.

5. Sociologists perform multiple roles.

5.1 Give some examples of how sociologists perform the researcher role.

5.2 Give some examples of how sociologists perform the policy analyst role.

5.3 Give some examples of how sociologists perform the interpreter role.

CHAPTER SUMMARY

1. What is sociology?

Sociologists study the social action and social organization in human societies. Research methods and theories help them to study societies scientifically. Sociologists look beyond individualistic and psychological explanations for behavior to the predictable broad patterns and regular occurrences of social life that influence individual attitudes and behaviors. They examine how these patterns vary across time, cultures, and social groups. C. Wright Mills coined the term *sociological imagination* to reflect the process of examining our experiences as influenced by the social world in which we live. The sociological imagination helps us to see that our actions and attitudes are far more than a product of our own feelings. In reality these actions and attitudes are influenced strongly by the social groups to which we belong, the particular time in history in which we live, and the social structure at multiple levels.

Sociologists strive to establish *social facts*, which are properties of group life that cannot be explained by the actions, feelings, or characteristics of individual persons. They examine such social facts as falling in love, crime rates, and prejudice. Sociologists also uncover the social forces that determine particular social facts. Some sociologists are interested in the *rates* of social phenomena: the number of cases found in a population or subpopulation for a given period. Examples include the death rate, the divorce rate, and the unemployment rate. Social facts are often used to explain other social facts; for example, the unemployment rate may affect the suicide rate. Because social facts are not always completely stable, sociologists find it difficult to establish scientific laws that apply to all people everywhere at all times.

2. What are the five key concepts in sociology?

Although sociologists employ many concepts to explain social reality, five have proved to be the most useful: social structure, social action, functional integration, power, and culture.

Social structure reflects the patterns of social relationships, social positions, and numbers of people. It can include such microstructures as the family as well as such macrostructures as entire societies. Social structure generally remains stable. Sociologists address the effects of social structure on individual attitudes and behavior.

Social action is based on an understanding of what individuals do in response to other people's actions. It underscores how people's relationships with other people affect individual behavior. Social relationships develop when someone's actions depend on the actions of other people. Communication lies at the heart of social action. It ranges from the development of interpersonal relationships to the large-scale coordination of social interaction found at the societal level. Even very private social actions, such as sexual behavior and dealing with the death and dying process, have a social component. That is, people's responses in such private situations are affected by their connections with other people.

Functional integration is simply the interdependence among the parts of a social system. Each part of a social system must contribute so that the larger social structure will work well. The contribution of each part is called its functions: These are the effects of some social group, event, or institution within a system of relationships to other such phenomena. For example, a college campus is a social structure that is based on functional integration; each of the different levels of social structure contributes to the daily functioning of the college as a whole. Many social structures also include dysfunctions, which are unintended outcomes with a counterproductive effect. For example, very large colleges and universities provide many useful functions, especially a wide diversity of special areas of study. Students, however, frequently feel more alienated in larger schools than in smaller schools.

Power occurs when one social actor (a person, group, or organization) can make others do its will, or at least can make sure that it will benefit from the actions of others. Direct power can be exercised by force, as when a terrorist group takes over a country. It can also be exercised indirectly by shaping a pattern of social structure, functional integration, or culture so that one social actor benefits more than others. The wide disparity between men's and women's wages, for example, reflects a larger social system that continues to favor males, particularly white males. Power also can occur at a very micro level, as when one third grader imposes his or her will on another, or at a very macro level, as when one country dominates other countries economically.

Culture includes the language, norms, values, beliefs, knowledge, and symbols that make up a way of life. These elements produce a distinct way of life for a given group of people. *Subcultures* emerge when one segment of a particular culture is very different from the rest. For example, American culture includes such subcultures as the Appalachian and the Amish. Many subcultures exist in American culture because of its history of diversity and open immigration.

These five key concepts help us to think critically. Critical thinking means going beyond accepting the obvious and asking how and why things occur. It also involves using multiple perspectives to examine a given social phenomenon.

3. Does the scientific method help sociological research?

The scientific method helps us to go beyond everyday, commonsense views of social reality and to take a more rigorous approach. The scientific approach involves several steps. The first is *abstraction* which involves setting aside the immediate appearance of things in order to search for aspects of their existence that allow us to understand them more precisely. For example, sociologists move beyond the journalistic analysis of the Los Angeles riots to examine them in the context of social structure, social action, functional integration, power, and culture. Abstraction enables social scientists to analyze social phenomena.

The next step is *analysis*, the careful and systematic study of the relationship among different parts of something. The Los Angeles riots, for example, must be understood in the context of culture and subcultures, imbalance in power relationships, unequal economic distribution, and prejudice and discrimination based on race. The different elements involved must be distinguished carefully before we can examine their combined effect on a particular outcome.

The third step is gathering *data*. Data are information that tells us about one or more of the abstract dimensions we have identified as significant in what we are studying. Social scientists are careful to examine data relevant to the questions they examine, and data must be collected as carefully and as systematically as possible. Many sociologists rely on surveys to identify possible causes and effects. For example, they might gather data on the timing of the various events in the Los Angeles riots, the racial distribution of the persons involved, people's beliefs and reactions to the police, and the nature of social connections as reflected in communication patterns. Systematically gathering data helps us to avoid commonsense views, which are based only on people's experiences and therefore are biased by those experiences.

Finally, the scientific method involves theories. A *theory* is an orderly, logical attempt to show how the relationships identified by analysis fit together with existing knowledge in a field. To explain the Los Angeles riots, for example, sociologists might employ relative deprivation theory, status inconsistency theory, and conflict theory. To be most productive, social scientific research must include a close relationship between the theories and the data. In fact, new research often helps to modify and clarify existing theories, while existing theories generally help to frame sociological research questions.

Sociology is only one of the social sciences. Others are psychology, economics, political science, and anthropology; each has its own particular focus. Psychology focuses primarily on individuals and small groups. It also examines biological makeup, learning, emotions, and other factors affecting people. Economics is concerned with the production and exchange of goods and services. Political science specializes in the study of government and public administration, ways of exercising power in a society, and international and domestic conflicts. Anthropology addresses the cultural dimensions of human life and makes a special contribution with its research on non-Western societies. Although each of these fields is distinct, the subject matter of all the social sciences overlaps. For example, education can be studied from the perspective of each of these social sciences, with each focusing on a different aspect of the educational institution.

4. How did sociology emerge as a discipline?

Sociology emerged as a discipline in the eighteenth and nineteenth centuries, a period of sweeping social changes. Until the eighteenth century, most Europeans lived in small agricultural villages. The family was the heart of village life, and nearly all families were farmers. Life was simple in these villages, and people were largely unaffected by developments in the larger social order.

The American and French Revolutions substantially affected this simple life. Monarchies everywhere were threatened by new ideas of individual rights, equality, and freedom. Capitalism was developing. The term *revolution* was coined to characterize these rapid social and economic changes. The Industrial Revolution had a major impact on social life: farm life declined and urban areas mushroomed. As a result, social interaction became far more impersonal. Also, the growth of colonial empires and international trade exposed Europeans to other people's customs and values, which usually were quite different from their own.

Sociology emerged from this social and intellectual turmoil. Before that time, the prevailing subject was social philosophy, which dealt with what society should be like. However, social philosophy could not explain the rapidly changing real world. What was needed was a science of society, a large body of factual information put into perspective by systematically tested theories. The term sociology was coined by Auguste Comte. Early sociologists took their scientific lessons from the physical sciences to examine social structure, social action, functional integration, power, and culture.

4

Rational-choice theory was an important framework for many of the early social sciences. Prominent among the founders of rational-choice theory were Adam Smith (1723-1790) and Jeremy Bentham (1748-1832). Smith emphasized the cost/benefit calculations in decision making. He viewed society as a self-regulating system, in which many different parts act in their own interest but are meshed together through market forces to form a whole that operates for the common good. Bentham emphasized that people are motivated to obtain pleasure and avoid pain. He disagreed with Smith's view that the sum of individual decisions, made on the basis of self-interest, automatically yields the greatest good for society as a whole. Bentham believed that scientifically planned government action would contribute to the public good. Rational-choice theory is still influential in several areas of sociology, particularly in public policy analysis, where it helps to identify who will gain or lose from any new public program.

Karl Marx (1818-1883) contributed much to sociology and economics. He believed that the most significant feature of industrial societies was their capitalist character; the means of production were owned privately and were used to maximize profits. This system generated conflict between the *capitalists* (the owners of the land, factories, and machines) and the *proletariat* (the workers who actually produce the economic goods). Marx believed that the interests of the two groups were inherently contradictory. Over time the workers would develop *class consciousness*, a sense of their shared interests and plight. This consciousness eventually would result in the overthrow of the capitalist system and the establishment of a classless society in which wealth would be distributed equally. Regarding the question of what holds society together, Marx's approach is power-oriented, but he also incorporates aspects of structure and action in his analysis of the relationship between individuals and society.

Emile Durkheim (1858-1917) was concerned with social solidarity, the underlying social forces that bind people together. He conceptualized two basic forms of social solidarity: *mechanical solidarity* is based on a strong sharing of beliefs, values, and customs; *organic solidarity* is based on a complex division of labor and characterizes modern societies. Durkheim stressed that the study of society takes place at a very different level from the study of individuals. He took a functionalist approach by arguing that society forms a whole that is greater than the sum of its parts, he pioneered sociology's use of the key concept of functional integration, and showed how different social activities and institutions worked together. In addition, Durkheim believed that shared values and practices characteristic of a culture helped to keep society together. He coined the term *anomie*, for a situation in which breakdowns of social norms or rules make it hard for people to identify who they are and what their lives mean. Durkheim believed that even people's most private feelings and behaviors are shaped by society.

Max Weber (1864-1920) thought that sociological explanations must derive from an understanding of why people choose the actions they do; accordingly he studied people's subjective beliefs, attitudes, values, and motives. He believed that sociologists must study and interpret such behaviors and attitudes from the perspective of the actor, an approach he called *verstehen*. Like Durkheim, Weber emphasized the importance of using scientific methods to study social facts. He believed that the most significant trend in modern times was an increasing rationalization of social action and social institutions. That is, Western society could be viewed in terms of a shift from traditional orientations to more rational orientations, in which people make a logical assessment of the consequences of their behavior. This increase in rationalization could be seen in the rise of science, the growth of government bureaucracies, and the development of capitalism. Weber particularly addressed the role of culture in understanding capitalism. In going beyond Marx, he argued that people's economic identities are not always the most important element in determining the outcome of a power struggle. He believed that we often care more about other social factors such as race, religion, and personal taste; these are the basis of *status groups*. Weber thought that status groups were particularly important for understanding political activity.

Other early sociologists thought that Marx, Durkheim, and Weber were too much concerned with large-scale social patterns. These other sociologists addressed the ways in which people construct face-to-face interactions; their approach is called *interactionism*. *Phenomenology* developed in Europe as one strand of interactionism. Phenomenologists study how people subjectively experience and understand their social world; they examine how individuals construct their own social realities. *Symbolic interactionism* combines phenomenology with pragmatism, which emphasizes how we learn from practical action. Two proponents of symbolic interactionism were George Herbert Mead (1863-1931) and W. I. Thomas (1863-1947). Both men emphasized that human behavior may be influenced by the facts of a particular situation, but is affected far more strongly by how people define those situations. In short, they emphasized the meanings that people attribute to a social situation. Mead believed that we learn our places in the world through social interaction; that is, we come to know ourselves by seeing how others react to us. Communication plays a key role in this interaction. In the communication process, people use symbols--words, gestures, facial expressions, and other sounds and actions that have common, widely understood interpretations. In short, behavior is shaped by *symbolic interaction*. Symbolic interactionists also focus on everyday behavior, such as the interaction on a first date.

These five founding theories--rational-choice theory, interactionism, and the views of Marx, Durkheim, and Weber--helped to launch sociology as a discipline and are still relevant to sociological analysis today. A sociologist's particular theoretical perspective substantially influences the research questions he or she addresses.

Three major perspectives have dominated the field. *Structural functionalism* emphasizes functional integration and social structure. *Conflict theory* criticizes the limitations of structural functionalism and argues that structural functionalism ignores the role of power and conflict. Finally, *symbolic interactionism* stresses the interpretation of culture and social action on a more individual basis. More recently, sociology has grown more specialized and more international, and hence has moved away from this simplified view of three approaches.

5. What is the relationship between sociology and public life?

Sociologists frequently contribute to discussions about public policy. In doing so, they perform three main roles: as researchers, as policy analysts, and as interpreters. As researchers, sociologists bring scientific data to bear on social issues. They carefully describe social phenomena and question commonsense assumptions. Their research is typically published in journals and books. Recently, sociologists have received more media exposure in their role as researchers.

Sociologists help to design, implement, and evaluate possible solutions to social problems in their role as policy analysts--for example, to help develop public policy responses to the poverty problem. As interpreters, sociologists help to make sense of social life and also help us to interpret and apply the lessons of scientific research. Theory plays a major role in their ability to provide interpretive frameworks.

REVIEW OF CONCEPTS

Match the concept with the definition.

Concepts

a. anomie
b. bourgeoisie
c. capitalists
d. class consciousness
e. conflict

f. conflict theory
g. critical thinking
h. culture
i. functional integration
j. interactionism

k. mechanical solidarity
l. organic solidarity
m. phenomenology
n. power
o. proletariat

p. scientific method   t. social structure   x. structural-functionalism
q. social action   u. sociological imagination   y. symbolic interactionism
r. social facts   v. sociology   z. theory
s. social solidarity   w. status groups

Definitions

____ 1. An approach to human behavior as constructed in interaction and interpreted through culture, stressing the collective attribution of meaning to social life. The most widespread theoretical orientation within interactionism.

____ 2. A sense of shared interests and problems among members of a social class.

____ 3. The rules, principles, and methods of science that are used for the systematic pursuit of knowledge.

____ 4. Solidarity that is based on common beliefs, values, and customs.

____ 5. The members of a capitalist industrialized society who have no control over the means of production--primarily the workers.

____ 6. Disruption in the rules and understandings that guide and integrate social life and give individuals a sense of their place in it.

____ 7. A way of looking at our personal experiences in the context of what is going on in the world around us.

____ 8. A philosophy that holds that people construct their own social reality in accordance with the ways they experience and understand their social world.

____ 9. Enduring properties of social life that shape or constrain the actions individuals can take.

____ 10. Altercations that occur when the exercise of power meets resistance.

____ 11. Relatively stable, enduring patterns of social relationships, or social positions, and of numbers of people; patterns over which individuals have little control.

____ 12. A systematic attempt to explain how two or more phenomena are related.

____ 13. The condition that results when underlying social forces bind people together.

____ 14. The ways in which the different parts of a social system are often so closely interrelated that what happens in one affects the others, and is influenced by them in turn.

____ 15. The attempt to develop an understanding that goes behind surface appearances to ask why and how events happen or conditions persist, whether social conditions could be changed, and in which different ways a given problem can be conceptualized.

____ 16. The learned norms, customs, values, knowledge, artifacts, language, and symbols that are constantly communicated among people who share a common way of life.

___ 17. The study of human society, including both social action and social organization.

___ 18. Behavior which is shaped by a person's understandings, interpretations, and intentions and which is in response to, coordinated with, or oriented toward the actions of others.

___ 19. The ability of a social actor to control the actions of others, either directly or indirectly.

___ 20. Members of the bourgeoisie.

___ 21. A general perspective in sociology that places its main emphasis on functional integration and social structure.

___ 22. Interdependence among a group of people that is based on an intricate division of labor.

Answers

1.	y	9.	r	17.	v
2.	d	10.	e	18.	q
3.	p	11.	t	19.	n
4.	k	12.	z	20.	c
5.	o	13.	s	21.	x
6.	a	14.	i	22.	l
7.	u	15.	g		
8.	m	16.	h		

REVIEW QUESTIONS

After studying Chapter 1, answer the following questions. The correct answers are listed at the end of the questions; each is followed by a short explanation. You are also referred to pages in the text-book for relevant discussion.

1. Which of the following best illustrates a sociological perspective?
   a. looking for biological explanations of homosexuality
   b. measuring people's IQ
   c. examining patterns of interaction in a cocktail lounge
   d. administering a personality test to explore why a student is having problems in school
   e. examining the decision-making process in a state legislature

2. C. Wright Mills's notion of the sociological imagination emphasized that
   a. history and biography—the individual and the particular period--need to be studied together.
   b. sociologists identify as many social facts as possible.
   c. sociologists come up with policy recommendations for the social problems they identify.
   d. sociology should be linked closely with psychology, economics, and political science.
   e. sociologists should employ empirical methods.

3. Which of the following is *not* a social fact?
   a. family size

b. age distribution
c. crime rates
d. occupational attainment
e. none of the above; all are social facts

4. If a sociologist were studying dating patterns on a college campus, which of the following is a social fact that he or she would most likely examine?
   a. balance of personality types
   b. the sex ratio on campus
   c. attractiveness of females
   d. athletic prowess of males
   e. both c and d

5. In addition to identifying social facts, sociologists also
   a. try to determine when the social facts first emerged.
   b. try to determine how important each fact is.
   c. try to determine the social forces that give rise to social facts.
   d. identify each social fact with a particular sociologist.
   e. identify the social costs of each social fact.

6. Susan decides to attend a particular college because her parents and older siblings attended that school. Which one of the five key concepts does this example reflect?
   a. social structure
   b. social action
   c. functional integration
   d. power
   e. culture

7. Navajos believe that a person's spirit remains after she or he dies, and that it can affect those who knew the person. Norms exist regarding appropriate behavior regarding someone who had died. This example reflects which one of the five key concepts?
   a. social structure
   b. social action
   c. functional integration
   d. power
   e. culture

8. The proportion of the United States citizens over the age of 80 has increased dramatically over the past decade and has affected other aspects of American life. This example reflects which one of the five key concepts?
   a. social structure
   b. social action
   c. functional integration
   d. power
   e. culture

9. The Los Angeles riots were in part a response to feelings of domination by those rioting. Police responded to control the riots. This example reflects which one of the five key concepts?
   a. social structure
   b. social action

   c. functional integration
   d. power
   e. culture

10. Professor Garcia studied female-only gangs and carefully linked his findings with existing knowledge about gangs to develop a framework for interpretation. Which of the steps in the scientific method does this example reflect?
   a. abstraction
   b. analysis
   c. gathering data
   d. constructing a theory
   e. addressing ethical issues

11. Professor Gabino observed the Los Angeles riots and identified various concepts to help her understand the riots more precisely. Which step in the scientific method does this example reflect?
   a. abstraction
   b. analysis
   c. gathering data
   d. constructing a theory
   e. addressing ethical issues

12. Professor Simms spent four months attending Alcoholics Anonymous meetings to collect information about the communication patterns among attendees. Which step in the scientific method does this example reflect?
   a. abstraction
   b. analysis
   c. gathering data
   d. constructing theories
   e. addressing ethical issues

13. The best antidote to common sense is
   a. economics.
   b. sociology.
   c. the sociological imagination.
   d. local theories.
   e. science.

14. When did sociology emerge?
   a. during the fifteenth and sixteenth centuries
   b. during the sixteenth and seventeenth centuries
   c. during the seventeenth and eighteenth centuries
   d. during the eighteenth and nineteenth centuries
   e. during the nineteenth and twentieth centuries

15. Which two dramatic political events transformed the traditional social order and provided the context for the development of sociology?
   a. the Insurrection and the Crusades
   b. the Crusades and the Spanish Inquisition
   c. the Spanish Inquisition and the American and French Revolutions

d. the American and French Revolutions and the Industrial Revolution
e. the Industrial Revolution and World War I

16. Who coined the term "sociology"?
    a. Adam Smith
    b. Jeremy Bentham
    c. Auguste Comte
    d. Emile Durkheim
    e. Karl Marx

17. Which one of the following statements best reflects rational-choice theory?
    a. People decide how much they are willing to give up to attain the level of education they want to get a particular job.
    b. People assess the relative amount of conflict in relationships and strive to alleviate that conflict.
    c. People link the structural and functional elements in their work relationships.
    d. People examine the underlying meanings behind everyday conversations.
    e. People strive to enhance the social solidarity of the communities in which they live.

18. Which one of the following statements best reflects Bentham's approach to rational-choice theory?
    a. The government turns over the control of education to the local communities.
    b. A capitalistic system provided the greatest good for the most people.
    c. A totalitarian system provided the greatest good for the most people.
    d. Governments that take scientifically planned action for reducing poverty will succeed in reducing poverty.
    e. Societies tend automatically to function smoothly and in the public interest.

19. The sociologist who stressed the increasing rationalization of social action and social institutions was
    a. Durkheim.
    b. Bentham.
    c. Mead.
    d. Weber.
    e. Marx.

20. Professor LaForge wishes to understand the process by which expectant parents come to define their role as parents and how they prepare for this role. Thus she attends the entire cycle of a childbirth class and spends time with groups of expectant parents, listening to their reactions. Which sociological approach is she following?
    a. *verstehen*
    b. positivism
    c. natural selection
    d. scientism
    e. social statics

21. Durkheim's views about social solidarity best reflect which one of the key concepts?
    a. social structure
    b. social action
    c. functional integration

d. power
　　e. culture

22. A sociologist studied how doctors and patients communicated with each other and emphasized how each interpreted the doctor-patient interaction. Which founding theory is represented?
　　a. Marx
　　b. rational choice
　　c. Durkheim
　　d. Weber
　　e. interactionism

23. Sociologists often are interviewed in the news media to bring a different and more analytical perspective on news events. Which role does this reflect?
　　a. policy analyst
　　b. researcher
　　c. consultant
　　d. clinical
　　e. interpreter

Answers

1. *c.* The sociological perspective examines behaviors and attitudes as influenced by interaction with others and by the larger social settings. See page 3.

2. *a.* Mills noted that the sociological imagination "enables us to grasp history and biography and the relation between the two within society." See page 4.

3. *e.* Social facts are properties of social life that cannot be explained by reference to the activities of characteristics of individual persons. All the examples reflect phenomena that require consideration of social settings in order to understand them accurately. See page 4.

4. *b.* The sex ratio reflects the relative balance of the number of men and women. It is part of the social setting on campuses and hence may influence dating behavior. See page 4.

5. *c.* Sociologists try to determine possible social forces as causes for the social facts they identify. See page 5.

6. *b.* Her decision is based on meaningful understanding of what she is doing and is a response to the actions of others. See page 6.

7. *e.* Culture is the language, norms, values, beliefs, knowledge, and symbols that make up a way of life. See page 7.

8. *a.* Social structure refers to patterns of social relationships of social positions, and of number of people. See page 5.

9. *d.* Power is the capacity of one social actor to get others to do its will or to ensure that it will benefit from the action of others. See page 7.

10. *d.* A theory is an orderly, logical attempt to show how the relationships identified by analysis fit together with existing knowledge in a field. Theories serve as frameworks for interpretation that help make sense of specific facts. See page 9.

11. *a.* Abstraction means standing back from the immediate appearance of things or activities in order to look for aspects of their existence that allow you to understand them more precisely. See page 8.

12. *c.* Data gathering is the actual gathering of information about the abstract dimensions we have identified as significant in whatever we are studying. See page 9.

13. *e.* The scientific method involves the systematic gathering of evidence to reduce the likelihood of overlooking facts and misunderstanding causes. See page 8.

14. *d.* Sociology emerged during the eighteenth and nineteenth centuries in Europe. This was a time of sweeping social changes, including the Industrial Revolution. See page 16.

15. *d.* The American and French Revolutions showed that old notions of authority were being replaced with new ideas of individual rights. The Industrial Revolution altered both the physical and the social landscape. See page 17.

16. *c.* The French thinker Auguste Comte coined the term "sociology" to describe a science of society. See page 17.

17. *a.* Rational-choice theory holds that in making decisions, people weigh the possible gains to be made from a particular action against the possible costs. See page 18.

18. *d.* Bentham believed that the public good could be achieved best by scientifically planned government action. See page 18.

19. *d.* Weber saw the history of Western society in terms of a shift from traditional to emotional to rational orientations. See page 21.

20. *a.* *Verstehen* is an empathic understanding of what people are thinking and feeling. Professor LaForge is stressing the importance of this subjective reality in her research. See page 21.

21. *c.* Functional integration refers to the interdependence among the parts of a social system. Durkheim was concerned with how societies were functionally integrated and argued that society forms a whole that is greater than the sum of its parts. See page 20.

22. *e.* The focus of the interactionist perspective is that people address and respond to others depending on how they interpret the social situation. They also focus on the communication process and the use of symbols. See page 22.

23. *e.* As interpreters, sociologists interpret what is going on in social life and help us make sense of the facts learned by scientific research and observed in daily interaction. See page 24.

EXERCISES

Exercise 1

Select an event or a feature of your life that is particularly important to you. You might select being a student, being male or female, a wedding you attended recently, a disagreement with your partner, your parents' divorce, your involvement in campus government, or something else.

1. Describe this event or feature. Provide details.

2. Describe and explain this event or feature using common sense.

3. Describe and explain this event or feature sociologically. Compare this account with the common-sense account.

Exercise 2

Find an article in a recent issue of a newspaper that might be of interest to a sociologist. The article might report on a specific event or issue, such as disagreement in a community over the location of a shopping center, a teachers' strike, or a woman joining a fire department. The article might be a "human interest" report detailing one person's particular experience, such as a near-death experience. Or the article might report on social trends, such as the increase in the proportion of people remaining single, declining birth rates, or changing attitudes toward work.

1. Compare the journalistic account with how a sociologist might analyze the event or issue.

2. Describe how social structure is or might be relevant in the example.

3. Describe how social action is or might be relevant in the example.

4. Describe how functional integration is or might be relevant in the example.

5. Describe how power is or might be relevant in the example.

6. Describe how culture is or might be relevant in the example.

Exercise 3

The sociological perspective helps us redefine and analyze our experiences. Two major decisions that you have made or will make involve your choice of a college major and your choice of a possible occupation.

1. Describe in some detail the sociological factors that contributed to your selection of a major or an occupation.

2. Describe how sociological factors, concepts and theories might be relevant in your chosen occupation. In answering this question, imagine yourself actually on the job.

Chapter 2
METHODS OF SOCIOLOGICAL RESEARCH

OBJECTIVES

After reading Chapter 2, you should understand the following main points and be able to answer the objectives.

1. As a science, sociology follows the scientific method.
   1.1 Show how Durkheim's study of suicide reflected both a sociological and a scientific approach to this topic.
   1.2 Distinguish Durkheim's types of suicide: egoistic, altruistic, anomic, and fatalistic.
   1.3 List the basic steps in the model research process.
   1.4 Describe the difficulties that sociologists often encounter in defining a problem.
   1.5 Distinguish dependent from independent variables by definition and example.
   1.6 Give one reason why sociologists review the literature.
   1.7 Define and give an example of hypothesis.
   1.8 Define and give an example of operational definition.
   1.9 Explain why sociologists often use multiple methods for gathering data.

2. Many difficulties emerge in sociological research.
   2.1 Differentiate validity from reliability.
   2.2 Present an argument that a correlation does not necessarily reflect a causal relationship.
   2.3 Define and illustrate spurious correlation.
   2.4 Explain why it is difficult to establish causal relationships in sociology.
   2.5 Show how sociological knowledge grows when theory spurs research and when research in turn generates new theories that produce more research.

3. Sociologists employ a variety of research methods.
   3.1 Distinguish quantitative research from qualitative research by definition and example.
   3.2 Define survey and give an example showing when this method would be appropriate.
   3.3 Describe how sociologists often use samples to draw conclusions about a population.
   3.4 Explain why it is more important to use a random sample than a large sample.
   3.5 Show how the wording and sequence of questions in a survey may affect the results.
   3.6 Compare a closed response and an open response question in the survey method.
   3.7 Compare interviews and questionnaires in terms of their advantages and disadvantages.
   3.8 Differentiate semistructured interviews from structured and unstructured interviews.
   3.9 Explain the basic logic of experiments.
   3.10 Compare laboratory experiments and field experiments in terms of their advantages and disadvantages.

3.11 State some of the ethical problems that emerge in experiments.
3.12 Define and give an example of ethnography.
3.13 Compare overt participant observation with covert participant observation in terms of the advantages and disadvantages of each.
3.14 Differentiate both overt and covert participation from nonparticipant observation in terms of advantages and disadvantages.
3.15 Explain why a sociologist might use content analysis.
3.16 Explain why sociologists do cross-cultural research.
3.17 Describe the relevance of historical studies for sociological research.
3.18 Explain why a sociologist might use secondary analysis.

CHAPTER SUMMARY

1. What does the scientific method involve?

Research in sociology begins when a sociologist wants to know why a particular social phenomenon occurs. Durkheim was an early French sociologist who wanted to know why people committed suicide. He was not satisfied with psychological explanations of suicide and decided to explore various sociological explanations. Using government statistics, he concluded that suicide is dependent on social circumstances. He identified four basic types of suicide. *Egoistic suicide* relates to social isolation and individualism: it occurs when people have weak ties with a community. Conversely, *altruistic suicide* occurs when people whose ties to their social groups are so strong that they commit suicide for the good of the group. *Anomic suicide* occurs when social normlessness occurs in times of stress and disruption. Finally, *fatalistic suicide* sometimes occurs when people face an inevitably bleak and depressing fate. Durkheim applied a sociological perspective to a phenomenon that was considered to be strongly psychological in origin. He also used empirical methods. Both approaches reflect his contribution to the development of sociology.

The first step in the model research process is defining the problem in a precise way. It is often difficult to determine clearly and precisely how to measure a particular phenomenon. Scientists study *variables*, factors capable of change. A *dependent variable* is a factor that is influenced by other factors, known as *independent variables*. A review of the literature enables us to determine what is known about a particular issue. It also helps us to resolve differences of opinion and to identify relationships among the factors as precisely as possible.

Sociologists frequently form hypotheses in their quest for explanations. A *hypothesis* is a tentative statement that predicts how two or more variables relate to one another. Researchers develop *operational definitions* to help define a concept in a measurable way. They use *indicators* in this process, something that can be measured empirically to get information about a more abstract variable related to the indicator but difficult to measure directly. To test hypotheses, researchers need data and employ statistics to analyze the data. The type of data required influences the choice of method that sociologists use to test their hypotheses. They need to gather enough information so they can understand the problem and test their hypotheses. Doing so is often difficult because researchers encounter problems in collecting data. Also, a given set of data is sometimes open to various interpretations. Once the data have been gathered, the next step is to analyze this information. Sociologists then form conclusions based on the results of the analysis.

2. What are some of the difficulties in sociological research?

Most of the difficulties in sociological research emerge because people are studying other people. Researchers strive to make findings that others can repeat and that achieve widespread acceptance.

Validity and reliability are the two key benchmarks employed. *Validity* is the degree to which a scientific study measures what it attempts to measure. *Reliability* is the degree to which a study yields the same results when repeated.

The specification of the relationships between variables is also difficult. Sociologists focus on identifying cause-and-effect relationships, relationships in which a change in a dependent variable is caused by a change in an independent variable. This goal is not easy to accomplish, however. There may be many factors at work, making it difficult to identify the key causal factors. In addition, a *correlation* between two variables (in which one changes as the other changes) may not always indicate a causal connection. A *spurious correlation* occurs when two variables are correlated but are not necessarily linked causally. Distinguishing meaningful from spurious correlations is central to sociological analysis.

People are not reducible to simple cause-and-effect equations, a fact that makes establishing causal relationships difficult. Furthermore, social variables may not remain constant over time or from place to place. The research process is not a one-step process but a developmental sequence in which theory spurs research. Research, in turn, generates new theories, which themselves produce more research.

3. *What are the basic designs in sociological research?*

Sociologists engage in quantitative and qualitative research. Those using *quantitative research* test for causal relationships by using statistics. Those using *qualitative research* examine some social phenomenon in detail and look for general patterns of social life, usually in nonstatistical ways.

The three basic designs in sociological research are surveys, experiments, and ethnography. *Surveys* involve systematically gathering answers to standardized questions from a specified sample of respondents. Respondents may be asked to answer questions by mail, over the phone, or in face-to-face interviews. Surveys are particularly useful for gathering information about events that cannot be measured directly.

One must clearly understand the sample and population employed in a survey. The *population* is the total number of people who share a characteristic that the sociologist wishes to study. For example, students at both public and private colleges and universities may constitute a population. A *sample* is a limited but representative subset of a population. For example, we might take a random sample of all students at private and public colleges and universities in the United States at a particular point in time. In a random sample, everyone within the population has an equal chance of being selected. A random sample is far more important than a large sample; small random samples almost always give more accurate results than large but nonrandom samples. In assessing published research, one must determine the nature of the sample employed. Frequently magazine surveys involve large numbers of respondents, but the samples tend to be nonrandom and include only those who subscribe to or purchase the magazine.

The wording and sequence of the questions in a survey may affect the validity and reliability of the data obtained. Using different words to measure the same concept may sometimes yield different results. The order in which questions are asked may also affect the responses. Issues raised in earlier questions can affect how respondents think about later questions. The form of the response is also relevant. In a *closed response* question respondents must choose from the set of answers provided by the researcher. In an *open response* question respondents answer in their own words. Using both forms for the same topic may produce different results.

Questionnaires are efficient for studying a large number of geographically scattered people. For some types of research, however, sociologists need more information than a short questionnaire provides; they turn to interviews in such situations. An *interview* is a conversation in which a researcher asks a series of questions or discusses a topic with another person. Interviews can be conducted in person or by phone. Effective interviewers listen carefully, record the responses accurately, know when to probe for more information, and know that the validity and reliability of interviews depend on the interaction between the interviewer and the respondent. Some interviews are *semi-structured*: the general and specific issues to be covered are identified in advance, but the respondents are free to talk about each topic in terms most meaningful to them. *Structured interviews* are those in which the wording and sequence of questions are carefully planned in advance. In an unstructured interview, the questions and the topic are not predetermined; the interviewer and the subject engage in free-flowing conversation.

The experiment offers the most effective technique for establishing cause-and-effect relationships. *Experiments*, particularly laboratory experiments, provide greater control over the independent and dependent variables and over the grouping of subjects into experimental and control groups. Laboratory experiments generally involve an artificial situation that can be regulated carefully by the researcher. That is, many factors can be held constant while the potential independent variable is isolated.

Laboratory experiments sometimes raise ethical questions. For example, researchers must frequently deceive subjects regarding the purpose of the experiment. Critics have raised questions about the right to deceive people or to cause them anxiety or humiliation in the name of science. Most colleges and universities have established clear guidelines on ethical principles. Researchers must 1) explain the experiment to the subject, 2) minimize lying, 3) warn subjects about potential hazards, 4) describe the use of the data, 5) maintain confidentiality, and 6) inform subjects fully before seeking consent.

Field experiments occur in real-world settings. Manipulating potential independent variables is more difficult in these experiments because the controlled conditions of the laboratory are absent. As a result, sociologists sometimes use natural social settings and naturally occurring phenomena to answer research questions. Occasionally they are able to separate subjects into experimental and control groups; sometimes such groups are established after the fact. Such limitations, however, impose restrictions on the extent to which the researcher can make causal assertions. Ethical issues also emerge in field experiments. For example, experimental groups operating with the independent variable may benefit in a way that the control groups do not. Deception, privacy, and other ethical issues also enter the picture.

In ethnographies, sociologists do not attempt to influence or change people's behavior. An *ethnography* involves simply observing people in everyday settings, usually over a long period, and providing detailed descriptions and interpretations of social life as it happens. In *overt participant observation*, the researcher participates in the social life of those who are being studied, and his or her role is made known to those people. Occasionally, however, such knowledge may affect the subjects' behavior. *Covert participant observation* remedies this problem because sociologists do not identify themselves as researchers; instead they try to act like members of the group they are studying. This method, however, raises serious ethical questions. Is it ethical to deceive people deliberately by pretending to belong to their group when the true intent is to study them? Privacy issues also emerge. A variation on covert participant observation is *nonparticipant observation*, in which sociologists do not participate in the activities of the group under study. They simply observe the group in its everyday setting.

4.   What other approaches do sociologists employ?

Sociologists employ *content analysis* to uncover information in both historical and contemporary materials. Content analysis involves various types of recorded communication, such as letters, diaries, laws, novels, and newspapers. It is especially useful in historical studies because it provides a way to organize and summarize systematically both the manifest and the latent content of the material. Content analysis may involve both qualitative research (research that depends on interpretations by the researcher) and quantitative research (research that employs statistics).

Comparative research enables comparisons between different societies, social groups, or social categories of people. It may involve any research method. The goal is comparison to help generate explanations. Comparative research applied to a society or social group other than our own is known as *cross-cultural research*. Such studies can be large or small scale, and the incidence of these studies is increasing.

Historical studies enable sociologists to examine the changes that take place in institutions, groups, and societies over time. Such studies are particularly appropriate in studying phenomena that occur infrequently. They are also useful in studying events that unfold over a long period. Finally, historical research enables sociologists to draw on documents created for other purposes. Secondary analysis is the analysis of data that were originally collected for another reason. It helps shed new light on historical events.

REVIEW OF CONCEPTS

Match the concept with the definition.

Concepts

a. altruistic suicide
b. anomic suicide
c. content analysis
d. correlation
e. correlation coefficient
f. covert participant observation
g. cross-cultural research
h. data
i. dependent variable
j. egoistic suicide
k. ethnographies
l. experiment

m. fatalistic suicide
n. globalization
o. hypothesis
p. independent variable
q. indicator
r. interview
s. mean
t. median
u. methodology
v. mode
w. nonparticipant observation
x. operational definition
y. overt participant observation

z. population
aa. qualitative research
bb. quantitative research
cc. random sample
dd. reliability
ee. sample
ff. secondary analysis
gg. spurious correlation
hh. standard deviation
ii. survey
jj. validity
kk. variable

Definitions

_____ 1. A research method that exposes subjects to a specially designed situation. The most effective technique for establishing cause and effect relationships among variables.

_____ 2. The number that falls in the middle of a sequence of figures.

_____ 3. A correlation between two variables that has no meaningful causal basis.

_____ 4. A statistical measurement of how far other recorded instances fall from the mean or from another central point.

_____ 5. Durkheim's term for suicide that results from social isolation and individualism.

_____ 6. A tentative statement that predicts how two or more variables affect or are related to one another.

_____ 7. Studies that describe social patterns in societies other than the researcher's own.

____ 8. The degree to which a scientific study measures what it attempts to measure.

____ 9. The figure that occurs most often in a series of data.

____ 10. A conversation through which an investigator seeks information from a research subject.

____ 11. In a survey, the total number of people who share a characteristic that is being studied.

____ 12. In an experiment, the quality or factor that is affected by one or more independent variables.

____ 13. The average obtained by adding all figures in a series of data and dividing the sum by the number of items.

____ 14. A decimal number between zero and one that is used to show the strength of a correlation.

____ 15. The degree to which a study yields the same results when repeated by the original researcher or by others.

____ 16. A research technique in which the investigator participates in the activities of those being observed and in which the investigator's role is made known.

____ 17. In an experiment, the quality or factor that affects one or more dependent variables.

____ 18. Reanalysis of data previously collected for other purposes.

____ 19. A measurable indicator for one of the variables in a hypothesis.

____ 20. A research technique in which people's activities are observed without their knowledge and in which the investigators never identify themselves as sociologists.

____ 21. Studies in which researchers observe people in their everyday settings, usually over an extended period.

____ 22. A sample drawn in such a way that every member of the population under study has an equal chance of being selected.

____ 23. Research that relies on statistical analyses of data.

Answers

1.	l	9.	v	17.	p
2.	t	10.	r	18.	ff
3.	gg	11.	z	19.	x
4.	hh	12.	i	20.	f
5.	j	13.	s	21.	k
6.	o	14.	e	22.	cc
7.	g	15.	dd	23.	bb
8.	jj	16.	y		

REVIEW QUESTIONS

After studying Chapter 2, answer the following questions. The correct answers are listed at the end of the questions; each is followed by a short explanation. You are also referred to pages in the textbook for relevant discussion.

1. The scientific method would be most useful in which of the following situations?
   a. to examine the effect of the Industrial Revolution on workers' morale
   b. to examine the effect of group size on intergroup conflict
   c. to determine who should obtain child custody in a divorce settlement
   d. to determine the validity of Catholics' belief in the infallibility of the Pope
   e. to determine whether kindness is a better value than generosity

2. The first step in the model research process is
   a. forming a hypothesis.
   b. forming a theory.
   c. choosing a research design.
   d. defining a problem.
   e. gathering the data.

3. Durkheim used what type of data in his study of suicide?
   a. historical documents
   b. government records
   c. interviews with those who attempted suicide
   d. interviews with the relatives of suicide victims
   e. content analysis of diaries of suicide victims

4. Indian widows throw themselves on the funeral pyres of their dead husbands. What type of suicide is this?
   a. egoistic
   b. altruistic
   c. anomic
   d. dysfunctional
   e. psychological

5. Professor Flint studied the incidence of cheating among students as influenced by class level. He was particularly concerned with identifying clearly what constitutes cheating. The professor was concerned with developing
   a. a theory.
   b. a hypothesis.
   c. an independent variable.
   d. a dependent variable.
   e. an operational definition.

6. Analysis of data primarily involves
   a. looking for patterns and relationships.
   b. looking for exceptional cases.
   c. comparing alternative theories.
   d. comparing alternative research designs.
   e. calculating statistics.

7. The more fire trucks show up at a fire, the more damage occurs. This is an example of a
   a. hypothesis.
   b. perfect positive correlation.
   c. perfect negative correlation.
   d. spurious relationship.
   e. cause-effect relationship.

8. Which of the following statements is *false* regarding sociological research?
   a. Social variables may vary over time or place.
   b. It is difficult to reduce human situations to simple cause-and-effect relationships.
   c. Every attempt should be made to keep social theory and social research separate.
   d. It is difficult to assign people systematically to experimental and control groups for natural-ly occurring events (such as being divorced).
   e. All are true.

9. In a study of gender, adjustment to retirement, and level of education, which variable(s) is (are) independent?
   a. gender
   b. adjustment to retirement
   c. level of education
   d. a and b only
   e. a and c only

10. Which of the following is the best example of a testable hypothesis?
    a. Prejudice and education are related.
    b. The meaning of prejudice for individuals is determined by the social context.
    c. Prejudiced people are not as good as unprejudiced people.
    d. The higher the level of education, the lower the degree of prejudice.
    e. Prejudice is caused by education.

11. Most students scored above 75 on the last exam, but two students scored below 50. Which of the following would be the most appropriate to show the central tendency in these scores?
    a. mean
    b. standard deviation
    c. median
    d. correlation
    e. mode

12. Shana weighs 109 pounds on the calibrated scale in her doctor's office, but every time she weighs herself on her bathroom scale, it shows 116 pounds. Which of the following statements is correct?
    a. Her scale is reliable but not valid.
    b. Her scale is valid but not reliable.
    c. Her scale is both reliable and valid.
    d. Her scale is neither reliable nor valid.
    e. Her scale is generalizable.

13. Putting questions on overpopulation before questions on personal use of birth control reflects which factor that may affect results on a survey?
    a. sequence

b. wording
c. double-barreled question
d. biased question
e. length of question

14. Johan took a random sample of residents in his all-male dorm for a survey on drinking. Which of the following best reflects the group he can describe with his results?
    a. all the residents he actually surveyed
    b. all residents in his dorm
    c. all residents in all men's dorms on campus
    d. all residents in both men's and women's dorms on campus
    e. all students on campus

15. Interviews of rape victims often cover several specific issues with specific questions, but allow the respondent a great deal of freedom to address the issues in whatever order she wishes and to talk about them in terms most meaningful to her. Which type of interview does this approach reflect?
    a. neutral
    b. semistructured
    c. unobtrusive
    d. structured
    e. unstructured

16. Professor Simpson wanted to study a church group without the members knowing he was studying them, so he joined the group. What type of ethnography is this?
    a. overt participant observation
    b. covert participant observation
    c. nonparticipant observation
    d. ethnomethodological
    e. interactionist

17. Which of the following strategies is most likely to employ previously collected data?
    a. content analysis
    b. field observation
    c. ex post facto study
    d. cross-sectional study
    e. secondary analysis

18. The 1990 Census is an example of which of the following methods?
    a. laboratory experiment
    b. field experiment
    c. survey
    d. content analysis
    e. unobtrusive measure

19. Professor Monroe wishes to isolate the causal effect of group test taking versus individual test taking on exam scores. Which of the following methods would be best?
    a. secondary analysis
    b. content analysis
    c. ex post facto study

d. experiment
e. survey

20. The best design for studying the changing role of women as shown in advertisements would be
    a. historical materials.
    b. experiment.
    c. survey.
    d. field observation.
    e. content analysis.

Answers

1. *b.* The scientific method relies on first measuring observable phenomena and then relating them. See page 29.
2. *d.* The first step in the model research process is defining the problem in a precise way. See pages 29-30.
3. *b.* Durkheim used government records that listed numbers of suicides and gave information about the people involved--their age, sex, nationality, religion, and marital status. See page 29.
4. *b.* Altruistic suicide occurs when people whose ties to their group are so strong that they commit suicide for the good of the people. See page 29.
5. *e.* When sociologists study relatively abstract concepts such as cheating, they must define the concept clearly in measurable terms. See page 32.
6. *a.* Data analysis primarily involves looking for patterns and relationships so that hypotheses relating independent and dependent variables can be assessed. See page 32.
7. *d.* A spurious relationship exists when two variables are correlated, but that correlation does not reflect a causal connection. That is, both variables are caused by another factor. In this case the size of the fire affects both the number of fire trucks and the damage. See page 37.
8. *c.* Research and theory are inseparable in sociology. See page 37.
9. *e.* Sex and level of education are both independent variables because both may influence adjustment to retirement, the dependent variable. See page 30.
10. *d.* Only this statement links the two variables as well as specifying the direction of the link. See page 31.
11. *c.* The median is the number that falls in the middle of a distribution of scores. Hence it is not affected by a few extremely high or low scores. See page 33.
12. *a.* Her scale yields the same weight on repeated measures and hence is reliable. This scale never yields her actual weight, however, and hence is not valid. See pages 36-37.
13. *a.* The sequence of questions--the order in which they appear--may affect responses to later questions. The questions on overpopulation may lead respondents to be less honest about their own use of birth control. See page 39.
14. *b.* A random sample allows generalizability but only to the group from which the sample was taken. Because he studied only one dorm, he can generalize only to residents of that dorm. See pages 38-39.
15. *b.* This approach reflects the semistructured interview because the researcher worked out the specific issues and questions in advance but allows the respondent considerable latitude in responding. See page 40.
16. *b.* In covert participant observation sociologists do not tell their subjects that they are being observed for an ethnography. See page 43.
17. *e.* Secondary analysis is used to analyze previously collected data. See page 47.
18. *c.* The census is compiled with both questionnaires and interviews, both of which reflect the

survey method. See page 38.

19. *d.* The major advantage of the experimental method is that it allows the researcher to study the impact of only one or two variables while holding other variables constant. See page 40.

20. *e.* Content analysis is used to examine recorded communication. See page 44.

EXERCISES

Exercise 1

Review the box "How to Read a Table" on page 34 in your text and then study this table.

Relationship between Gender and the importance attached to having lots of money in a random sample of 16,000 Tenth Graders in public and private High Schools in the United States in 1990, in Percentages *

IMPORTANCE OF HAVING LOTS OF MONEY	GENDER Males	Females	TOTALS
Not Important	5.2	8.8	7.0
Somewhat Important	41.2	56.4	48.9
Very Important	53.6	34.8	44.1
TOTALS	100.0	100.0	100.0

* Significance at .001 level

These data are part of the National Education Longitudinal Study of 1988 sponsored by the National Center for Education Statistics and conducted by the National Opinion Research Center. Students were in the eighth grade in 1988 and the tenth grade in 1990.

1. What do you know about the sample and the population? How well can the results be generalized?

2. What conclusions can you draw about the validity of the study from the source of the data?

26

3. State a hypothesis that these data can address. Identify the independent and dependent variables.

4. Compare males and females in terms of importance attached to having lots of money; do this for each category importance. What differences, if any, exist in each category?

5. What general relationship appears, if any? Do the results support your hypothesis?

6. How would you explain these results?

7. Are the results statistically significant? What does your answer mean in determining how extensively the results can be generalized?

8. What other independent variables may influence importance of money? Which of these variables would be the most important to control for in the relationship between gender and importance of money? Why?

Exercise 2

Select a topic of interest to you, perhaps one that is currently receiving attention on your campus or in the news. Identify possible independent or dependent variables.

1. Develop a hypothesis you wish to test.

2. Select three of the following methods and briefly outline how you would test this hypothesis using each one: survey, experiment, ethnography, historical studies, content analysis.

Method A:

Method B:

Method C:

3. Develop operational definitions for your independent and dependent variables for one of the methods.

4. Describe the main advantage and disadvantage of each of the three methods you selected in terms of your study. Which method would be best? Why?

Exercise 3

Prepare an outline to argue both sides of this question: Is sociology a science?

Chapter 3
CULTURE

OBJECTIVES

After reading Chapter 3, you should understand the following main points and be able to answer the objectives.

1. Culture is the sum of the learned customs, beliefs, values, knowledge, artifacts, and symbols that are communicated constantly among a set of people who share a common way of life.
   1.1 Define culture and list its various elements.
   1.2 Describe the relationship between culture and behavior.

2. People use the elements of culture to create, sustain, and change their way of life; the elements of culture are values, norms, symbols, language, and knowledge.
   2.1 Compare material and nonmaterial culture.
   2.2 Define values and give a few examples.
   2.3 Show how values reinforce each other and also how they can conflict.
   2.4 Contrast norms with values and give examples of norms.
   2.5 Show how norms vary.
   2.6 Compare folkways, mores, and laws, and give examples of each.
   2.7 Discuss how symbols are used in social life.
   2.8 Define language and describe its use in social contexts.
   2.9 Illustrate how language affects social action and social structure.
   2.10 Discuss the varieties of knowledge and their role in social life.

3. Cultural integration is the degree to which parts of a culture form a consistent and interrelated pattern.
   3.1 Show how cultural integration reflects the key concept of functional integration.
   3.2 Link the concept of assimilation to cultural integration and diversity.
   3.3 Explain how the elements of culture are interwoven to form a complex whole.
   3.4 Distinguish dominant culture from subculture.

4. The case of the Hispanic subculture in the United States illustrates processes of subcultural change.
   4.1 Describe distinctive features of the Hispanic subculture.
   4.2 Explain why Hispanics have been among the least assimilated into the dominant culture.
   4.3 List three sources of subcultures other than ethnicity and religion.
   4.4 Differentiate counterculture from culture and subculture.
   4.5 Distinguish between ethnocentrism and cultural relativism.

5. The production of culture perspective calls attention to the interplay between individuals who actively create culture and the social structures that influence those creations.
   5.1 Discuss the assumptions behind the production of culture perspective, particularly as they relate to the key concepts.
   5.2 List the factors determining whether a new element will become part of a culture.
   5.3 Identify the role of cultural gatekeepers.
   5.4 Describe the role of public taste in the production and acceptance of culture.

6. The growth of electronic media for communication has had a profound impact on the content and distribution of culture.
   6.1 Discuss the consequences of new electronic media for communication.
   6.2 Evaluate the claim that television has changed *how* we view the world as well as the content of those views.
   6.3 Demonstrate how the mass media have contributed to the internationalization of culture.
   6.4 Show how the internationalization of culture has played a critical role in important world events.

CHAPTER SUMMARY

1. What is culture, and what role does it play in society and in its members' lives?

Culture can be defined as the learned norms, values, knowledge, artifacts, language, and symbols that constantly circulate among people who share a way of life. The content of culture ranges from our beliefs about what is important in life to the common everyday habits that we take for granted. Culture is inherently social; that is, we create and express the elements of our culture and constantly communicate to each other our understanding of our social world.

2. What are the elements of culture?

All human cultures have the same basic elements: knowledge, language, symbols, values, norms, and artifacts. Sociologists often distinguish between the material and the nonmaterial aspects of culture. *Material culture* includes all the physical objects, or artifacts, that people make and to which attach meaning. *Nonmaterial* culture includes human creations that are not embodied in physical objects, such as values, norms, and knowledge and the like. A *value* is a general idea that people should care about what is good or bad. People's values affect their way of life. Competition, for example, is a core American value. Values often reinforce each other, such as efficiency and progress. Other values are in conflict, such as humanitarianism and individual success.

Values provide a framework for developing norms of behavior. A *norm* is a specific guideline for action; it is a rule that says how people should behave in a particular situation. Norms can be implicit or very explicit, and can vary greatly from society to society and from group to group. They also change over time. Generally they are situational--they apply to particular circumstances and settings. Norms vary in the importance that people assign to them and in the way people react to violators. *Folkways* are norms that are simply everyday habits and conventions; people follow them without even thinking about them. *Mores* are the norms that people consider vital to their well-being and to their most cherished values. Strong sanctions are applied to violators of mores. *Laws* are a special kind of norm that has been formalized or institutionalized; these rules have been written into a code of laws, and police and courts have been formally assigned the task of enforcement and punishment. Laws are rules that are enacted by a political body and are enforced by the power of the state.

3. Why are symbols, language and knowledge essential features of human societies?

Symbols, language, and knowledge are three other elements of culture. Each is essential to human societies because they allow us to create meaning and abstract ideas, to communicate them to others, and to record them for succeeding generations. *Symbols* are objects, gestures, sounds, or images that represent something other than themselves. They do not always look like, sound like, or otherwise resemble what they symbolize. The meanings attached to symbols are often very arbitrary, and are simply a matter of tradition and consensus.

Language is a system of verbal and (sometimes) written symbols with rules about how those symbols can be combined to convey complex meanings. Language permits the creation, communication, and preservation of abstract cultural ideas, and it lies at the root of the transmission of culture. Sociologists are interested both in the structure of language and in the role of language in social action (how people use language to coordinate their activities and to create and confirm social understandings). *Social markers* are behavior patterns that give clues to the meaning of a social situation by providing indications about who people are, to what groups they belong, and what their understanding of a situation is. That is, social markers help to identify where a person or group fits into a social structure.

Knowledge may be defined as the body of facts, beliefs, and practical skills that people accumulate over time. Some knowledge is simply procedural; other knowledge consists of information about people, places, and events. Ours is the "information society" because of the rapid accumulation of new knowledge and the fundamental importance of the growth of knowledge for economic, political, and social life.

4. What are the relationships among dominant cultures, subcultures and countercultures?

The elements of culture described above are woven together into a complex whole. *Cultural integration* is the degree to which the parts of a culture form a consistent and interrelated pattern. Cultures can be more or less integrated, but in all cases there is at least some interdependence among the set of beliefs, values, and artifacts. This interdependence is evident in situations where changes in one realm of culture force changes in other realms. Cultural integration can be enhanced by *assimilation,* the process by which newcomers to America (and other "outsiders") give up their culturally distinct beliefs, values, and customs and take on those of the dominant culture. The degree of cultural integration varies considerably across cultures and time. Cultures that are very heterogeneous and loosely integrated involve a certain amount of internal contradiction.

The *dominant culture* consists of those values, beliefs, traditions, and outlooks which members of certain groups impose on other members of society. American society includes many groups whose lifestyles and attitudes make them different from the mainstream dominant culture. If members of such groups identify themselves in terms of their distinctive norms and values, sociologists say that they belong to a *subculture.* Subcultures form around common ethnic or religious heritages, occupational traditions, or socioeconomic status.

One rapidly growing ethnic subculture in the United States is that of Hispanic-Americans, whose distinctive value system includes a strong emphasis on a person's inner worth and on the closeness of family and one-to-one friendship ties. These values lead to behavior patterns that differ from those in the dominant Anglo-American society. Hispanics have been among the least inclined to become assimilated into the dominant culture.

Tensions often develop between members of the dominant culture and those of one or more subcultures, particularly those subcultures which oppose dominant norms and values. *Countercultures* are subcultures that are not merely distinct from the dominant culture; they are oriented towards challenging that culture or deliberately trying to change it.

5. How are the values and norms of another culture to be evaluated?

Cultural ideas vary widely from society to society. People often view their own culture as correct and good, and those of others as strange or even immoral; this feeling is known as *ethnocentrism*. Ethnocentrism can be a source of unity within groups but can cause friction or conflict between groups with different cultures.

The *cultural relativist* position requires one to deliberately suspend judgment about the cultural ideas of other societies. Any element of culture is relative to a particular time, place, and set of circumstances. Unlike ethnocentrism, cultural relativism encourages understanding and tolerance between groups.

6. How do new cultural patterns become part of social life?

The production of cultural perspectives suggests that the elements of culture are not created all at once; rather, new patterns of ideas and beliefs take hold gradually as old ones gradually disappear. These changes in cultural elements are shaped by social structures in which new ideas and beliefs are created and nurtured. Cultural innovators--those who try to introduce new ideas or beliefs into a society--are embedded in social contexts that either facilitate or retard the creation and subsequent adoption of their innovations. The fate of a cultural innovation is determined in part by the degree to which it conforms to shared ideas and expectations that are part of the existing culture.

Cultural innovations can live or die at the hands of *cultural gatekeepers*, the people who regulate the flow of new cultural elements into society. These gatekeepers help to determine which cultural innovations will receive exposure through traditional channels of distribution. Public taste is also important for the acceptance or rejection of new elements of culture, although the importance of "consumer demand" is often exaggerated. Cultural gatekeepers can manipulate taste by flooding society with certain cultural products while keeping others out of sight.

7. How have the modern electronic media changed the content and communication of culture?

It is difficult to understand the profound changes in American culture without appreciating the role played by electronic inventions that enable people to collect, process, and exchange information: radio, the telephone, the tape recorder, television, the motion picture, the computer, the VCR, and the camcorder. The development of these technologies depended on the prior invention of language itself, and built on earlier advances in communication such as writing and printing.

The telephone and the computer, as well as modern electronic media such as radio and television, have greatly accelerated the speed with which information can spread to large numbers of people located far apart. These media have made people more aware of their worldwide mutuality and interdependence.

The impact of television on cultural change has perhaps been the most profound of all. Both the content and the form of a message are shaped by the medium of communication. Because television is a visual as well as an auditory medium, material selected for broadcast on the nightly news must be visually exciting, sensational, and action-filled. TV news stories typically last one minute or less.

What are the effects of the growing dominance of television in communicating information? Some people suggest that TV causes people to blur the distinction between serious news items and entertainment; important public issues or personal tragedies are often handled by TV as if they were soap operas. Other people suggest that TV has blurred the distinction between face-to-face interaction and indirect communication at a distance. Television has also created new social situations: people realize that when the camera points at them, their behavior is being watched by millions. Finally, TV also can reinforce certain cultural stereotypes. The presentation of racial or ethnic groups is often idealized, thus leading to misleading or incomplete portrayals of their lives.

The growth of the mass media has resulted in the *internationalization* of culture. A single global culture has replaced distinctive local cultures. Although the internationalization of culture is not new, the process has become much more rapid than in the past. Large-scale immigration is another social force contributing to the internationalization of culture in recent times. Finally, the international culture has played a critical role in important world events.

REVIEW OF CONCEPTS

Match the concept with the definition.

Concepts

a. assimilation
b. counterculture
c. cultural gatekeepers
d. cultural integration
e. cultural relativism
f. culture
g. dominant culture

h. ethnocentrism
i. folkways
j. knowledge
k. language
l. laws
m. material culture
n. mores

o. nonmaterial culture
p. norms
q. social marker
r. subculture
s. symbol
t. values

Definitions

_____ 1. The idea that any element of culture is relative to a particular time, place, and set of circumstances.

_____ 2. Any pattern of behavior that provides indications about who people are, what groups they belong to, and what their understanding of a situation is.

_____ 3. A group whose norms, attitudes, values, and lifestyle clash directly with or are opposed to those of the dominant or mainstream culture.

_____ 4. All the learned customs, beliefs, values, knowledge, artifacts, and symbols that are communicated constantly among a set of people who share a common way of life.

_____ 5. The group whose values, norms, traditions, and outlooks are imposed on the society as a whole.

_____ 6. Norms that people consider vital to their well-being and to their most cherished values.

_____ 7. A system of verbal (and usually also written) symbols with rules about how those symbols can be strung together to convey more complex meanings.

_____ 8. Specific guidelines for action that say how people should behave in particular situations.

_____ 9. The degree to which parts of a culture form a consistent and interrelated whole.

_____ 10. Human creations, such as values, beliefs, rules, customs, systems of government, and language that are not embodied in physical objects.

____ 11. People who regulate the flow of new elements of culture into society.

____ 12. Everyday habits and conventions.

____ 13. A group of people whose perspective and lifestyle differ significantly from those of the dominant culture and who identify themselves as different; members share norms, values, and attitudes.

____ 14. The tendency to view one's own cultural patterns as good and right and to judge others by those standards.

____ 15. All the physical objects or artifacts that people make and to which they attach meaning.

____ 16. The body of facts and beliefs that people accumulate over time.

____ 17. Rules that are enacted by a political body and enforced by the power of the state.

____ 18. General ideas that people share about what is good or bad, desirable or undesirable.

____ 19. The process in which newcomers take on many of the cultural patterns of the host society and give up their own distinctive cultural patterns.

____ 20. An object, gesture, sound, image, or design that represents something other than itself.

Answers

1.	e	8.	p	15.	m
2.	q	9.	d	16.	j
3.	b	10.	o	17.	l
4.	f	11.	c	18.	t
5.	g	12.	i	19.	a
6.	n	13.	r	20.	s
7.	k	14.	h		

REVIEW QUESTIONS

After studying Chapter 3, answer the following questions. The correct answers are listed at the end of the questions; each is followed by a short explanation. You are also referred to pages in the textbook for relevant discussion.

1. Which of the following is *not* an element of culture?
   a. norms
   b. symbols
   c. values
   d. natural environment
   e. language

2. Which of the following things would be considered part of culture?
   a. a Buick

b. an advertisement for Buicks
c. the plays of Shakespeare
d. Bermuda shorts
e. all of the above

3. Which of the following is an example of nonmaterial culture?
   a. a television set
   b. a stone hatchet
   c. a copy of the Bible
   d. the Empire State Building
   e. the law against child molesting

4. Which of the following is a value?
   a. People should thank their hosts before leaving a party.
   b. People should cooperate.
   c. Students should not throw tomatoes at a lecturing instructor.
   d. Drivers should not exceed the posted speed limit.
   e. Pedestrians should not jaywalk.

5. Which is a *false* statement about values?
   a. No value applies in every social situation; there are always exceptions.
   b. Values are reflected in seemingly trivial day-to-day activities, such as playing a game.
   c. All values in a group or a society must be consistent and compatible.
   d. Conflicts between values create pressure for social change.
   e. Values change as social events and circumstances change.

6. At the funeral of a close friend, a man suddenly bursts out laughing and cannot stop. An usher asks the man to leave because he has violated
   a. a law.
   b. a norm.
   c. a value.
   d. a social marker.
   e. knowledge.

7. Which of the following is a *false* statement about norms?
   a. Norms are always made explicit, as in written laws or Biblical commandments.
   b. Norms can vary greatly from society to society.
   c. Norms vary from group to group within a society.
   d. Norms are rules that apply to specific circumstances and settings.
   e. Ordinarily, people follow norms more or less automatically.

8. The rule against wearing very tall hats in crowded movie theaters is an example of
   a. a folkway.
   b. mores.
   c. a law.
   d. cultural relativism.
   e. ethnocentrism.

9. Sociologists would describe the cross on the altar of a Christian church as a symbol because
   a. it is a physical object.

b. it is used in a ritual.
c. it stands for something other than itself.
d. it is treated with respect.
e. it is valuable.

10. Which of the following is a *false* statement about symbols?
   a. The meaning given to a symbol is frequently arbitrary, a matter of tradition and convention.
   b. The meanings of symbols can easily be changed.
   c. The meaning of a symbol must be the same for all people in a social group.
   d. Some symbols can stand for a wide variety of ideas or beliefs.
   e. In different cultures, different symbols are used to represent the same concept.

11. Which of the following is *not* an immediate consequence of the development of language in human society?
   a. ability to imagine the future and preserve the past
   b. ability to pass on knowledge to new generations
   c. ability to control fertility
   d. ability to learn about and from the experiences of others
   e. ability to formulate complex plans

12. The youth movement of the 1960's rejected dominant American values of materialism, competitiveness, hard work, and individualism. The youth movement is an example of
   a. dominant culture.
   b. subculture.
   c. counterculture.
   d. material culture.
   e. cultural gatekeepers.

13. Which of the following is a subculture?
   a. Hispanic-Americans
   b. adolescents
   c. medical students
   d. inmates in a prison
   e. all of the above

14. Which of the following is *not* part of the traditional values of the Hispanic-American subculture?
   a. spiritual values being more important than material values
   b. emphasis on a person's inner worth
   c. deep personal attachments among family members and friends
   d. reliance on public agencies and social services in times of need
   e. transcendent qualities such as justice, loyalty, and love

15. In the process of assimilation
   a. the values of the subculture change, but the norms and practices of the dominant society do not.
   b. the norms and practices of the dominant society change, but the values of the subculture do not.
   c. the values of the subculture change, and so do the norms and practices of the dominant

culture.
   d. there is little change in values, norms, or practices.
   e. people are always unhappy.

16. Scientific articles are being produced at the rate of one every two minutes and even scientists have trouble keeping up with recent developments. This example reflects which element of culture?
    a. language
    b. norms
    c. values
    d. symbols
    e. knowledge

17. When European and American slave traders began to seize slaves from various African societies, they assumed that they were helping these people by removing them from their savage, barbaric life and showing them how "civilized" people could, and did, live. The attitude of the slave traders toward traditional African culture is an example of
    a. ethnocentrism.
    b. cultural relativity.
    c. cultural integration.
    d. cultural gatekeepers.
    e. a cultural universal.

18. The designer Oscar de la Junta is reviewing some fashion sketches prepared by a young man who would like to work for Oscar. The style is dramatically different from anything that Oscar has ever seen, and he decides that he hates it. He banishes the young designer from his office and tells him that he has no future in the fashion industry. The young man gives up his dream, and now he waits tables in Greenwich Village. In this instance, Oscar is playing the role of
    a. a univocal symbol.
    b. a multivocal symbol.
    c. a cultural gatekeeper.
    d. an enforcer of the law.
    e. a folkway.

19. Which was *not* listed among the cultural consequences of television?
    a. increased speed in the communication of ideas
    b. increased audience for the communication of ideas
    c. change in the boundaries between public and private spheres of life
    d. increased ability to distinguish serious news from entertainment
    e. breakdown of the distinction between face-to-face interaction and indirect communication at a distance

20. Two factors noted as contributing to the increasingly rapid process of the internationalization of culture have been
    a. the computer and the acceptance of English as a standard language
    b. the acceptance of English as a standard language and the increased level of education
    c. the increased level of education and the spread of democracy
    d. the spread of democracy and the electronic media
    e. the electronic media and large-scale immigration

1. *d.* Culture is a social creation; it is not provided by the natural or the physical environment. Culture is defined as all learned customs, beliefs, values, knowledge, artifacts (things made by people), and symbols that are constantly communicated among a set of people who share a common way of life. See page 52.

2. *e.* For sociologists, culture signifies a society's entire learned way of life. Culture includes both the tangible and the intangible things that a given group of people has created and to which they attach similar meanings. See page 53.

3. *e.* Nonmaterial culture consists of abstract human creations (such as laws, values, beliefs, or ideas) that are not embodied in physical objects. The other choices are all examples of material culture: physical objects that people make and to which they attach meanings. See page 53.

4. *b.* Values are general ideas that people share about what is good or bad, desirable or undesirable. The abstract value of cooperation can be interpreted in different ways, depending upon the particular situation. The other choices are all examples of norms: specific guidelines for how people should act in particular situations. See page 54.

5. *c.* Within the American system of values, there are contradictions between conformity and individuality and between equality and racial superiority. To deal with inconsistent values, people sometimes apply different values in different situations. The contradictions within a value system sometimes create pressure for social change. See page 55.

6. *b.* Norms are specific guidelines for action that specify how people should behave in particular situations. At funerals, participants are expected to show grief or sadness, not to laugh. The man violated this normative expectation and was "punished" for doing so. See page 55.

7. *a.* Most often, norms are unspoken customs that people follow implicitly. That is, most of the normative rules governing everyday life are not formalized or written down into an official code. We grasp norms implicitly in the process of learning culture. See pages 55-56.

8. *a.* Most people would automatically remove a tall hat when they sit down to watch a movie; common sense tells us that leaving the hat on might obstruct the view of people sitting behind us. Folkways are everyday habits or conventions that people follow without giving much thought to the matter. See page 57.

9. *c.* In the Christian religion, the cross symbolizes the crucifixion of Jesus Christ; it stands for pain, suffering, faith, and the hope of salvation. A symbol is an object, gesture, sound, image, or design that represents something other than itself. See page 58.

10. *c.* The meaning of a symbol may be somewhat different for different people in a society. A wedding band might signify a lifelong commitment for some, while for others it might signify a relationship that will last only as long as both partners are satisfied. See page 59.

11. *c.* Many other cultural and technical developments beside language were necessary for the control of fertility. The other choices are all immediate consequences of the development of language, which is defined as a system of verbal (and often written) symbols with rules about how those symbols can be combined to convey more complex meanings. See page 59.

12. *c.* A counterculture is a group whose norms, attitudes, values, and lifestyle clash directly with or are opposed to those of the dominant or mainstream culture. Hippies rejected deferred gratification, sexual restrictiveness, and "the establishment." See page 65.

13. *e* A subculture is a group of people whose perspective and lifestyle differ significantly from those of the dominant culture and who identify themselves as different. Members of a subculture share norms, values, and attitudes. See page 63.

14. *d.* Hispanic-Americans value an intense sense of family obligation and loyalty. The strong

commitment to mutual assistance within the family means that elderly people usually live at the family home and are seldom placed in nursing or retirement institutions. See pages 63-64.

15. *c.* Assimilation is a two-way street. To some extent the norms and practices of American society are a mix of the cultural traditions of a variety of subculture groups, and they are constantly changing as new groups are assimilated. See page 62.

16. *e.* Knowledge is the body of facts, beliefs, and practical skills that people accumulate over time. Modern society is accumulating knowledge at a fantastically rapid pace. See page 61.

17. *a.* Ethnocentrism is the tendency to view one's own cultural patterns as good and right and to judge others by those standards. Ethnocentrism enabled the slave traders to rationalize or justify behavior that today would be condemned by almost everybody. See page 65.

18. *c.* Cultural gatekeepers are people who regulate the flow of new elements of culture into society. Unless someone steals the patterns of the young designer, these new fashion ideas might never hit the streets. See page 67.

19. *d.* Among other things, the growing dominance of TV has blurred the boundary between serious news and entertainment. We expect matters of politics, education, and economics to be as entertaining as a weekly sitcom or game show. This situation results, in part, from the requirement that TV package news or information into short, visually dramatic segments; on TV it is difficult to develop a coherent, well-documented, and well-reasoned analysis. See page 71.

20. *e.* The electronic media enables cultural items to circle the globe rapidly. Large-scale immigration has brought together many different cultures but has helped develop a single global culture in which everyone participates. See page 71.

EXERCISES

Exercise 1

This exercise asks you to consider both sides of a controversial question of public policy, a question that demands a sociological perspective.

Hispanic Americans are one of the largest subcultures in American society. Many Hispanics in the United States speak only Spanish; this is true for children as well as for adults. Suppose that the legislature in the state of Texas--which has a large Spanish-speaking population--is considering a bill that would provide special funds for bilingual elementary education. The bill would finance schooling in both English and Spanish for Grades 1 through 6, and would cost a great deal of money. The debate in the legislature is intense: some say that the program is a waste of time and money; others say that the program is essential.

You have been called in as an expert in cultural sociology. You are asked to prepare a brief statement on the advantages and disadvantages of funding a program of bilingual education. Organize your report so that it describes the *advantages* and *disadvantages* of the program for the following four groups:

1. The Hispanic population of Texas.

2. The non-Hispanic taxpayers of Texas.

3. Teachers in Texas elementary schools.

4. Managers of businesses and corporations in Texas.

On the basis of your report, try to decide whether you think it is likely that the Texas legislature would pass a bill to fund bilingual elementary education. What political or economic forces would play a role in that decision?

Exercise 2

You have accepted a job as counselor for foreign students at your college or university. Your first assignment is to prepare a "survival manual" for those students who arrive from abroad on your campus with little understanding of American culture and behavior patterns. Assume that all the foreign students understand English well enough to read it and speak it. Tell them what they need to know in order to get along during their first few days at your college or university. Remember that these arriving students are largely ignorant of the local folkways and symbols that may be peculiar to your campus, and that they have only a "textbook" familiarity with the values, norms, and laws of American society at large.

1. Provide information about the local folkways and symbols of your college or university.

2. Provide information about broader norms and values of American society.

3. What do the two lists above tell you about the dominant or distinctive features of American culture?

4. If your survival manual were not available to these foreign students, how might they acquire the information that you provided?

Exercise 3

The distinction between ethnocentrism and cultural relativism is easy to make in the abstract, but often it becomes difficult to apply in particular cases. This exercise asks you to consider the behavior patterns listed below *first* from an ethnocentric perspective and *then* from a cultural relativist perspective. That is, evaluate the behavior pattern first from the perspective of your own values and beliefs and then from the presumed values and beliefs of someone (or some society) that engages in that behavior. For any of these behavior patterns, can you make the case that your ethnocentric evaluation should be more universal? That is, can you devise a set of principles (values, knowledge) that might convince anyone in any society that *your* evaluation of the behavior is the "right" or the "best" one?

1. Genocide of a racial or ethnic minority.

2. Spitting in public places.

3. Control of television programming by the government.

4. Permanent elimination of all nuclear weapons.

5. Homosexual relationships between consenting adults.

6. Free health care to all who need it.

7. Theft of a book from a university library.

8. Permanent lifetime employment at one corporation or organization.

Chapter 4
INTERACTION AND SOCIAL STRUCTURE

OBJECTIVES

After reading Chapter 4, you should understand the following main points and be able to answer the objectives.

1. Social interaction is the process of people orienting themselves to others and acting in response to each other's behavior.
    1.1   Summarize the four social forces that transcend the intentions and desires of individuals.
    1.2   Use the example of the job seeker to illustrate the relationship between interaction and social structure.
    1.3   Compare micro and macro levels of sociological analysis.
    1.4   Define social interaction.
    1.5   Show how social interaction is affected by patterns of social structure and culture.

2. Sociologists are mainly interested in the meanings that people give to their social interactions.
    2.1   Describe how social interaction is shaped by shared knowledge.
    2.2   Discuss processes of defining the situation; give several examples.
    2.3   Explain the significance of the Thomas theorem.
    2.4   Outline the role of the negotiated order when considering definitions of the situation.

3. Four theoretical orientations have been used to examine social interaction: symbolic interaction, the dramaturgical approach, ethnomethodology, and social exchange.
    3.1   Describe symbolic interaction, especially the importance of symbolic gestures and role-taking.
    3.2   Discuss the advantages and disadvantages of Goffman's dramaturgical approach, especially the role of impression management.
    3.3   Define ethnomethodology; describe an ethnomethodological experiment.
    3.4   Discuss the social exchange perspective and show how it is rooted in rational-choice theory.
    3.5   Evaluate these four theoretical perspectives on social interaction.

4. Networks are webs of relationships among a set of people who are linked together, directly or indirectly, through their various communications and dealings.
    4.1   Define network and social relationships.
    4.2   Describe how sociologists study nodes and ties in networks.
    4.3   Use the example of a job search to illustrate the sociological importance of networks.
    4.4   Define the following characteristics of social networks: density, reachability, range and centrality.

4.5 Explain how networks translate small-scale interaction into large-scale structures.

4.6 Summarize the role of power in networks.

5. Statuses and roles are part of the structure of society; they define behavior expected of people in different circumstances.

5.1 Define status and status set; give examples.

5.2 Give examples of the following kinds of statuses: ascribed, achieved, master, salient.

5.3 Define role; give several examples.

5.4 Define role set and differentiate role strain from role conflict.

6. Patterns of heterogeneity and inequality in the large-scale society significantly affect individuals' choices and their interactions.

6.1 Explain the usefulness of a social structural focus.

6.2 Describe two patterns of social distribution: heterogeneity and inequality.

6.3 Discuss how heterogeneity and inequality affect social integration.

6.4 Define society and social institution.

6.5 List the functions served by social institutions.

6.6 Compare the functional and power perspectives on social structure.

CHAPTER SUMMARY

1. What is social interaction?

Social action is shaped by several social forces that go beyond the intentions and desires of individuals. First, all interactions are ordered by socially defined expectations about how people should act in a given situation. Second, social behavior is ordered by the characteristics that people bring to an interaction. Third, interpersonal connections--networks--also shape social behavior. Finally, social interactions occur within a much broader social structural context, which also affects their direction and outcome. In examining social forces, sociologists employ two basic approaches, microsociology and macrosociology. *Microsociology* examines small-scale, everyday patterns of behavior and face-to-face interactions. *Macrosociology* examines large-scale social arrangements, focusing on their structure and their long-term effects. Some topics, such as the webs of relationships called networks, are examined from an approach that lies between these two.

Social interaction is the process of people orienting themselves to others and acting in response to each other's behavior. The fact that this process is social means that more than one person is involved; the fact that it is interaction means that all parties are influencing one another. People interact with others in order to accomplish some goal; their behavior in such interactions is always directed toward specific other people. Power differences may affect social interaction, particularly in competitive or coercive situations. Social interaction is influenced very strongly by social structure and culture.

2. How do processes of defining the situation affect social interaction?

Social interaction always occurs in some setting, but the meaning of that setting must be defined by the participants. The shared knowledge that we have internalized provides us with a sound basis for people knowing what is expected of us and helps us to make sense of a particular situation. The sociologist W. I. Thomas said that if people "define situations as real, they are real in their consequences." This observation, which became known as the Thomas theorem, says that once we define a situation, that definition determines not only our actions but also the consequences of our actions.

Many social situations that we experience are at least somewhat ambiguous. Hence we often test our actions and modify them on the basis of the feedback we receive in our struggle to produce a more precise collective definition of what is going on. The *negotiated order* approach suggests that shared expectations impose limits on interactions, but these limits are not immutable. There is room for improvisation and negotiation. However, negotiations often create new rules that in turn impose constraints on future interactions.

3. What are the four sociological views on interaction processes?

When two people are engaged in face-to-face conversation, they are involved in social interaction. In their interactions with others, people influence one another's attitudes, feelings, and behavior. How do people create a shared social world through these social interactions? Sociologists have developed four perspectives on this question.

First, *symbolic interactionism* suggests that people achieve interaction by using symbols to convey common meanings attributed to events or objects. According to George Herbert Mead and his followers, the meaning of social reality is constructed through symbolic interaction. The meaning of a *symbolic gesture* extends beyond the act itself. The same gesture or phrase can have different meanings in different social contexts. One important part of social interaction is *role-taking*: we often put ourselves in the place of those with whom we interact, and thus come to know their feelings and intentions more clearly. The role-taking process allows us to anticipate other people's response to a contemplated action: sometimes we choose not to act in a certain way because in anticipating the response of other participants, we decide that this response is not desired. According to Mead and other symbolic interactionists, we play out roles in our mind before we speak, as we imagine how others are likely to respond.

Second, in the *dramaturgical approach* of Erving Goffman, life is viewed as a theatrical performance with "actors" following "scripts" (or roles) on various "stages." According to Goffman, this "performance" is a process of managing the impressions that one hopes to make on others. Different behavior occurs in different regions of social space, as people try to create impressions that are appropriate for one occasion or another. The goal of the dramaturgical approach is to reveal the images that people create as they present a carefully constructed "self" to others in social interaction.

Third, *ethnomethodology* exposes the taken-for-granted routine assumptions that allow people to create order in everyday activities. Ethnomethodology is an attempt to understand how people make sense of their social interactions. Harold Garfinkel reveals the assumptions governing routine behavior by devising experiments that intentionally violate these assumptions. At moments when the expected social world seems to break down, we can appreciate the unstated, often unnoticed, rules that ordinarily hold it together.

Fourth, *social exchange* theorists such as Blau and Homans see social interactions as rational calculations of mutually beneficial transactions: "You scratch my back and I'll scratch yours." Social exchange theory is a form of rational choice theory, which holds that people weigh the anticipated gains and losses before choosing a course of behavior. However, the rational choice model does not adequately explain such apparently irrational behavior as love. Homans and others draw on the school of psychology known as *behaviorism* to explain the emotional and habitual aspects of social interaction. According to this perspective, people tend to repeat behavior for which they have been rewarded in the past and to avoid behavior for which they have been punished. The combination of rational choice and operant conditioning helps to shape many patterns of social interaction.

4. What are networks, and why are they important for understanding social interaction and social structure?

Most people have many different kinds of relationships with many different people. The people whom we know and interact with regularly also interact among themselves to some extent. This web of social relationships among people who are linked together (directly or indirectly) through their various communications and dealings is called a *network*. Without much effort, you can draw pictures of the networks to which you belong. Our linkages and connections, the networks in which we participate, influence our opportunities.

Sociologists have developed several useful conceptual tools to examine social networks. The units involved in these networks are usually individual people, and are known as *nodes*. Nodes also can be collective actors such as groups and organizations. The *ties* connecting these nodes can also vary from network to network. Ties can vary in content (such as degree of friendship and frequency of interaction), strength (stronger ties involve more frequent contact), reciprocity (the degree to which people list each other as important), and symmetry (the equivalence of nodes in such characteristics as age, education, and sex).

How do networks as a whole differ from one another? They may vary in terms of *size*, the number of nodes in a network. They may vary in *density*, the ratio of actual ties to all possible ties (or whether all possible connections are "filled"). They may vary in *reachability*, the number of direct ties through which a person must pass to reach any other node in the network. They may vary in *range*, a given person's absolute number of ties with others in the network. They may vary in *centrality*, the proportion of all possible links a person actually has made.

Social power also plays a role in networks. Power is not an attribute of an individual, but of a social relationship. Because most social relationships in a network involve the exchange of valued items, differences in power among those in a network depend on the degree to which some of those persons control valued resources. Control of valued resources depends largely on where a person is located in the network.

5. What are the elements of social structure?

A *social status* is any position in the social structure that determines where a person fits into the organized whole of a group, organization, or society. Most social statuses contain varying levels of power as well as of rights, responsibilities, and interests. Everyone occupies several different statuses at any given time; a *status set* reflects the full array of these positions.

Sociologists are interested in how people move into social statuses. *Ascribed statuses*, such as being male or female, are assigned to people without any effort on their part. *Achieved status* is a position that one attains through personal effort (such as an occupation). These two statuses are frequently linked because what people achieve is shaped partly by their ascribed characteristics. A *master status* is a particular status (either ascribed or achieved) that determines many of a person's other statuses and shapes his or her identity throughout life. A *salient status* is a social position that dominates in a particular social context.

Every status carries a socially prescribed *role*--a set of expected behaviors, obligations, and privileges. People learn how to play their roles by watching and interacting with others in a process known as *socialization*. Roles are not straitjackets, however. Individuals are free to interpret the roles they play, and to give them their own personal styles. Roles also change over time.

Roles exist in relation to each other. A single status may involve several roles, known as a *role set*. People occasionally have difficulty in meeting the obligations of a role set. *Role strain* occurs when the obligations of a role associated with a single status are too demanding for an individual's resources. *Role conflict*, on the other hand, occurs when as a result of competing or incompatible demands and roles stemming from two different social statuses. When role strain or role conflict becomes so great that people leave one or more of their social statuses, *role exit* occurs: this is the process of disengaging from a role that was central to one's identity, redefining relationships with former role-set partners, ceasing to think of oneself in the former role, and reestablishing an identity in a new role.

The number of people occupying different statuses in a population is another critical element of social structure that influences social interaction. The overall composition of a population creates opportunities for, and places limits on, the formation of social relationships. Societies differ in their degree of heterogeneity and inequality. *Heterogeneity* reflects how the population is distributed among such categories as sex, race, religion, and ethnicity. *Inequality* reflects how people are ranked by wealth, income, or power. A high degree of heterogeneity may promote intergroup relations, such as intermarriages. When more people are spread more evenly among a variety of categories, more opportunities exist for contact with people from different categories. Such contact may develop into social relationships. The degree of inequality in a population also affects social relations among people of different social classes.

A *society* is an autonomous group of people who inhabit a common territory, have a common culture, and are linked to one another through routinized social interactions and interdependent statuses and roles. Many sociologists have considered what integrates a society. Some believe that *functional integration* among social institutions is important. A *social institution* includes the behavior patterns and status/role relationships that fulfill certain basic societal needs. Social institutions serve several functions: reproducing new members and teaching them the customs and beliefs shared by those who live in their world (the role of the family), mobilizing scarce resources to produce the goods and services that people want (economic institutions), protecting people from external threats (political institutions), teaching people about certain statuses and roles (educational institutions), motivating people to perform their roles by giving life meaning and purpose (religious institutions), and acquiring and communicating new knowledge and using knowledge to obtain raw materials and transform them into usable goods (the institutions of science and technology). Some sociologists believe that functional integration occurs when all these institutions are doing their jobs. Others believe that societies never function smoothly because conflict is an inherent feature in societies. Sociologists generally agree, however, that institutions serve as important centers of change within societies. Both the shape of social institutions and the relationships between them have changed over time. More important, social institutions are a major source of continuity and stability in societies.

REVIEW OF CONCEPTS

Match the concept with the definition.

Concepts

a. achieved status
b. ascribed status
c. dramaturgical approach
d. ethnomethodology
e. impression management
f. macrosociology
g. master status
h. microsociology
i. negotiated order

j. network
k. nodes
l. role
m. role conflict
n. role exit
o. role set
p. role strain
q. role-taking
r. salient status

s. social institutions
t. social interaction
u. social relationships
v. social status
w. society
x. status set
y. symbolic gesture

Definitions

_____ 1. The clash between two competing roles.

_____ 2. The process of people orienting themselves to others and acting in response to each other's behavior.

_____ 3. Erving Goffman's term for the efforts people make to control how others see and respond to them.

_____ 4. A position in a social structure that determines where a person fits within the social order.

_____ 5. The large-scale analysis of sociological data derived from studies of the structure and effects of overall social arrangements.

_____ 6. The web of relationships among a set of people who are linked together, directly or indirectly, through their various communications and dealings.

_____ 7. A status that a person attains largely through personal effort.

_____ 8. The small-scale analysis of data derived from studies of everyday behavior and face-to-face social interaction.

_____ 9. A shared definition of a situation arrived at by "testing out" actions and modifying them based on feedback from others.

_____ 10. A sociological perspective that views social interaction as resembling a theatrical performance in which people "stage" their behavior in such a way as to elicit the responses they desire from other people.

_____ 11. The status of a person that largely determines his or her social identity.

_____ 12. Difficulty in meeting the obligations of a role associated with a single social status.

_____ 13. A status assigned to people without effort on their part.

_____ 14. The process of disengaging from a role that was central to a person's identity.

_____ 15. A viewpoint on social interaction developed by Harold Garfinkel that focuses on the ways in which people make sense of everyday interaction.

_____ 16. A status that dominates in a certain social context.

_____ 17. Patterned behaviors and status/role relationships that fulfill basic societal needs.

_____ 18. The connected social units within a social network.

_____ 19. Relatively enduring patterns of interaction between two or more people.

_____ 20. A set of behaviors, attitudes, obligations, and privileges expected of anyone who occupies a particular status.

_____ 21. The cluster of different roles associated with a particular status.

1.	m	8.	h	15.	d
2.	t	9.	i	16.	r
3.	e	10.	c	17.	s
4.	v	11.	g	18.	k
5.	f	12.	p	19.	u
6.	j	13.	b	20.	l
7.	a	14.	n	21.	o

REVIEW QUESTIONS

After studying Chapter 4, answer the following questions. The correct answers are listed at the end of the questions; each is followed by a short explanation. You are also referred to pages in the textbook for relevant discussion.

1. Which one of the following is *not* one of the social forces affecting social action?
   a. Interactions are ordered by socially defined expectation about behavior.
   b. Social behavior is ordered by the characteristics people bring to an interaction.
   c. Interpersonal connections shape social behavior.
   d. Interactions occur within a broader social structural context.
   e. Social behavior is very much determined by instinctive influences.

2. Which of the following is an example of the microsocial level of analysis?
   a. institutionalized racism
   b. hierarchy of wages
   c. stereotypes
   d. the political system
   e. interaction among people at a bar

3. Which of the following is a *false* statement about social interaction?
   a. Social interaction can occur without the exchange of words.
   b. Behavior in social interaction is always framed by socially defined expectations.
   c. Social interaction is purposive.
   d. Power differences exist in social relationships
   e. Social interaction is often complementary or cooperative but seldom competitive or coercive.

4. Which sociological perspective on interaction processes would be most interested in how people size up a situation before charting a course of action?
   a. dramaturgy
   b. social exchange
   c. symbolic interaction
   d. macrosocial perspective
   e. ethnomethodology

5. A man dyes his hair green and pink before he goes to a local punk hangout. This concern for creating a certain impression would be of greatest interest to which perspective on interaction processes?

a. the dramaturgical approach
b. social exchange
c. symbolic interaction
d. macrosocial perspective
e. ethnomethodology

6. A maitre d' at a fancy French restaurant accidentally burps while seating guests at a table. Although the burp is audible to everyone, no one says anything or looks at the maitre d'. This example illustrates
   a. opportunity structure.
   b. studied nonobservance.
   c. backstage region.
   d. deniable communication.
   e. social exchange.

7. The ethnomethodological perspective is best illustrated by which of the following?
   a. attempts to upset routine behavior by intentionally violating taken-for-granted rules of everyday life
   b. the idea that social interaction is a series of reciprocal and mutually beneficial exchanges
   c. people trying to control potentially embarrassing situations through impression management
   d. people "testing out" their behavior and modifying it in accord with feedback from others
   e. The idea that the meanings imputed to events or settings determine the kind of behavior that people will choose.

8. Joe arranged a date for his roommate Jim; a short while later, Jim helped Joe study for a sociology exam. This exchange illustrates
   a. an institution.
   b. impression management.
   c. opportunity structure.
   d. a norm of reciprocity.
   e. defining the situation.

9. Becky went to a party and upon arrival she decided that the other people there thought of her as inferior to them. She then found herself acting in an "inferior" manner--spilling her drink, using improper grammar, and having little to say. Which of the following does this example best reflect?
   a. the Thomas theorem
   b. symbolic gestures
   c. role-taking
   d. reciprocity
   e. impression management

10. Women tilt their heads more than do men when speaking to someone in an authority position. The tilt often reflects deference. Which one of the following does this example reflect?
    a. negotiated order
    b. social gesture
    c. role strain
    d. impression management
    e. ethnomethodology

11. When he looked for a job, Karl went to his father, who in turn went to a business colleague, who in turn went to a salesman, who in turn went to a secretary at a company that had a vacancy. Karl had to cover four steps or links to reach the secretary at the company with the job opening. This story illustrates which property of social networks?
    a. density
    b. heterogeneity
    c. reachability
    d. inequality
    e. range

12. Network analysis would be appropriate for investigating all *but* which one of the following?
    a. study of how "connections" (who you know) help people find jobs
    b. definition of the situation by two people involved in a job interview
    c. analysis of the bridge between the micro and macro levels of analysis
    d. exploration of how various resources (such as information, influence, money) flow from individual to individual
    e. examination of links among corporations in a certain industry

13. "Female" is an example of
    a. a status.
    b. a single role.
    c. an institution.
    d. a network.
    e. a society.

14. Which is the best example of an ascribed status?
    a. income
    b. educational attainment
    c. marital status
    d. race
    e. religion

15. When you walk into the classroom, the status of student becomes most important for determining your behavior and interactions. This situation illustrates which of the following concepts?
    a. salient status
    b. role strain
    c. master status
    d. ascribed status
    e. opportunity structure

16. A teacher's obligation to lecture students on interesting and useful topics is an example of
    a. a status.
    b. a single role.
    c. role set.
    d. opportunity structure.
    e. master status.

17. Which of the following is a *false* statement about social roles?
    a. We learn roles through socialization.
    b. Roles are not cast in stone; within certain limits, people are free to interpret the roles they

play.
c. Roles exist in relation to other roles.
d. Sometimes the obligations associated with a role are too demanding for a person's resources.
e. The set of roles in a status makes consistent demands and expectations.

18. Sam is an elementary school teacher whose own child is sick today. He's trying to decide whether to stay home with his child or go to school and teach his pupils. This example reflects
    a. role strain
    b. role conflict
    c. role-taking
    d. role overload
    e. role exit

19. Some sociologists search for ways in which large-scale social patterns contribute to the integration of society and to its smooth operation. Which perspective is this?
    a. structural
    b. action
    c. dramaturgical
    d. functional
    e. power

20. According to Peter Blau's theory of social distribution, which of the following conditions is most likely to increase rates of intergroup marriage?
    a. low heterogeneity
    b. high homogeneity
    c. low inequality
    d. high heterogeneity
    e. values and motivations that urge people to marry those from different social backgrounds

21. Which is *not* a need that every society must confront?
    a. to teach new members the customs, beliefs, and values shared by those in the society
    b. to mobilize scarce resources in order to produce and distribute goods and services
    c. to create a government that is responsive to the needs of all people
    d. to protect people from external threats of invasion
    e. to motivate people to perform social roles by giving their lives meaning and purpose

22. All societies must teach people about certain roles and statuses, especially those that pertain to being a citizen and a worker. Which specialized institution performs this function?
    a. the family
    b. economic institutions
    c. political institutions
    d. educational institutions
    e. religious institutions

Answers

1. *e.* Social action is not determined by instincts, but by the social structures and contexts within which action occurs. See page 76.
2. *e* The micro (or small-scale) level of analysis focuses on small details of face-to-face interac-

52

tion. The other choices illustrate macrosocial analysis of large-scale structures of societies as a whole. See page 77.

3. *e.* Social interaction is often competitive or coercive, such as in work settings. See page 77.

4. *c.* Symbolic interactionists like George Herbert Mead look at the meanings that people attach to various objects and events and at the symbols they use to convey these meanings to others. Mead emphasized that during social interaction, we mentally play out a role by anticipating responses of others to different courses of behavior; we choose the behavior most likely to achieve the response we desire. See pages 80-81.

5. *a.* The dramaturgical perspective views social interaction as resembling a theatrical performance in which people "stage" their behavior in order to create a certain impression of themselves for others. In this case, hair dye was part of his "makeup." See pages 81-82.

6. *b.* Goffman says that people involved in a social interaction are motivated to support each other's presentation of self. The customers pretend not to notice an unexpected behavior that is clearly not part of the frontstage role of maitre d'. Such studied nonobservance allows all participants to proceed successfully with their collective performance. See page 82.

7. *a.* Garfinkel's ethnomethodological experiments deliberately violate taken-for-granted assumptions in order to show how people come to grasp shared understandings that provide order to their interactions. See pages 84-85.

8. *d.* According to the social exchange perspective, the norm of reciprocity stipulates that we should give and receive equivalently in our interactions with others: "You scratch my back and I'll scratch yours." See pages 85-86.

9. *a.* Since Becky defined the situation as real, it became real in its consequences. This is known as the Thomas theorem. See page 79.

10. *b.* Tilting one's head is a social gesture--the meaning of the gesture (deference) extends beyond the gesture itself. See page 80.

11. *c.* Reachability refers to the number of steps required for any person in a network to reach someone else in that network. See page 89.

12. *b.* Network analysis has little to say about how people in interaction define their situation. Instead, network analysis explores patterns in the link or relationships among people, and attempts to show how those patterns affect behavior and opportunities of members of the network (whether these are individuals or "collective" units such as corporations). See page 89.

13. *a.* "Female" is a position in a social structure; thus it is a social status. Social statuses determine where people "fit" in a society. See page 92.

14. *d.* An ascribed status is assigned to people without effort on their part. Usually, ascribed statuses are assigned at birth and are not easily changed in the course of a lifetime. The other answers given as choices are achieved statuses. See page 93.

15. *a.* The salient status is that which dominates behavior and interaction in a certain social context. When the student leaves the classroom and goes to the bowling alley with friends, the status of student is less important as a determinant of behavior in that setting. See page 93.

16. *b.* A social role is a set of behaviors, attitudes, obligations, and privileges expected of anyone who occupies a particular status. The correct choice is one part of the role set (or status) of teacher. See page 94.

17. *e.* Role conflict occurs when carrying out the demands of one role makes it impossible to carry out the demands of another. See page 95.

18. *b.* Sam is experiencing conflict between his role of parent and his role of teacher. Since two different social statuses are involved, he is experiencing role conflict. See page 95.

19. *d.* The functional integration approach examines the consequences of behavior and social institutions for the perpetuation of the social order. Sociologists who adopt the functionalist perspective would be most likely to ask how specialized institutions (for example, political

institutions) satisfy distinctive societal needs (in this example, the protection of people from external threats such as invasion and from internal threats such as crime). See page 97.

20. *d.* High heterogeneity means that the population is differentiated into distinctive racial, ethnic, religious, or economic groups. High rates of heterogeneity encourage people to interact with those who are different from themselves; this interaction in turn increases the likelihood of intergroup marriage. See page 96.

21. *c.* Although it is true that every society needs some form of government, some totalitarian societies have been ruled successfully by dictators who refused to listen to the needs of the people. See pages 97-98.

22. *d.* Educational institutions are charged with the responsibility of equipping people with the values and skills necessary for performing successfully the roles of citizen and worker. Societal integration depends on the ability of specialized institutions--such as educational systems--to meet such basic needs. See page 98.

EXERCISES

Exercise 1

A status is a position in a social structure that determines where a person fits within the social order. In face-to-face interaction, we tell other people what statuses we occupy by means of certain visual cues. Some cues are almost impossible to hide; in American society it is difficult to hide your race, sex, and (possibly) age. Such ascribed characteristics are often the ones most visible to others. We also communicate achieved statuses by using a variety of visual cues, some intentional and others unintentional. To gain a sense of the range of visual cues of social statuses, collect magazines and newspapers on different subjects, choosing those that contain many advertisements with pictures of people.

1. Select a variety of photographs from different magazines. For each one, make a list of the social statuses occupied by the person in the picture.

2. Try to summarize your findings by dividing the visible statuses into ascribed and achieved. Are any of the statuses likely to serve as the subject's master status? Which ones? Why?

3. What kinds of social statuses are typically *impossible* to tell only from a photograph?

4. If your magazines are directed to very different audiences (such as *True Confessions* and *Sports Illustrated*), compare the kinds of visual cues of social status that turn up frequently in each type of magazine.

5. How are these status cues manipulated in order to sell certain products?

Exercise 2

Find a public place on your campus that is busy with social interaction--a place where people meet to talk in small groups. It might be at a student union, in a dorm cafeteria, or in the hallway of a classroom building. Without being intrusive, watch carefully the patterns of social interaction of small groups containing *both males and females*.

1. Who typically initiates social interaction, males or females? Who typically ends it?

2. Are there differences between males and females in how long each "holds the floor" (dominates the conversation)?

3. Compare males and females in terms of gestures and language style.

4. Now examine groups made up of *either all males or all females*. How do patterns of social interaction in same-sex groups differ from those in mixed groups?

5. Does this analysis of face-to-face interaction tell you anything about the expectations associated with gender roles in contemporary American society?

Exercise 3

This exercise is based on data from the U.S. Bureau of the Census.

	1970	1980	1986
Total married couples	44,597,000	49,714,000	51,704,000
Interracial married couples	310,000	651,000	827,000

1. What would you do to determine whether the *rate* (or proportion) of interracial married couples has increased or decreased between 1970 and 1986?

2. Formulate several hypotheses ("hunches") about the changing rate of interracial marriage between 1970 and 1986. How would you explain the pattern suggested by the above statistics?

3. If you adopted a social structural perspective, what additional information (or data) would you collect to explain these changes?

4. If you adopted a social exchange or rational choice perspective, what additional information (or data) would you collect in order to explain these changes?

5. If you adopted a social network perspective, what additional information (or data) would you collect in order to explain these changes?

Chapter 5
SOCIALIZATION

OBJECTIVES

After reading Chapter 5, you should understand the following main points and be able to answer the objectives.

1. We learn about our social identity through social interaction with others.
   1.1 Illustrate how socialization reflects cultural values and role patterns.
   1.2 Show how societies shape their children in the image of their own culture.
   1.3 Show how socialization is linked to the five key concepts.

2. Social scientists have long debated the relative importance of biological makeup (nature) and the social environment (nurture).
   2.1 Explain the views of sociobiologists.
   2.2 Show how the environment affects inborn potential but also how inborn traits affect social interaction.
   2.3 Explain why the nature of the human animal both allows and requires socialization.
   2.4 State the implications of the research on isolation as it applies to the nature-nurture debate.
   2.5 Describe how socialization affects adults as well as children.

3. The various perspectives shed light on the socialization process.
   3.1 Define self.
   3.2 Summarize Cooley's ideas on the social origin of self, particularly his idea of the looking-glass self.
   3.3 Describe Mead's contributions regarding the effects of early social interaction on self-awareness, including his use of significant symbols.
   3.4 Describe Mead's use of the "I" and the "me."
   3.5 Explain the role of significant others in the development of self.
   3.6 Define generalized other.
   3.7 Summarize Freud's view of socialization, including his use of the id, the ego, and the superego.
   3.8 Differentiate Freud's view of socialization from those of Cooley and Mead.

4. Socialization processes vary by social class.
   4.1 Summarize the research on how values differ by social class.
   4.2 Identify a key factor responsible for class-based differences in values.

5. There are many agents of socialization.
    5.1 Differentiate intentional from unintentional socialization.
    5.2 Identify some of the specific aspects of family life that contribute to socialization.
    5.3 Identify some of the specific aspects of interactions with peers that contribute to socialization.
    5.4 Identify some cross-cultural differences in peer-group socialization.
    5.5 Identify some of the specific aspects of mass media that contribute to socialization.
    5.6 Identify some of the specific aspects of schools that contribute to socialization.

6. Adult socialization (secondary socialization) builds on primary socialization experiences.
    6.1 Illustrate how desocialization and resocialization contribute to socialization.
    6.2 Describe how desocialization and resocialization occur in total institutions.
    6.3 Describe how occupational socialization occurs.
    6.4 Summarize the rule of anticipatory socialization.

CHAPTER SUMMARY

1. What is socialization and why are sociologists interested in the socialization process?

Socialization involves instilling the basic elements of culture in a society's new members; every society shapes its children in the image of its own culture. Socialization enables people to participate effectively in their communities. There are two basic aspects of socialization. First, socialization creates individuals who are part of a human community. It enables people to live within their groups and to be effective members of the society into which they are born. Second, socialization is the process by which a society reproduces itself in a new generation. It helps transmit the values and traditions of the past to the next generation.

2. How important are nature and nurture for socialization?

Many years ago some scientists argued that infants are blank slates and that their experiences determine who we become; experience cannot change what nature ordained. Today scientists recognize that both factors are essential; the interaction between biological and environmental forces determines the development of a human being.

Sociobiologists argue that biological factors establish the basic blueprint for human development. They believe that humans have evolved behavioral traits that help them survive and flourish. Most sociologists reject the extreme claims of sociobiologists and instead believe that environmental pressures tend to encourage different forms of human social action.

Certain traits are fixed genetically, such as hair color and sex. In most cases, however, genes do not dictate how a child will develop, but instead establish a range of possible outcomes. How much of a child's potential is realized depends on the environment.

Personality development reveals a particularly complex pattern of gene-environmental interactions. Personality includes the characteristic modes of thinking, feeling, and acting that individuals develop because of experience. Most studies of gene-environment interaction focus on how the environment affects inborn potentials, but studies of *temperament* (behavioral predispositions) show how inborn traits affect social interaction. That is, children with different temperaments evoke different responses from other people and can cause children to seek or avoid activities. In short, biology provides the raw material for development, but experience shapes that raw material. This interaction of genes and environment also contributes to culture through the development of shared patterns of social behavior.

The nature of the human animal both allows and requires socialization. Human babies are very helpless; therefore they must learn a great deal from experience. Evidence for the importance of socialization comes from extreme situations in which infants and young children were isolated. Finally, the effects of socialization are felt not only by children but also by their parents and by others; immigrants are particularly likely to feel the effects of socialization.

3. Which perspectives and theorists help us understand socialization?

Charles Horton Cooley (1864-1929) was one of the first theorists to consider the social origins of self. The self is the notion that each individual has a unique and distinct identity; it emerges from interactions with others. Cooley developed the idea of the *looking-glass self*: we acquire our sense of self by seeing ourselves reflected in other people's attitudes and behaviors toward us and by imagining what they think of us. The looking-glass self has three parts: 1) what we imagine others see in us, 2) how we imagine they judge what they see, and 3) how we feel about those judgements. The looking-glass self, then, is a mixture of observation, imagination, and subjective interpretation. Perhaps most important, it is a social construction. Cooley also distinguished primary relationships (family and close friends) from secondary relationships (casual acquaintances).

George Herbert Mead (1863-1931) traced the development of self-awareness to early social interaction. He stressed the use of *significant symbols*, the signs, gestures, and language used to interact with others. Through symbolic interaction, children learn to anticipate what others expect and to evaluate and adjust their own behavior accordingly. Mead believed that the self includes two parts: the "I" and the "me." The "I" is the active, spontaneous, idiosyncratic self, and is the product of individual distinctiveness. The "me" is the social self, a product of socialization. Together these two elements help to define an identity--the self.

Regarding the development of a "me," Mead proposed that this aspect of the self develops in early childhood as a result of role-playing. Children frequently take the roles of people who are important in their social world (significant others). As they mature, they begin to move from simple play involving one role to games involving the interaction of many roles. Eventually they see themselves as part of society and internalize the standards, attitudes, and beliefs of parents and others. Mead referred to this internalized sense of self as the *generalized other*.

Perhaps the theory of socialization with the greatest impact is that of Sigmund Freud (1856-1939). In his view, socialization is a lifelong battle among three forces: the id, the ego, and the superego. The *id* is a reservoir of innate biological drives aimed at obtaining physical pleasure. The *ego* is the rational part of the self which mediates between the id and reality. The *superego* reflects the conscience and embodies the moral standards of society. Freud thought that the ego's job was to find safe ways to satisfy the id without causing guilt to the superego. All three of these parts strive for control. People are not born with an ego or a superego; these components develop through social interaction. Although Cooley and Mead viewed socialization as the gradual merger of the individual and society, Freud viewed it as a constant battle between society and a person's biological inclinations and drives.

4. How does socialization vary by social class?

Values regarding socialization vary by social class. Melvin Kohn has studied this area and has identified consistent class differences and values. Those in the higher social classes are more likely to value traits that involve self-direction, while those in the lower social classed are more likely to value traits that involve conformity to external authority. As a consequence, working-class parents emphasize manners, neatness, being a good student and obedience. Middle-class parents emphasize consideration, interest in explaining why things happen, responsibility, and self-control. The first set of traits stressed conformity to an external authority; the second stresses conformity to one's own internal standards.

Behaviors also differ by social class. Because working-class parents value conformity, they focus on the immediate consequences of a child's actions. In contrast, middle-class parents are more likely to be concerned with children's motives than with the actions as such.

Kohn believes that class-based differences in values and behaviors emerge from parents' work experiences. Work that provides opportunities for independent thought and initiative fosters middle-class values, while work that restricts these opportunities fosters working-class values. Hence success in the working-class world depends on following procedures and orders, while success in the middle-class world depends more on autonomous thinking.

5. How does the family act as an agent of socialization?

The family is perhaps the most important source of socialization, given its central role in the early developmental period. It plays this central role because it introduces children to intimate relationships and gives them their first experience of being treated as distinct individuals. In essence, the family is the child's first reference group, the first group whose norms and values the child adopts as his or her own and uses to evaluate his or her behavior. The family also introduces children to group life.

Several factors in family life affect socialization. For example, fathers and mothers have different parental styles. Fathers tend toward physical play and unfamiliar games, while mothers tend toward vocal interaction and familiar games. The number of siblings and the birth order also have substantial effects. Interactions with siblings enable children to learn about cooperation and conflict as well as negotiation and bargaining. Finally, the family introduces the child into society, helping him or her to find an identity in the larger social world.

6. How do other agents of socialization operate?

Sociologists have long recognized that peers play a critical role in children's initiation to society. Peer groups provide experience with egalitarian relationships. The absence of a power imbalance enables peers to teach other skills and to provide resources in ways in which parents frequently cannot. Children select peers; they do not select their parents. This selection opportunity enables children and young adults to test some of their preferences for certain types of friends. Peers also teach each other about subjects that adults consider sensitive or taboo (such as sex) and develop their own distinctive norms and values. During adolescence the influence of peers increases, while the influence of parents decreases. Adolescents often experience conflict with the power and expectations of their parents and other adults. However, adolescents generally remain responsive to their parents' desires regarding goals and values. Peer values generally reinforce parental values. Cross-cultural research has highlighted differences in peer group socialization in different societies.

Children are exposed increasingly to a variety of mass media. The media play a substantial role in contemporary socialization and have become increasingly important over the last several decades. Children in the United States today spend more time watching television than in school. Parents as well as others have become increasingly concerned with the role of television and other mass media, but a review of the research on the impact of television on children yields mixed results. Generally the research shows that watching programs which emphasize positive values often stimulates positive behaviors, whereas viewing violence and other negative types of programs encourages aggression and other types of negative behaviors. At a minimum, it is clear that television can have a major effect in that children interact with television in much the same way as they interact with other elements in their social environment.

Education has become an increasingly important source of socialization in the last century as society became less rural and more urban. School serves as a transition point between the home and the adult world. Schools teach certain official values (such as intellectual skills), but they also include a hidden curriculum that teaches useful skills (such as how to live in a bureaucratic setting). Success in school depends largely on how well students learn to play the role of student. Recently, schools have started changing the traditional structure of education to enhance cooperative problem solving and group efforts.

7. What role does socialization play in adulthood?

Adult socialization can take several forms. Some life transitions simply build on existing norms, values, and roles; others require *resocialization* or the internalization of an alternative set of norms and values. For example, army recruits and mental patients must be resocialized to their new roles. *Desocialization* requires stripping oneself of the self-image and values acquired previously and replacing them with a new outlook and self-image. The example of college athletes noted in the text shows that the processes of resocialization do not necessarily benefit individuals or society.

Total institutions, such as prisons, are organizations that deliberately close themselves off from the outside world and lead a very insular life that is formally organized and tightly controlled. Newcomers to total institutions undergo *mortification*: they are stripped of clothes and personal possessions and are given standard clothing. They perform meaningless tasks, endure abuse and are deprived of privacy. These procedures are designed to destroy newcomers' feelings of self-worth and to prepare them for deference to their superiors.

Occupational socialization involves learning the norms, values, and beliefs appropriate for a new occupation or organization. Considerable variation occurs in the type and extent of occupational socialization. People often prepare themselves for a new work role through *anticipatory socialization*, the alterations in values and perceptions that people experience when they know they will experience a significant change in social roles. Some organizations expect almost complete resocialization, while others expect much less. Whether one is socialized individually or in groups also makes a difference.

Socialization into a first major job often involves four tasks: 1) coming to terms with the organization, 2) learning to cope with resistance to change within the organization, 3) resolving ambiguity in one's job, and 4) learning how to get ahead. Employees' levels of involvement affect the extent to which they internalize the values of a particular organization or occupation.

REVIEW OF CONCEPTS

Match the concept with the definition.

Concepts

a. anticipatory socialization
b. desocialization
c. ego
d. generalized other
e. id
f. looking-glass self

g. mortification
h. occupational socialization
i. resocialization
j. self
k. significant others
l. significant symbols

m. socialization
n. sociobiologists
o. superego
p. temperament
q. total institutions

Definitions

____ 1. Goffman's term for the process of desocialization that occurs in total institutions.

____ 2. The notion held by each of us that we possess a unique and distinct identity--that we are set apart from other objects and people.

_____ 3. The process of shedding one's self-image and values; usually followed by resocialization to a different set of values.

_____ 4. According to Sigmund Freud, the rational part of the self that finds socially acceptable ways of satisfying biological cravings.

_____ 5. Organizations deliberately closed off from the outside world where behavior is tightly controlled.

_____ 6. Freud's term for the conscience, the part of the personality that internalizes the society's views of right and wrong.

_____ 7. The mental rehearsals, concrete plans, and changes in beliefs, norms and values that individuals use to prepare for a significant change in social roles.

_____ 8. An internalized general impression of what society as a whole expects.

_____ 9. Scientists who hold that humans have certain genetically evolved behavioral traits that provide a survival advantage and so have tended to endure.

_____ 10. Cooley's term to explain how others influence the way we see ourselves. We gain an image of ourselves by imagining what other people think about our appearance and behavior.

_____ 11. People who are emotionally important in one's life.

_____ 12. The behavioral predisposition with which a child is born.

_____ 13. Freud's term for the reservoir of innate biological drives, aimed at obtaining physical pleasure.

_____ 14. The internalization of a new and different set of norms and values.

_____ 15. According to Mead, conventionalized gestures and words acquired in infancy and early childhood that arouse desired responses in others and make social interaction possible.

_____ 16. The process by which new members of a society are instilled with the fundamental elements of their culture; the means by which we become members of human society.

_____ 17. The process of aligning the norms, values, and beliefs of a new worker with those of the organization or occupation.

Answers

1.	g	7.	a	13.	e
2.	j	8.	d	14.	i
3.	b	9.	n	15.	l
4.	c	10.	f	16.	m
5.	q	11.	k	17.	h
6.	o	12.	p		

REVIEW QUESTIONS

After studying Chapter 5, answer the following questions. The correct answers are listed at the end of the questions; each is followed by a short explanation. You are also referred to pages in the text-book for relevant discussion.

1. Which one of the following statements portrays most accurately the relationship between heredity and environment?
   a. Biology is more important than environment.
   b. Environment is more important than biology.
   c. Biology sets the basic blueprint for human development.
   d. Environment sets the basic blueprint for human development.
   e. It is difficult to determine the effects of biology and environment.

2. Sociobiologists maintain that
   a. people are simply animals.
   b. people have evolved physical characteristics to enhance survival.
   c. people have evolved behavioral traits to enhance survival.
   d. human infants are basically a blank slate waiting to be written on.
   e. sociology and biology should merge to form a new discipline.

3. Studies of early childhood isolation have shown that
   a. physical isolation often speeds up the development process.
   b. there is little difference between animals and human beings raised in isolation and those raised with normal contact.
   c. isolation has serious consequences for development in other species, but human beings can survive isolation with no serious consequences.
   d. human contact is an essential part of human development.
   e. the effects of isolation vary by social class and length of isolation.

4. Cooley believed that the looking-glass self involves
   a. imagining how we look to others.
   b. imagining how we think they think we look.
   c. interpreting how we think they think we look.
   d. a and b only.
   e. a, b, and c.

5. At a hockey game, the cheer, claps, and boos of the crowd are examples of
   a. significant others.
   b. generalized others.
   c. significant symbols.
   d. sociological terms.
   e. rude behavior.

6. "I know I shouldn't go to the movie. I have homework to do. It's a week night, but why not? I'll go." Mead would say that a certain part of the self is at work here. It is
   a. the me.
   b. the significant other.
   c. the generalized other.
   d. the I.

e. the self.

7. Children develop a me, according to Mead and his followers, primarily by
    a. obeying their parents.
    b. disobeying their parents.
    c. role playing.
    d. merging the id with the ego.
    e. merging the ego with the superego.

8. An example of the looking-glass self would be
    a. a vain person.
    b. a person in a career where appearance is important, such as a model.
    c. a person who associates only with people in the same economic class.
    d. a person who feels inferior after making a mistake and being told that he or she is stupid.
    e. a person who believes everything he or she is told about himself or herself.

9. Which of the following does *not* view socialization as a gradual, complementary merger of individual and society?
    a. Cooley
    b. Mead
    c. Freud
    d. Erikson
    e. Kohlberg

10. Toilet training relates to which aspect of Freud's view of self?
    a. id
    b. me
    c. ego
    d. I
    e. superego

11. Which one of the following values does *not* characterize middle-class socialization?
    a. consideration
    b. interest in how and why things happen
    c. responsibility
    d. self-control
    e. manners

12. Kohn's research on how values and behaviors differ by social class shows that these differences are related directly to
    a. the size of the family.
    b. parents' experiences at work.
    c. the parents' experiences as children.
    d. the religion of the parents.
    e. the size of the community.

13. The most important agent of socialization is
    a. the family
    b. schools
    c. peers

d. mass media
e. religion

14. Parent try consciously to mold (socialize) their children, but
    a. much socialization is unintentional.
    b. there are other factors influencing children, such as social class, parents' education, and the like.
    c. it is not possible consciously to socialize someone.
    d. a and b.
    e. a and c.

15. The key aspect of peers as an agent of socialization that sets them apart from parents is that
    a. there are more of them.
    b. they have less authority.
    c. they provide a relationship among equals.
    d. they are more emotional.
    e. they are more willing to talk.

16. Which of the following accurately represents the relative influence of parents and peers on adolescents?
    a. adolescents generally reject their parents' preferences.
    b. adolescents generally reject their peers' preferences.
    c. peers have more influence than do parents.
    d. parents have more influence than do peers.
    e. peer values generally reinforce parental values and adolescents are responsive to both.

17. The research on the effects of television on children shows that television
    a. is watched too much.
    b. has both positive and negative effects.
    c. has positive effects but not negative effects.
    d. has negative effects but not positive effects.
    e. has no effects.

18. As job structure has changed from assembly-line jobs to those requiring independence and self-motivation, schools have changed by
    a. emphasizing cooperative problem solving and group efforts.
    b. emphasizing more freedom in the classroom.
    c. organizing schools into smaller classrooms.
    d. hiring a new type of teacher.
    e. emphasizing training for bureaucratic life.

19. A person is convicted of a crime and goes to prison, where she must learn a completely different set of norms and values. She experiences
    a. desocialization.
    b. resocialization.
    c. antisocialization.
    d. primary socialization.
    e. superego socialization.

20. Frank will become a Wall Street lawyer upon graduation next year. He practices what the new experience will be like by talking to employees and developing behaviors he thinks characterize such lawyers. Frank is experiencing
   a. regressive socialization.
   b. resocialization.
   c. desocialization.
   d. mortification.
   e. anticipatory socialization.

Answers

1. *c.* Biology sets the basic blueprint for human development in language, physical skills, and emotions. See page. 106.
2. *c.* Sociobiologists argue that humans have evolved certain behavioral traits that help them survive and flourish. See page 106.
3. *d.* Research both on institutionalized children and on a few cases of isolated children shows that children who are not handled and played with develop slowly, if at all. See page 107.
4. *e.* In the looking-glass self, we start by imagining the way we appear to others, then we identify with how we imagine others judge that appearance, and finally we interpret those judgments for our own self-image. See page 108.
5. *c.* Significant symbols are conventionalized gestures that people understand. See page 109.
6. *d.* The I is responsible for our spontaneous responses. See page 109.
7. *c.* Children develop a me--perceiving themselves as distinct persons whom others observe and judge--by role playing. Taking on the roles of significant others helps children see themselves from another person's point of view. See page 110.
8. *d.* In the looking-glass self, we interpret ourselves by imagining how we appear to others. See page 108.
9. *c.* Freud stressed the conflict between society and the biological drives of sex and aggression in his view of socialization. He also argued that socialization was forced on children. See pages 110-111.
10. *e.* The superego develops through the child's encounter with the demands of society as conveyed by his or her parents. Toilet training is just one example of how the superego is formed. See page 110.
11. *e.* Working-class parents emphasize manners as part of the emphasis on conformity to external authority. See page 112.
12. *b.* Kohn found that work which provides opportunity for independent thought, initiative, and judgment tends to foster middle-class values. See page 112.
13. *a.* The family is the most important agent of socialization because it introduces children to personal relationships, it is the child's first reference group, and it introduces children to group life. See page 114.
14. *d.* All parents' behaviors, even unconscious reactions, influence children, as do the other factors in a child's life. See pages 113-114.
15. *c.* At home and at school children are always subordinate to adults; with peers they relate to social equals. This feature provides unique opportunities for sharing, learning, and growth. See page 115.
16. *e.* Adolescents respond to both parents' and peers' preferences. Peer values generally reinforce parental values. See page 117.
17. *b.* The research on the effects of television on children shows that it has both positive and negative effects. Television viewing has been found to influence sharing and cooperation as well as aggressive behaviors. See page 118.

18. *a.* In order to help prepare workers for jobs requiring the ability to think independently and to be self-motivated, schools have changed the traditional structure of schools to emphasize cooperative problem-solving and group efforts. See page 119.

19. *b.* Becoming a prisoner involves resocialization because a different set of norms and values must be internalized. See pages 119-120.

20. *e.* Frank is experiencing anticipatory socialization, in which he starts to "recast" himself in anticipation of the socialization he is about to undergo.

EXERCISES

Exercise 1

Study the table on the next page, paying particular attention to the role of each significant other for males and for females over time.

1. Order by rank the importance of the significant others and explain the results.

2. Examine how the percentages for each significant other differ by gender. Explain the results.

3. Describe how the percentages change over time. Explain the results.

4. Compare parents, peers, and the school as agents of socialization.

Percentage of the Same Students at Each Grade Level Who Name at Least One Person in Each of the Following Categories of Significant Others as Being Important in Their Lives (Males = 255 and Females = 306)

Categories of Significant Others	Sex	Grade 8 %	Grade 9 %	Grade 10 %	Grade 11 %	Grade 12 %
Parent(s)	Males	97	96	96	95	93
	Females	99	98	96	98	98
Age Level Relatives	Males	62	60	46	52	57
	Females	76	75	70	78	75
Adult Relatives	Males	38	40	27	35	31
	Females	55	57	47	53	52
Friends, Same Sex	Males	44	48	26	33	27
	Females	54	68	46	62	53
Friends, Opposite Sex	Males	15	18	14	22	26
	Females	30	32	33	57	25
Local Adults	Males	19	20	15	20	24
	Females	27	32	23	23	16
Teachers in General	Males	38	37	24	20	18
	Females	34	34	12	16	16
Other Academic Persons (Counselors, Coaches, Principals)	Males	9	9	6	13	15
	Females	12	6	3	7	7
Unclassified (e.g. God, Famous People, Dogs, Me, etc.)	Males	28	22	18	25	16
	Females	12	17	13	15	12

Source: W. B. Brookover and E. L. Erickson, *Sociology of Education* (Homewood, IL: Dorsey, 1975), p.306.

Exercise 2

The "Who am I?" test is used frequently to identify the socializing influences in our lives. Please write 20 answers to the question "Who am I?" in the spaces below. Answer for yourself, *not* as if you were giving the answers to someone else. Write them in the order that they occur to you. Take 10 to 12 minutes and stop when that time has passed, even if you have not completed all 20 responses.

1. I am

2. I am

3. I am

4. I am

5. I am

6. I am

7. I am

8. I am

9. I am

10. I am

11. I am

12. I am

13. I am

14. I am

15. I am

16. I am

17. I am

18. I am

19. I am

20. I am

1. Try to group your responses into two or more categories. People often group them into statuses and roles (female, Catholic, wife) or evaluations with respect to others (smart, attractive, cynical). Analyze your responses in terms of these categories or other categories.

2. The first responses typically reflect those most important to a respondent. Is this the case with your responses? Why are these most important to you?

3. Describe what the results show about your current and earlier socialization experiences. Identify the key persons responsible for your socialization.

4. Compare your responses with those of five other students. Describe and explain differences and similarities.

Exercise 3

Describe your socialization into the college-student role. Identify significant others, discuss anticipatory socialization, analyze the socialization experiences provided by the college (such as freshman orientation), and differentiate formal versus informal sources of socialization. Draw on issues raised in the chapter.

Chapter 6

THE LIFE COURSE: FROM CHILDHOOD TO OLD AGE

OBJECTIVES

After reading Chapter 6, you should understand the following main points and be able to answer the objectives.

1. The life course highlights the interaction between socialization and the social context.
    1.1 Using the baby-boom generation and children of the Great Depression as examples, show how individuals and age groups both reflect and affect society.
    1.2 Define life course.
    1.3 Define birth cohort and describe how sociologists use birth cohort as an analytical tool.
    1.4 Differentiate age from aging and age structure.
    1.5 Show how the five key concepts help analyze the life course.
    1.6 Define age grading and give examples of how age grading varies among cultures and across time.
    1.7 Give examples of how norms regarding age-appropriate behavior are woven throughout our social fabric.
    1.8 Demonstrate how rites of passage mark transition.
    1.9 Compare transitions in contemporary and in traditional societies.
    1.10 Show how changes in the life course are both a cause and an effect of wider social change.
    1.11 Synopsize Erikson's psychosocial theory of lifelong development.

2. Being a child depends on levels of physical, mental, and emotional maturity as well as on historical circumstance.
    2.1 Explain why childhood was not recognized in the Middle Ages and why it was recognized during the Renaissance period.
    2.2 List the three causes of the disappearance of childhood.

3. Adolescence also reflects social conditions.
    3.1 Define identity.
    3.2 Describe the history of the concept of adolescence.
    3.3 Identify the predominant theme of adolescence.
    3.4 Explain why teenagers begin sexual activity earlier than before.
    3.5 List some of the factors that influence the transition to adulthood.

4. Adulthood is also characterized by many changes.
    4.1 Identify the crises that adults experience, according to Erikson.
    4.2 Compare the approach of Erikson to that of Levinson.

71

4.3 Draw some comparisons between the life course of men and that of women.

5. Aging is connected closely with social change and social structure.
    5.1 Compare the myths about aging with the realities.
    5.2 Describe how widowhood is different for men and women.
    5.3 Explain why the proportion of working men over 65 has declined.
    5.4 Profile the economic situation of older people.
    5.5 Profile the political involvement of older people.
    5.6 Explain the significance of the work of Kubler-Ross.

CHAPTER SUMMARY

1. How do sociologists view the life course?

Sociologists examine how individuals and age groups both reflect and affect society as they live their lives and interact with the larger social world. *Birth cohorts,* such as the baby boomers and the children of the Great Depression, share essential aspects of the society in which they live because they were born in the same year or period of years. Such cohorts become a product of their particular time and place. Each age cohort experiences the various stages in the *life course*, the collective biography of groups of people as they move through life. The life course involves a series of generally predictable changes that people experience. The sociological approach emphasizes how growth and aging are shaped by, and help to shape, social structure and historical circumstances.

The examples in the text regarding the baby boom generation and the children of the Great Depression highlight two important aspects of the sociological approach to the life course. First, sociologists recognize that the experiences of people moving from birth to death occur in distinctive historical, institutional, and cultural contexts. Second, sociologists are interested in the social changes that occur as successive generations of people pass through the stages of life. In their analysis of the life course, sociologists distinguish between age, aging, and age structure. *Age* is the number of years since a person was born; it involves various social definitions regarding what is required of and appropriate for people of different ages. *Aging* is the process of growing older, which begins on the day we are born. *Age structure* is the number of people in a society at each stage of the life course. In other words, it is the distribution of a population by age.

Age affects the flow of people into and out of various social roles and statuses. It also governs the distribution of valued resources in society, such as money, power, and prestige. This process of classifying people into social categories according to their age is known as *age grading*. Age grading was not always as prevalent as it is today. The trend toward increased age grading can be seen in several spheres of social life, such as education and age at marriage. Norms regarding appropriate ages for major life events are also subject to change. Finally, the scheduling of major life events varies from one society to another. Growing up in a developing society is very different from growing up in a Western society. In developing societies, age is a major characteristic used to allocate statuses and roles, rights, and obligations. In most modern societies, age is simply one of several characteristics used to make these allocations. Negative stereotyping based on age, called *ageism*, persists. Ageism may result in *age discrimination*: the denial of rights, opportunities, and services to a person exclusively because of his or her age.

Age is different from other ascribed statuses, such as race and gender, because it is a *transitional status*: people move periodically from one age category to another. This process of moving through the life course is called aging. As they age, people face different sets of expectations and responsibilities, enjoy different rights and opportunities, and possess different amounts of power and control. As a result, transitions from one age status to another are very important and are often marked by *rites of passage*: public ceremonies that record the transition. Examples include religious confirmations and graduation ceremonies. Rites of passage are important for both the individual and the society. Through the use of stories and symbols that explain the meaning of the change in age, the individual and the society are reminded of the rights and responsibilities that go along with the new status.

Age structure refers to the distribution of a population by age--the number of people at each age level. People in different birth cohorts often have very different life experiences. The size of the cohort is a major factor affecting these experiences. The proportion of Americans age 65 or older has been increasing steadily, primarily for two reasons: the average life expectancy has increased constantly and the baby boom generation is now becoming older. These changes in age structure can have profound effects on American social life. For example, the graying of the population will affect the practice of medicine and the progression of the baby boom generation may tax government programs that provide benefits for the elderly.

Sociologists generally look at four major stages: childhood, adolescence, adulthood, and old age. Erik Erikson built on these four major stages in developing his ideas about the social experiences that people undergo during the course of their lives. He proposed that people face eight challenges as they pass through the life course; each challenge must be met in either a positive or a negative fashion.

2. What characterizes childhood as a stage in the life course?

According to Erikson, the challenge experienced by infants is the resolution of basic trust versus mistrust while they are totally dependent on others. As toddlers, they begin to seek independence from adults and must face the choice between autonomy and shame of doubt. At about age 5, children begin to initiate interactions with peers and to take on more responsibilities; this challenge is known as initiative versus guilt. When they reach school age, children try to acquire skills and information and to relate to a larger social circle; this challenge results in industry versus inferiority.

The idea that childhood is a special stage in life is a fairly recent cultural invention dating only from the Renaissance. Until that time, children moved very quickly into their adult roles. By the eighteenth century, childhood came to be viewed increasingly as a time to learn, explore, and play, although this status began to apply to children from middle- and working-class backgrounds much later than to children from upper-class backgrounds. Between the 1870s and the 1930s (when child labor became increasingly unacceptable), children came to be valued less for their wages and their economic contributions than as emotional and sentimental assets. Several factors help to count for this shift: economic forces and technological change, the relatively high earnings of adults, and a moral redefinition of childhood.

Some recent scholars argue that childhood has disappeared again. As evidence, they show that children engage in many adult behaviors much earlier now than in the past. Several factors account for this disappearance of childhood. First, parental authority has declined. Second, television has exposed children to information that once was the exclusive domain of adults. Third, the modern child care industry has lessened the specialness of childhood. Not everyone laments this disappearance of childhood, some people believe that we should not shield children from the complexities of life and believe that complete economic dependence lessens the development of self-worth. Others argue that the notion of protected childhood is inconsistent with the realities of modern family life.

3. What characterizes adolescence as a stage in the life course?

According to Erikson, adolescents face the challenge of identity versus role confusion. *Identity* is an understanding of who one is and where one is going.

Adolescence is an even more recent invention than childhood. Near the end of the nineteenth century the period between childhood and adulthood came to be identified as a particularly dangerous and vulnerable stage in development. G. Stanley Hall, who wrote at the turn of the century, argued that young people should be given a chance to experiment and explore before being pushed into the adult world. His ideas both reflected and predicted social conditions. Education was transformed from a luxury to a necessity as America became increasingly industrialized and urbanized. Adolescence took shape as an analytical concept particularly in the 1940s and 1950s, when the segregation of young people in schools fostered the development of an adolescent society or subculture with its own tastes and standards. The social events of this period helped to foster this development: these included increased access to cars, greater affluence, and changing practices in dating and other forms of social interaction.

The age at which children become adolescents is slowly moving downward. For example, the average age at the first sexual experience has declined considerably, although there is still much variability in the age at which particular teenagers begin having sex. Several factors explain this variability. First, some teenagers mature physically earlier than do others. Second, parents' sexual and marriage patterns influence their children's sexual behavior. Third, sociocultural factors affect the age at which a person has his or her first sexual experience. Fourth, peer influence helps to determine the age at which teenagers begin having sex.

Adolescents face contradictory messages: some cultural signals encourage them to grow up faster, but the lack of opportunities makes it difficult to assume complete independence. As a result, the adolescent years are being stretched out at both ends. Recent years have seen increased variation in the timing and sequence of events involved in becoming an adult.

4. What characterizes adulthood as a stage in the life course?

Erikson observed that the challenge for young adults (ages 20 to 40) is intimacy versus isolation. In middle adulthood (ages 40 to 60) the challenge is generativity versus stagnation. At this stage of life, adults frequently must balance the desire to make substantial contributions to the world with feelings of boredom and resignation.

Daniel Levinson pioneered the systematic study of the adult cycle. He believes that the adult male life cycle is divided into stable periods in which a man reviews and evaluates his past choices and considers the future. Transition periods are difficult. Levinson argues that all men progress through the same stages in the same order. The first stage occurs during the twenties. When young men begin to make their own choices and to define their place in the adult world. At age 30, seriousness increases because the decisions are now more permanent and farther-reaching in their consequences. The midlife transition occurs between ages 40 and 45. Early signs of aging set in, and many men have reached a plateau in their career. At this stage many men experience a time of reassessment. Evidence suggests that the "ages-and-stages" approach may not apply as well to women as to men because the timing of childbearing can vary dramatically. This variation in turn affects decisions about work and career. We still do not know exactly how the influx of women into the labor force and the tendency of younger women to combine family roles with jobs will alter the female life course in adulthood. One thing is certain, however: family roles are more central for women than for men at all stages.

5. What characterizes the last stages of the life course?

In Erikson's model, the last stage of life (over 60) is marked by the challenge of integrity versus despair. One can either integrate the lived life into a coherent whole or can regret the past and feel helpless about the future.

Life for older Americans is not as bad as many people believe. People over 65 are very satisfied with their present lives. Most of those age 85 and older still maintain independent households and are not a drain on their children's time and finances. Yet they stay in close contact with their children. Most older people also draw on a wide network of friends for social support.

Because women in the United States live seven to eight years longer than men, there are five times as many widowed women as widowed men. Women tend to marry older men; therefore they are much more likely to be widowed during a large part of their old age. The experience of widowhood is different for men and for women. Men may find it more difficult to adjust because they lose not only a wife but also a system of domestic support. Widowhood also clashes with men's self-definitions as independent and resourceful. Because there are so many more unmarried older women than unmarried older men, men are much more likely to remarry.

The proportion of elderly men who remain employed has dropped steadily over the last several decades. Several factors account for this decline. Technological changes have eliminated some jobs once filled by older men. Also, government retirement programs and private pension programs in effect have defined 65 as the "official" age for retirement. In fact, most people still choose to retire at or before age 65.

Although most people are very content with retirement, retirement can be stressful, especially for men. Men are more likely than women of the same generation to derive their core identity from their job. However, the satisfaction with retirement varies considerably depending on socioeconomic conditions and on the characteristics of the job left behind. People from higher-status occupations are more likely to report enjoyment in retirement.

Older people are economically much better off today than in the past, in part because of Social Security and Medicare. The proportion of the aged living below the poverty line has fallen dramatically. Economic inequality still persists, however. Poverty also increases with age, in part because of rising medical expenses.

Many of the elderly are politically active. In terms of conventional political participation, older Americans are among the most active people in the nation. Yet some evidence shows that the elderly as a group cannot exercise much power.

The meaning of death for individuals as well as for society has changed as a result of increased longevity and the growing size of the aging population. Now that death is occurring at a later age, more people are able to contemplate their own deaths. Ernest Becker believed that the denial of death inhibits preparation for dying, thereby making the final transition even more difficult. He maintained that fear of dying and failure to accept the inevitability of death are major sources of unperceived stress in modern societies. Elisabeth Kubler-Ross identifies five stages in the process of dying: denial, bargaining for a reprieve, anger, depression, and finally acceptance of the inevitable. She argues that dying persons should be enabled to work through the stages. These changing conceptions of death and dying have altered the responses of societies and social institutions to dying persons. In addition, new medical technologies have raised concerns about the autonomy of the dying and about the right to refuse treatment and to choose the manner and place of one's death.

REVIEW OF CONCEPTS

Match the concept with the definition.

Concepts

a. age
b. age discrimination
c. age grading
d. ageism
e. age structure
f. aging
g. birth cohort
h. hospice
i. identity
j. life course
k. rites of passage
l. transitional status

Definitions

___ 1. A status that is not permanent, but changes over time.

___ 2. A system of negative beliefs about the capacities, skills, and health of the elderly.

___ 3. Classifying people into different social categories according to age.

___ 4. The sense of "who you are"; a sense of continuity of self-image in past, present, and future.

___ 5. The number of people in a society at each stage of the life course.

___ 6. Public ceremonies that celebrate and publicize the transition from one stage of life to the next.

___ 7. The number of years since a person was born.

___ 8. The category of people who were born in the same year or period, and who age together.

___ 9. The socially defined sequence of stages in the life cycle, from birth to death. Each stage entails characteristic tasks, expectations, and privileges.

___ 10. A homelike facility that provides care and support for the terminally ill and their families.

Answers

1.	l	5.	e	8.	g
2.	d	6.	k	9.	j
3.	c	7.	a	10.	h
4.	i				

REVIEW QUESTIONS

After studying Chapter 6, answer the following questions. The correct answers are listed at the end of the questions; each is followed by a short explanation. You are also referred to pages in the textbook for relevant discussion.

1. The examples of the baby boom and children of the Great Depression best illustrate which of following?
   a. The definition of success has changed.
   b. The definition of adulthood has changed.
   c. Cohorts at the beginning of the century had greater effects on society than did later cohorts.
   d. Individuals and age groups both reflect and affect society.
   e. Cohorts have increasingly affected government policy.

2. Which one of the following in *not* an example of birth cohort?
   a. all those born in the five years after World War II

b. all those who entered kindergarten in 1980
c. all those who were married in the 1960s
d. all those who graduated from high school in 1968-1970
e. all those born in the recession years of the early 1980s

3. Samantha plotted the number of people at various ages for Peru to help her understand population implications for that country. Which concept was she using?
   a. age structure
   b. aging
   c. age
   d. population density
   e. age grading

4. All societies classify individuals into social categories based on age. This phenomenon is known as
   a. age grading
   b. age segregation
   c. age segmentation
   d. age classification
   e. age differentiation

5. The number of stages in the life course and the boundaries between the stages
   a. vary considerably across cultures but not much across time.
   b. vary considerably across time but not much across cultures.
   c. vary considerably across both time and cultures.
   d. are identifiable primarily in modern complex societies.
   e. are relatively recent observations made by social scientists.

6. In comparison to traditional societies like the Masai, the boundaries between stages of the life course in American society today are
   a. more strictly defined.
   b. more loosely defined.
   c. more evident for men than for women.
   d. more clearly defined for later stages.
   e. more clearly defined for earlier stages.

7. Professor Shantz believes that old students cannot learn as well as young students and hence denies old students the extra help provided to young students. These two factors reflect (respectively)
   a. aging and transitional status
   b. transitional status and age structure
   c. age structure and ageism
   d. ageism and age discrimination
   e. age discrimination and age grading

8. Bar and bat mitzvahs, graduations, marriages, and ceremonial dances are examples of
   a. social symbols.
   b. particularistic socialization.
   c. the effect of religion as an institution.
   d. gestures.

e. rites of passage.

9. Erikson's stages reflect
   a. different ages in socialization.
   b. a basic conflict between one's psychological and sociological experiences.
   c. a basic conflict at different points in time between an individual need and society's ability to satisfy it.
   d. a basic conflict between the id and the superego, reflected in various ways at various stages in the life course.
   e. a gradual increase in the social maturity of individuals as they transverse the life course.

10. Childhood as a stage of its own in the life course was first recognized
    a. in early Roman times.
    b. in the 1500s in East Asia.
    c. in the Middle Ages.
    d. in the Renaissance
    e. in the Industrial Revolution

11. Infants generally learn that the world is a safe place where their needs will be met. But if nurturing is not consistent, they may see the world as a harsh place where they must fend for themselves. Which of Erikson's stages is represented?
    a. basic trust vs. mistrust
    b. autonomy vs. shame and doubt
    c. initiation vs. guilt
    d. industry vs. inferiority
    e. intimacy vs. isolation

12. A four-year-old begins to explore the neighborhood on her own and to make friends. Her parents are very supportive, which helps develop feelings of self-worth in the child. Which of Erikson's stages is represented?

    a. basic trust vs. mistrust
    b. autonomy vs. shame and doubt
    c. initiation vs. guilt
    d. industry vs.inferiority
    e. intimacy vs. isolation

13. A seven-year-old learns skills in how to interact with others and acquires basic information at school. He makes new friends. Because his ventures are supported by his parents and teachers, he develops pride. Which of Erikson's stages is represented?
    a. basic trust vs. mistrust
    b. autonomy vs. shame and doubt
    c. initiation vs. guilt
    d. industry vs. inferiority
    e. intimacy vs. isolation

14. Adolescence as a stage of its own in the life course was first recognized
    a. in early Roman times.
    b. in the 1500s in East Asia.
    c. in the Middle Ages.

d. in the sixteenth century.

e. in the nineteenth century.

15. Which social trend contributed particularly to the notion of adolescence as we know it today?
    a. Adolescents were needed as laborers in the Industrial Revolution.
    b. Adolescents suffered noticeably in the Depression years.
    c. Adolescents were needed in World War II.
    d. Adolescents were segregated in schools in the 1940s and 1950s.
    e. Adolescents became more recognized as the baby boom cohort became adolescents.

16. An adolescent experiences difficulty in determining who she is and has no idea what she wants for her future. Which of Erikson's stages is represented?
    a. identity vs. role confusion
    b. intimacy vs. isolation
    c. generativity vs. stagnation
    d. industry vs. inferiority
    e. initiation vs. guilt

17. Which of the following most accurately summarizes the transition to adulthood today as compared to earlier?
    a. Children become adolescents earlier now.
    b. Adolescents remain adolescents longer.
    c. Children become adolescents later now.
    d. Adolescents become adults sooner.
    e. a and b.

18. A 25-year-old man has few friendships and has not married. He fears a loss of self. Which of Erikson's stages is represented?
    a. generativity vs. stagnation
    b. intimacy vs. isolation
    c. identity vs. role confusion
    d. industry vs. inferiority
    e. integrity vs. despair

19. Levinson built on Erikson's discussion of stages by
    a. applying Erikson's ideas to women.
    b. applying Erikson's ideas to nonwhites.
    c. consolidating Erikson's stages into three basic stages across the life course.
    d. discrediting Erikson's stages.
    e. focusing on the transitions experienced in adulthood.

20. The available evidence on the stages of the adult female life cycle suggests that
    a. there are no such stages for women.
    b. the stages progress at a much more rapid rate than for men.
    c. the stages and the transitions are the same for women as for men.
    d. women do not go through specific stages in as predictable a way as do men.
    e. there are more stages among older women than among older men.

21. Which one of the following is *not* a myth regarding the elderly?
    a. Physical and mental decline occur inevitably.

b. Sexuality becomes nonexistent.
c. Senility is pervasive and untreatable.
d. They are inflexible.
e. All of these are myths.

22. Which one of the following is *false*?
    a. People over 65 are dissatisfied with their present lives.
    b. Most over 85 maintain independent households.
    c. Most of the elderly stay in close contact with their children.
    d. Widowhood is more difficult for men to adjust to.
    e. The proportion of elderly men remaining employed has declined.

23. Kubler-Ross's work on the five stages of dying stressed that
    a. women and men experience death differently.
    b. people should not be told they are dying.
    c. professionals other than physicians should be involved with dying people.
    d. dying is viewed differently in different cultures.
    e. people need to know they are dying and to work through the stages of dying.

Answers

1. *d.* Both examples help us to see how individuals and age groups both reflect and affect society. See page 131.
2. *c.* A birth cohort includes those who were born close to the same time and who thus experience life events at relatively similar times. People who married in the 1960s would include a variety of people born at many different points in time. See page 129.
3. *a.* In plotting the number of people in Peru at each stage of the life course, she was establishing the age structure of Peru. See page 131.
4. *a.* Age grading is the process in which all societies engage to classify people into various social categories based on age. See page 132.
5. *c.* How many stages in the life course a society recognizes and how the boundaries are defined vary considerably from culture to culture and from one historical period to another. See pages 132-133.
6. *b.* The boundaries between stages in the life course are defined more loosely in modern societies than in traditional societies. See page 133.
7. *d.* The first part reflects negative stereotyping based on age--ageism. The second reflects the denial of rights, opportunities, and services based on age--age discrimination. See page 133.
8. *e.* Rites of passage have marked transitions from one stage in the life course to another for generations in all cultures. See page 141.
9. *c.* Erikson proposed a psychosocial theory of development across eight stages of the life course. At each stage the individual faces a basic conflict between one of his or her predominant needs and society's ability to satisfy it. See page 137.
10. *d.* Before the Renaissance people recognized that children were immature, but childhood was not considered a special and separate stage of life. See page 144.
11. *a.* The first stage, according to Erikson, is basic trust vs. mistrust. See page 137.
12. *c.* At age four or five, children experience initiation vs. guilt as they begin to extend their mastery over their own bodies to the world around them. If they are supported, the results are positive. See page 137.
13. *d.* Children of school age experience industry vs. inferiority as they struggle to acquire skills

and information and to relate to a larger social circle. Depending on the response, pride or inferiority may result. See page 137.

14. *e.* Adolescence was first recognized as a separate stage in the life course in the nineteenth century. See page 140.

15. *d.* Adolescence as we know it today really took shape in the 1940s and 1950s when the segregation of young people in schools fostered the development of an adolescent society. See page 140.

16. *a.* Adolescents commonly experience identity vs. role confusion in their quest for self-definition and for clarity about their futures. See page 140.

17. *e.* Many cultural signals tell children to grow up sooner--to become adolescents sooner. Yet the lack of opportunities (the right job or mate, affordable housing) makes it difficult to assume adult independence earlier, so adolescents often remain dependent on their parents longer. See pages 142-143.

18. *b.* Young adults (ages 20-40) must fuse their identities partially with those of other people, forming deep friendships and starting a family. The danger is that they will fail to commit themselves because they fear loss of self. This crisis is intimacy vs. isolation. See page 143.

19. *e.* Levinson found that the adult male life cycle is divided into stable periods. The transitions from one stable period to another, however, are often difficult. See page 144.

20. *d.* The evidence shows that the "ages and stages" approach may not apply as well to women. The timing of childbearing accounts for this difference and affects a woman's decisions about work and career. See page 145.

21. *e.* All of these are myths regarding the elderly. In reality, physical decline generally does not occur until the eighties. Many elderly people are sexually active if partners are available. Senility involves a variety of problems, many of which are treatable. Older people are no less flexible than younger people. See page 147.

22. *a.* Public opinion polls consistently show that people over 65 are extraordinarily satisfied with their present lives. See page 147.

23. *e.* Kubler-Ross identified five stages of dying: denial, bargaining, anger, depression, and acceptance. She argued that dying people need to work through these stages. See page 150.

EXERCISES

Exercise 1

You are a member of a birth cohort. That is, you were born at a particular historical time and thus share a similar historical experience with others born in approximately the same period. Identify the particular economic, political, and social conditions of your birth cohort that have affected and will affect your cohort at the various stages of life.

1. Economic conditions.

2. Political conditions.

3. Social conditions.

Erikson proposed eight stages in the life course. Give examples of each, based on your own experiences or on others' experiences.

1. Trust vs. mistrust (infancy).

2. Autonomy vs. shame (toddlers).

3. Initiation vs. guilt (early childhood).

4. Industry vs. inferiority (school age).

5. Identity vs. role confusion (adolescence).

6. Intimacy vs. isolation (young adulthood).

7. Generativity vs. stagnation (middle adulthood).

8. Integrity vs. despair (old age).

Exercise 3

Review the advertisements in the last few issues of *Newsweek, Time,* or *U.S. News and World Report.* Also review the advertisements in a few issues of the same magazine published ten years ago and twenty years ago. Examine how the aged are portrayed in each time period. Examine the occupational roles portrayed, the activities portrayed, whether the persons appear happy or sad, the social contexts in which they appear, the products being advertised, and the messages conveyed. Attach copies of the most relevant advertisements (be sure to label each with its source and date).

1. Current issues.

2. Issues of ten years ago.

3. Issues of twenty years ago.

Chapter 7
DEVIANCE AND CRIME

OBJECTIVES

After reading Chapter 7, you should understand the following main points and be able to answer the objectives.

1. Deviance is behavior that members of a social group define as violating their norms.
   1.1 Define deviance.
   1.2 Show how deviance is related to the five key concepts.
   1.3 Explain how deviance is relative to a particular time, place, or context.
   1.4 Show how the social definition of deviance applies to inner-city gangs.
   1.5 Identify the social functions provided by deviance.
   1.6 Discuss the relationship between power and the social definition of deviance.
   1.7 Explain how labeling theory accounts for deviance.
   1.8 Distinguish primary deviance from secondary deviance.

2. Some sociologists explain deviance in terms of unusual biological or psychological characteristics of the individual deviant; these characteristics make deviants and criminals different from the conforming population.
   2.1 Discuss the biological factors that may be related to deviant and criminal behavior.
   2.2 Describe the psychological theories of deviance and crime.

3. Other sociologists assume that deviants and conformists are essentially the same kind of people. They explain deviance by situational and societal factors that lead ordinary people to engage in behavior which is defined as deviant.
   3.1 Summarize the differential association theory of deviance.
   3.2 Summarize the structural strain theory of deviance.
   3.3 List Merton's five responses to stress caused by the inability to pursue culturally approved goals; give an example of each response.

4. Social control refers to society's efforts to regulate itself, including mechanisms by which social norms are upheld and by which their actual or potential violation is restrained.
   4.1 Define social control.
   4.2 Discuss the internalization of normative standards.
   4.3 Distinguish between informal and formal sanctions.

5. Crime is the violation of a norm that has been entered into the law and is backed by the power and authority of the state.

5.1 Define crime.
5.2 Describe how and why definitions of crime change.
5.3 Summarize the research on violent crimes.
5.4 Define victimless crimes.
5.5 Explain how organized crime develops.
5.6 Differentiate white-collar from corporate crime.

6. Evidence suggests that police, the courts, and prisons have not been effective in reducing the high rates of crime in American society.
   6.1 Assess the suggestions of Currie to control crime.
   6.2 Drawing on Skolnick and Bayley's research, describe how police can be more effective in reducing crime.
   6.3 Discuss the criminal justice funnel.
   6.4 Describe the confusion surrounding the purposes of prisons in American society.

CHAPTER SUMMARY

1. What is deviant behavior?

Deviance may be defined as behavior that members of a social group consider to violate their normative standards. Whether a given act is deviant depends on the time, place, and social context in which it occurs and on the people who define and apply the norms. Thus deviance is relative to a specific social situation. For example, what is considered deviant varies between ethnic groups, social classes, occupational groups, and sexes. Definitions of deviance may change because the norms of societies and groups change. As a result, changes in the definitions of deviance themselves may bring about social change. The text uses the case of inner-city gangs to highlight the social definition aspect of deviance.

2. How do the functionalist and power perspectives explain deviance?

Deviance can serve various social functions. For example, a group or community defines what behavior is acceptable when it defines certain other kinds of behavior as deviant. Also, deviance tends to unite members in opposition to the deviant, thereby reaffirming their social solidarity. Finally, deviance may serve as a catalyst for social change. Whether deviance leads to reaffirmation of existing norms or serves as a catalyst for new norms depends in part on the type of society in which that deviance occurs. A high degree of consensus regarding acceptable behavior typically exists in simple, traditional societies, where the punishment of deviance leads to increased commitment to the status quo. Social change and renegotiation of norms are often the result of deviance in complex, modern societies because of the many competing lifestyles and moral points of view.

The power perspective comes into play when we ask whose norms prevail in a given society. In American society, both wealth and race help determine who holds the power to influence definitions of deviance. Typically, the label of deviant is applied to those with relatively little power. People are generally slow to label the very powerful as deviant, even when they are responsible for significant damage to individuals in society. However, the relatively powerless who are more likely to be labeled deviant are not necessarily poor and nonwhite. For example, women who protest sexual harassment are often labeled deviant.

Karl Marx believed that a small ruling class of economic elite individuals determines moral norms (and hence definitions of deviance) because such norms can be used to support the existing economic order. He believed that the strength of society's response to norm violation depends on how severely the violation threatens established power relations. As a result, said Marx, law reflects the interests of the governing class. The entire criminal justice system reflects the values and interests of those in power, who control the legislatures, the police, and the courts. Our system of justice is not blind to differences in social power. Even in such a system, however, the power of the elite is never absolute.

3. How does the labeling perspective explain deviance?

Various social agents label people deviant when they violate social norms. Being labeled in this way has long-term consequences for one's social identity. Sociologists distinguish primary deviance from secondary deviance. *Primary deviance* is an initial violation of a social norm; no inferences are made regarding a person's character on the basis of such an act of deviance. *Secondary deviance* includes norm violations that have become part of a person's lifestyle because that person thinks of himself or herself as deviant as a result of other people's opinions. Most of us engage in primary deviance, as when we violate the speed limit. Secondary deviance occurs when primary deviants are singled out and labeled criminal. Such people then are typically excluded from the mainstream of life. This social rejection tends to encourage the labeled people to define themselves as deviant and to adopt a deviant lifestyle. As a result, they take on the role that other people expect of them. Chambliss's study of two cliques of boys at one high school suggests that the same behavior can cause very different labels to be attached to the perpetrators. Although both groups violated social norms in a dangerous and costly way, the Saints (from well-off families) were defined as future leaders just "having a little fun," while the Roughnecks (from less affluent families) were defined as future criminals starting their careers as juvenile delinquents. The labeling of people as deviant affects their later opportunities. For example, an "ex-con" may find it more difficult to find a steady job than would someone with no criminal record. In extreme cases, the labeled individual begins to follow a deviant career by fully adopting a deviant lifestyle and by identifying with a deviant subculture.

4. How do sociologists explain deviance?

Over the years, many attempts have been made to explain who behaves in deviant fashion in terms of people's inherent natures. In the nineteenth century, for example, Lombroso thought that people were born to be criminals, and that criminals' skulls possessed characteristics of savage apes. His theory later was disproved because it was found that the skulls of criminals did not differ significantly from those of non-criminals. The historical settlement of Australia also raises questions about the existence of born criminals. A significant proportion of early immigrants to Australia were convicted criminals; yet crime rates in Australia today are not unusually high. This fact suggests that the settlers' criminal tendencies were not passed on biologically to subsequent generations.

Sigmund Freud argued that in the process of growing up, most people learn how to inhibit their innate drives toward pleasure and aggression. Freud believed that deviance occurs when children lack an appropriate adult with whom to identify, an adult whose moral norms and values they can adopt as their own. Other psychological explanations emphasize the role of parental discipline in forming later attitudes towards rule-breaking behavior. Punishing children for aggression, for example, results in more (not less) aggressiveness. These findings underscore the utility of the social-learning perspective.

Differential association, a more social structural theory, suggests that deviance is learned through the transmission of certain values and norms among members of a subculture. In everyday language, this theory holds that a person becomes a thief because he "hangs around with a bad crowd." Such people are socialized to accept the norms and values of a juvenile gang, for example, even though the rest of society considers the gang's norms and values to be deviant. Through differential association the attitudes and norms of the deviant subculture become even more deeply entrenched. The label "differential association" suggests that people who engage in deviant behavior spend more time associating with those who reject mainstream norms and values than with those who conform to them. Deviant subcultures, such as a gang, offer their members role models, emotional support, and ideological justifications while protecting them somewhat from the negative evaluations and sanctions imposed by the wider society.

The *structural strain* theory assumes that social norms define culturally acceptable legitimate goals as well as culturally acceptable means for achieving those goals. Robert Merton suggests that rates of deviant behavior will be higher among those groups who fail to achieve culturally approved goals by conforming to culturally approved means. In other words, rates of deviance will be higher among groups that experience a discrepancy or disjunction between societal expectations and legitimate opportunities for achieving those expectations.

According to Merton, the source of deviance is found in the structural strain that results from a gap between culturally defined goals and legitimate means for achieving them. What happens when individuals internalize culturally approved goals but cannot reach these goals by acting in normatively approved ways? In such a situation, says Merton, an individual responds in one of five ways. All but the first involve deviance: 1) *conformity*--seeking legitimate goals by legitimate means; 2) *innovation*--pursuing legitimate goals by deviant means; 3) *ritualism*--abandoning legitimate goals by following culturally prescribed means; 4) *retreatism*--abandoning both legitimate goals and legitimate means; and 5) *rebellion*--rejecting culturally approved goals and means and replacing them with a new set of goals and means.

Merton's theory is partly a rational choice model of why some people behave in defiant fashion. He noted that deviance is a rational option when a certain social structural condition exists, namely, a lack of legitimate channels by which to achieve culturally desirable goals. His approach also has a social psychological component because the absence of legitimate means for achieving culturally desirable goals produces frustration (which in turn generates deviance).

5. What types of social control are used to suppress deviance?

Social control refers to society's efforts to regulate itself; it includes those mechanisms by which social norms are upheld and by which their actual or potential violation is restrained. In other words, social controls are processes used in encouraging people to conform to norms that define acceptable or preferable behavior.

Social control operates on both an internal and an external level. On the internal level, individuals learn through socialization the norms and laws that define proper behavior. Internalization is the process through which cultural standards become part of an individual's personality structure. Properly socialized people police themselves, and social control becomes self-control.

Not all people are properly socialized, however, and some never internalize the important values and norms of a society. Thus some other mechanism is also necessary to prevent high rates of deviance. External social control consists of *sanctions*--penalties for violating norms or laws, or rewards for conforming to them. *Informal sanctions* reflect the unofficial pressure to conform to norms and values. In everyday situations, people reward or punish others as a way of controlling their behavior. For example, we might make fun of someone who dresses in clothes that are years out of date, just as we might compliment someone who dresses in the latest styles. *Formal sanctions* come into play when informal sanctions do not work; formal sanctions are officially imposed pressures to conform, such as fines or imprisonment. Formal sanctions are needed more in large, complex societies than in small, closely knit communities.

6. What is crime, and what are the major types?

A *crime* is a violation of a norm that has been entered into the law and is backed by the power and authority of the state. Not all deviance is criminal behavior, and not all criminal behavior is always considered deviant. An act is criminal if 1) it violates a law and 2) it carries the threat of formal sanctions such as fines or jail terms. Like deviance, crime is defined in relation to specific historical and cultural settings. Some behavior formerly defined as criminal, such as alcoholism, is now defined as an illness.

The Federal Bureau of Investigation differentiates crimes with criminal intent (crimes against people and against property) from crimes not involving criminal intent (such as white-collar crime and prostitution). *Violent crimes* include murder, assault, and rape, but still reflect only about 10 percent of all crimes with criminal intent. American society is more violent than other societies. The most likely victims of violent crimes are black males of lower socioeconomic status. The widespread availability of firearms has been cited as one of the causes of high rates of violent crimes. Crime rates are higher among the poor and in larger cities than elsewhere.

Victimless crimes have no apparent victims. Examples include drug use, gambling, and prostitution. Yet, such acts are designated as criminal because the community as a whole (or powerful groups within it) regard them as morally repugnant. Some people, however, argue that victimless crimes really have victims.

Organized crime has been defined as a continuing conspiracy that operates for power and profit. Participants in organized crime seek immunity from the law either through threats or through corruption. Organized crime specializes in providing illicit goods and services (drugs, prostitution, gambling), though the profits from these activities are sometimes laundered through investments in legitimate businesses. Crime syndicates often develop among immigrants who are not familiar enough with the mainstream culture to participate in its economy and who are suspicious of the police and other authorities who do not speak their language.

White-collar crime is committed by individuals of high social status in the course of their occupations. Examples include embezzling, stealing from an employer, and evading personal income taxes. This type of crime differs from "common" crime in three ways: 1) it relies on manipulation of records and on concealment rather than on force or the threat of force; 2) it is more costly; and 3) comparatively light sentences are meted out to the offenders. White-collar crimes are committed for personal gain.

Corporate crimes are illegal acts committed on behalf of a formal organization. Their primary goal is to boost company profits. Because corporations are not persons they cannot be jailed. Corporate crimes are generally handled outside the court system by government regulatory agencies; in most cases, sanctions are slight.

7. Has the American criminal justice system been successful in controlling crime?

Although rates for certain crimes have declined, crime rates in the United States are higher than those in comparable countries. One reason is the ineffectiveness of informal social controls, resulting from increasing fragmentation of our society. Also, for members of many racial and ethnic groups, discrimination makes it difficult to attain culturally valued goals through legitimate means; hence they turn to deviant means instead. Elliot Currie argues that the crime rate will be reduced only by major social structural changes such as significant rearrangements of resources and opportunities among members of American society.

In most cases, enlarging the police force does not reduce crime, but certain reorganizations of police activities have been successful. For example, increases in crime rates can be slowed when routine bureaucratic functions are turned over to civilians (thus freeing police officers from these time-consuming tasks) and when local communities are mobilized to assist the police in law enforcement activities.

The American criminal justice system has been described as a "funnel": only a very small percentage of the many crimes committed in this country result in arrests, convictions, and prison sentences. In many cases, the victim will not testify against the accused criminal, so the case is thrown out of court for lack of evidence. Sometimes the accused person pleads guilty to a crime less serious than that originally charged, a process known as *plea bargaining*. Poor nonwhites are disproportionately likely to be funneled through the criminal justice system.

Public support for imprisonment has been increasing, even as rates of imprisonment continue to climb. In fact, prison systems have not been able to keep up with the flood of inmates. Many of the problems surrounding the prison system stem from a confusion of purposes. Some people argue that prison sentences should deter people from committing crimes; others think they should rehabilitate criminals; still others believe that prison sentences should serve as punishment and to protect the public. It is generally agreed, however, that the prison system is inadequate. Some states are experimenting with alternatives to prison sentences, such as public service and house arrest, but imprisonment remains the most likely fate for those convicted of serious offenses.

REVIEW OF CONCEPTS

Match the concept with the definition.

Concepts

a. conformity
b. corporate crimes
c. crime
d. deviance
e. differential association
f. formal sanctions
g. informal sanctions
h. innovation
i. internalization
j. labeling theory
k. organized crime
l. plea bargaining
m. primary deviance
n. rebellion
o. retreatism
p. ritualism
q. sanctions
r. secondary deviance
s. social control
t. victimless crimes
u. violent crimes
v. white-collar crime

Definitions

____ 1. The process by which individuals are socialized into the patterns of behavior that prevail in a particular group with which they associate the most.

____ 2. Official pressure to conform to social norms and values specifically enforced by organizations such as police departments, courts, and prisons.

____ 3. The process in which a district attorney offers to reduce charges if a suspect will plead guilty and relinquish the right to a trial.

____ 4. Society's efforts to regulate itself; those mechanisms by which social norms are upheld and by which their actual or potential violation is restrained.

____ 5. Seeking culturally approved goals by culturally approved means (Merton).

____ 6. Unofficial pressures to conform including disapproval, ridicule, and the threat of ostracism.

____ 7. Creating new goals and the means for pursuing them (Merton).

____ 8. The initial violation of a social norm, about which no inferences are made regarding the motives or the character of the person who committed the act.

___ 9. Crimes that lack victims, except perhaps the people who commit them.

___ 10. Crime committed by high-status individuals in the course of their occupations.

___ 11. Rewards for conforming to a social norm or penalties for violating it.

___ 12. A pattern by which people come to define themselves as deviants and undertake life patterns as a reaction to their being labeled deviants by others.

___ 13. Crimes such as murder, assault, and rape that involve an act of physical violence against the victim.

___ 14. Pursuing culturally approved goals by deviant means (Merton).

___ 15. The process by which cultural standards become part of an individual's personality structure.

___ 16. Illegal activity committed on behalf of a formal organization.

___ 17. A violation of a norm that has been entered into the law and is backed by the power and authority of the state.

___ 18. Abandoning culturally prescribed goals and means (Merton).

___ 19. A continuing conspiracy operating for profit and power and seeking immunity from the law through fear or corruption; specializes in providing illegal goods and services.

___ 20. The theory that people come to acquire a deviant social identity and pursue a deviant lifestyle because others have labeled them deviant and cut them off from the social mainstream.

___ 21. Adhering rigidly to norms, yet abandoning related goals (Merton).

___ 22. Behavior that the members of a social group define as violating their norms.

Answers

1.	e	9.	t	16.	b
2.	f	10.	v	17.	c
3.	l	11.	q	18.	o
4.	s	12.	r	19.	k
5.	a	13.	u	20.	j
6.	g	14.	h	21.	p
7.	n	15.	i	22.	d
8.	m				

REVIEW QUESTIONS

After studying Chapter 7, answer the following questions. The correct answers are listed at the end of the questions; each is followed by a short explanation. You are also referred to pages in the text-book for relevant discussion.

1. Ivan Boesky's insider trading is an example of which type of crime?
   a. index crime
   b. corporate crime
   c. victimless crime
   d. organized crime
   e. white-collar crime

2. Which of the following is a true statement about deviance?
   a. Taking the life of another person is always considered deviant behavior.
   b. Deviance contributes nothing to the maintenance of the social order.
   c. Deviance is relative to a particular time, place, and context, and depends on who defines and applies social norms.
   d. The social norms that define deviance have remained the same throughout the history of the United States.
   e. Deviance is always disruptive to the social order.

3. Which one of the following is *false* regarding the functional view of deviance?
   a. Defining deviant behavior helps a group define acceptable behavior.
   b. Deviance helps unite members of a society in opposition to the deviant.
   c. Uniting against deviants helps reaffirm a society's social solidarity.
   d. The moral norms against which deviance is measured are established by economic elites.
   e. Deviance may serve as a catalyst for social change.

4. Breaking the speed limit is an example of
   a. organized crime.
   b. white-collar crime.
   c. secondary deviance.
   d. primary deviance.
   e. differential association.

5. The labeling perspective is an outgrowth of which perspective?
   a. social interactionist
   b. power
   c. functionalist
   d. biological
   e. differential association

6. Which of the following is *not* a consequence of being labeled a deviant?
   a. Previously favorable impressions made on other people are wiped out.
   b. It is more difficult to become accepted as a member of conventional society.
   c. The labeled deviant usually tries to avoid contact with others who engage in the same deviant activity.
   d. The deviant label becomes a self-fulfilling prophecy.
   e. The labeled deviant often embarks on a deviant career.

7. When Charles Goring measured the skulls of criminals and the skulls of ordinary citizens, he found
   a. that the skulls of criminals had higher cheekbones and larger jawbones than did the skulls of ordinary citizens.
   b. that the skulls of ordinary citizens had higher cheekbones and larger jawbones than did the skulls of criminals.
   c. fewer neurological disorders among criminals than among ordinary citizens.
   d. proof for Cesare Lombroso's theory that criminal's skulls looked more like skulls of apes than did those of ordinary citizens.
   e. no physical differences between the two groups of skulls.

8. Which is the best conclusion to draw from biological research on criminals and deviants?
   a. Aggressiveness has no biological cause; it is completely cultural in origin.
   b. We need more information on how neurological, genetic, and environmental factors interact to affect behavior.
   c. The history of Australia, which originated as a penal colony, proves conclusively that crime has no biological determinants.
   d. Biological explanations of crime and deviance are likely to disappear in the near future.
   e. There is a close connection between skull shape and criminal activity.

9. Freud's approach would suggest which of the following as an explanation of deviance?
   a. Deviance is caused by the inability to attain approved goals through legitimate means.
   b. Deviance is caused by genetic abnormalities.
   c. Deviance is caused by an underdeveloped superego.
   d. Deviance is caused by socialization into a deviant subculture.
   e. Deviance is caused by the labeling of certain actions as violations of norms.

10. Joe found it impossible to hang onto a steady job. He was finding it increasingly difficult to earn enough money to support his wife and three children. In desperation he broke into a gas station and stole the safe. Joe's deviance is best explained by which theory?
    a. Lombroso's theory of the born criminal
    b. structural strain
    c. differential association
    d. Marxist theories
    e. labeling

11. Paula is a student in law school. She becomes disillusioned with her chosen career because she feels that lawyers are only trying to get rich at the expense of others. She decides that only by overthrowing the American government can people establish a society that rejects wealth and profit making as its ideals. She drops out of law school and joins a group of anarchists who plan to blow up the White House. Paula's response illustrates which of Merton's five types?
    a. conformity
    b. innovation
    c. ritualism
    d. retreatism
    e. rebellion

12. If someone accepted the culturally prescribed goals of the society but rejected the legitimate means for pursuing them, Merton would classify this deviance as
    a. conformity.

b. innovation.
c. ritualism.
d. retreatism.
e. rebellion.

13. Billy is looking to make some cash by stealing a car. On a busy street he notices a parked Toyota with its doors unlocked. He could take that one easily, but he thinks there would be too many witnesses around; besides, the resale value of the car would not bring in much. An hour or so later, he sees a Mercedes parked on a deserted side street. The car is locked, so it would be more work to break into, but no one is around, and the car would fetch top dollar. Billy goes to work on the Mercedes. This story best illustrates which theory of deviant behavior?
    a. biological theories
    b. rational choice models
    c. functionalist theories
    d. social stress
    e. Marxist theories

14. Harold really needed a new watch. While walking through a large department store he saw a display of fine watches, but unfortunately all of them were too expensive. Although there were no salespeople around the display, and although it might have been easy to shoplift one of the watches, the thought of stealing never entered Harold's mind. This incident illustrates the success of
    a. formal social control.
    b. brainwashing.
    c. internalization.
    d. sanctions.
    e. plea bargaining.

15. One day in class, John was chewing bubble gum. Every few minutes he blew a huge bubble, and it exploded with a loud pop. The professor stared at John with a nasty expression, and John was so embarrassed that he swallowed the gum. The professor's action is an example of
    a. informal sanctions.
    b. formal sanctions.
    c. internalization of social norms.
    d. rewarding John's conforming behavior.
    e. rational choice.

16. A 15 year-old girl is arrested and convicted for prostitution. The judge assigns her to a rehabilitation center for female juvenile delinquents. This story illustrates
    a. white-collar crime.
    b. secondary deviance.
    c. formal sanctions.
    d. informal sanctions.
    e. corporate crime.

17. The Johns-Manville Corporation exposed its workers to harmful levels of asbestos dust. This action illustrates which type of crime?
    a. violent crime
    b. victimless crime
    c. white-collar crime

    d. corporate crime

    e. organized crime

18. Prostitution is an example of which type of crime?
    a. violent crime
    b. victimless crime
    c. white-collar crime
    d. corporate crime
    e. organized crime

19. Which of the following statements is a correct description of the control of crime in American society?
    a. The rate of violent crime is lower than in other comparable countries.
    b. Police are more successful in lowering crime rates when they remain distant from the communities that they patrol.
    c. Many felons are never convicted because their victims are afraid to testify against them.
    d. The criminal justice funnel insures that all convicted felons--regardless of race or economic status--serve their full prison sentence.
    e. Prisons have succeeded in providing useful rehabilitation services.

20. Which one of the following is *true*?
    a. Public support for imprisonment is increasing and rates of imprisonment have risen.
    b. Public support for imprisonment has declined and rates of imprisonment have risen.
    c. Public support for imprisonment is increasing and rates of imprisonment have declined.
    d. Public support for imprisonment has declined and rates of imprisonment have declined.
    e. We do not have sufficient data to make a conclusion.

Answers

1. *e.* Boesky's goal was personal wealth rather than corporate profits; as an entrepreneur, he enjoyed a high status in American society, and his insider trading occurred in the context of this occupation. See page 155.
2. *c.* Deviance is behavior or a set of characteristics considered in violation of social norms. The definition and the application of norms vary, depending on the time, place, and context, and on who has the power to distinguish acceptable from unacceptable behavior. See page 157.
3. *d.* The establishment of moral norms against which deviance is measured is part of the power perspective, not the functionalist perspective. See pages 160-162.
4. *d.* Primary deviance is an initial violation of a social norm, about which no inferences are made regarding a person's character. See page 162.
5. *a.* The social-interactionist approach holds that people's self-concepts are the product of how they think others perceive them. This external assessment is part of the labeling approach. See pages 162-163.
6. *c.* People who are labeled deviant sometimes adopt a deviant lifestyle and form an identity with others who engage in the same behavior. For example, a prostitute might start to hang around with other prostitutes in order to find emotional support and rationalizations for her career. See page 162.
7. *e.* There is little evidence linking physical traits such as skull shape to deviant or criminal behavior. See page 164.
8. *b.* Some evidence exists to show that some forms of deviance, such as mental disorders, are

at least partly biological in origin, but we need more research. See page 164.

9. *c.* According to Freudian psychology, the failure to acquire an appropriate superego or conscience may lead to deviance because the individual cannot reconcile internal drives (such as aggression) with social demands. See pages 164-165.

10. *b.* Structural strain theory suggests that when conformity to social norms fails to satisfy a person's legitimate desires, that person eventually will be forced to seek satisfaction through deviant means. See page 166.

11. *e.* Rebellion is the rejection of legitimate or approved goals and means, and the substitution of new ones. Paula rejects the American emphasis on monetary success and uses deviant means (violence) to attain alternative goals. See page 167.

12. *b.* Innovation is the use of deviant means to pursue culturally prescribed ends or goals. Rates of such deviance are higher for social groups who are systematically denied opportunities to pursue prescribed goals through approved or legitimate means. See page 166.

13. *b.* Billy is weighing the risks and potential rewards in stealing a car; his decision to steal the Mercedes entails fewer risks (of getting caught) and promises the highest payoffs. See page 167.

14. *c.* Internalization is the process by which cultural standards (norms, rules, and laws) become part of an individual's personality structure. Thus, it was "natural" for Harold to wait until he had enough money to buy the watch. See page 168.

15. *a.* Informal sanctions are the unofficial pressures to conform to norms and value, based on a desire to live up to the expectations of others. In this case, the professor is not *formally* charged with responsibility for maintaining normatively proper behavior. See page 168.

16. *c.* Formal social controls are the official pressures to conform to social laws and norms, specifically enforced by organizations such as police departments, courts, and juvenile detention centers. See page 184.

17. *d.* Corporate irresponsibility in this case victimized the employees of Johns-Manville. See page 174.

18. *b.* Victimless crimes have no apparent victims. There is no complainant. But some argue that such crimes do have victims; prostitutes may spread AIDS, for example. See page 171.

19. *c.* The criminal justice funnel refers to the fact that only a small percentage of crimes results in arrests, convictions, and prison sentences. Many victims are unwilling to provide evidence needed for arrest and conviction because the accused person is a friend or family member, because they are afraid of revenge, or because they have no confidence in the police or the courts. See page 176.

20. *a.* Data show that public support for imprisonment is increasing and that rates of imprisonment have risen. See page 177.

EXERCISES

Exercise 1

A rash of crimes in a major city leads to several letters to the editor in the local newspaper, each offering an explanation of the problem as well as suggested solutions. For each of the following letters, answer these questions:

1. Which sociological theory of deviance is suggested by the letter?
2. What are the sociological assumptions or value judgments made by the letter writer?
3. What evidence is offered by the letter writer to support his or her explanation? Does the evidence support the conclusions?

4. Do you think the solution proposed by each letter would be effective in reducing the crime rate? Justify your answer.

LETTER A

Dear Editor,

The crime problem in our city has gotten out of hand. I do not feel safe walking the streets, day or night (and I live in the suburbs). Maybe I have a solution. I have, for several years now, studied the mug shots on the FBI wanted posters in my local post office. I have noticed that an overwhelming number of suspects have pronounced foreheads and thick, bushy eyebrows. The city police should pay special attention to people exhibiting such traits.

1. Theory:

2. Assumptions/value judgments:

3. Evidence:

4. Effectiveness:

LETTER B

Dear Editor,

I am particularly upset by the recent wave of violent street crime, and it seems to me that these crimes are committed by the same small group of ex-cons who get out of jail and right away return to a life of crime. Here is a modest proposal that just might work. Let's revive the "scarlet letter" and put an orange mark or something on their hands as they are released from jail or prison. That way, law-abiding citizens would avoid these criminals, and they would be forced to live only with their own kind. Then they would not be able to corrupt our innocent teenagers by encouraging them to embark on a life of crime. Also, this permanent mark would be a visible reminder to them of their wrongdoing, and make them think twice about mugging someone on the street.

1. Theory:

2. Assumptions/value judgments:

3. Evidence:

4. Effectiveness:

LETTER C

Dear Editor,

My neighbor was held up at gunpoint and lost his wallet and his watch. It could have been much worse; at least he is still alive. How could this happen? I think the problem is that these deviants do not know right from wrong, and they have no sense of morality. What better place to learn morality than in church? I think all convicted criminals should be required to attend the church of their choice for a minimum of five years after their jail term.

1. Theory:

2. Assumptions/value judgments:

3. Evidence:

4. Effectiveness:

Exercise 2

In *Women Who Kill* (New York: Holt, Rinehart and Winston, 1980), Ann Jones writes: "Crimes of violence committed by women--about 10 percent of all violent crimes--have not increased significantly in the last twenty years . . . The rate of murders committed by women has remained steady at 15 percent of all murders for as long as anyone has kept records anywhere. But rates of arrests for all crimes between 1967 and 1976 rose 15 percent for men and 64 percent for women. Among Juvenile women, arrests increased 68 percent for women" (p. 4).

1. Translate the statistics reported by Ann Jones into your own words.

2. Keep in mind that women make up just over 50 percent of the American population. Why do women commit only 10 percent of the violent crimes? Use the following theories to help you answer this difficult question: biological explanations, psychological explanations, rational choice theory, structural strain, differential association, labeling theory, and Marxist perspectives.

3. In trying to explain why only 15 percent of all murders are committed by women, can you identify any factors or causes that are ignored by all of these theoretical perspectives?

4. Why have arrest rates (for all crimes) increased more rapidly for women than for men? Do any of the above theoretical perspectives help you answer this question?

Exercise 3

Pretend that you have just witnessed the following deviant or criminal acts. For each case, answer the following questions: What action would you take? Would you ignore the act, intercede on behalf of the victim, reprimand the offender immediately, or notify the appropriate authorities? Why would you react in this way? What do your reactions suggest about the effectiveness of informal social controls for reducing rates of crime and deviance?

1. Littering:

2. Cheating on a test:

3. Sale of marijuana:

4. Stealing a library book:

5. An apparent "date rape":

6. Taking "cuts" in a long line:

7. Armed robbery in a store:

8. Vandalism in a dormitory:

9. Homosexual relations in a public bathroom:

10. An obviously drunk person getting behind the wheel of a car:

11. A student embezzling funds from a club treasury:

Chapter 8
GROUPS AND ORGANIZATIONS

OBJECTIVES

After reading Chapter 8, you should understand the following main points and be able to answer the objectives.

1. A social group is a set of individuals who identify with one another and who interact in informally structured ways based on norms, goals, and values that they share implicitly.
   1.1 Define social group; give several examples.
   1.2 List the differences between social groups and formal organizations.
   1.3 Show how the five key concepts are relevant to examining groups and organizations.
   1.4 Describe how group experiences affect lives of members.
   1.5 Contrast social groups and aggregates; give examples of each.
   1.6 Discuss the four characteristics of all social groups.

2. Group dynamics are the recurrent patterns of social interaction among members of a social group.
   2.1 Define group dynamics.
   2.2 Explain how group size influences group dynamics.
   2.3 Compare dyads and triads in terms of group dynamics.
   2.4 List three differences between the group dynamics of large groups and of small groups.

3. Patterns of conformity and control, formation of leadership roles, and processes of decision making are also part of group dynamics.
   3.1 Compare conformity to norms and use of force as two mechanisms of social control in social groups.
   3.2 Contrast instrumental leadership and expressive leadership.
   3.3 List the four stages in group decision making.
   3.4 Define groupthink; discuss its causes and consequences.

4. There are many types of social groups; our membership in these different kinds of groups affects our attitudes, behavior, and feelings.
   4.1 Distinguish between in-groups and out-groups.
   4.2 Explain how boundaries around social groups are created, and why they are important.
   4.3 Contrast primary groups and secondary groups; give examples of each.
   4.4 Explain why Cooley called primary groups "primary."
   4.5 Define reference group; describe its two functions.

5. All social groups depend upon commitments of time and resources from members in order to survive.
  5.1 Explain the importance of commitment for the survival of a social group.
  5.2 Define greedy group; give several examples.
  5.3 Describe the following commitment mechanisms and illustrate each with an example from the Amish: sacrifice, investment, renunciation, communion, mortification, and transcendence.

6. Formal organizations have become a prominent feature of the modern social landscape because they are especially effective at controlling large numbers of people, integrating diverse operations, and overcoming rivals or reducing opposition.
  6.1 Define formal organization.
  6.2 List the three problems solved by bureaucratic innovations.
  6.3 Discuss von Moltke's bureaucratic innovations; explain why they were copied later by other military leaders.
  6.4 Explain how Swift's integration of diverse operations enabled him to defeat his competitors.
  6.5 Define co-optation; discuss its role in the success of the Tennessee Valley Authority.

7. Bureaucracies maximize effectiveness in attaining organizational goals, in reaching goals at the lowest cost, and in controlling uncertainty.
  7.1 List three benefits of bureaucracy.
  7.2 Discuss the five elements of Weber's ideal-type bureaucracy.
  7.3 Describe the sources of bureaucratic variation.
  7.4 Contrast formal structure and informal structure.
  7.5 Describe how the informal structure both enhances and impedes the attainment of organizational goals.

8. Bureaucracies may be efficient and rational, but this form of social organization also has several limitations and at least one alternative.
  8.1 Define ritualism; give examples.
  8.2 Define Parkinson's Law; give examples.
  8.3 Describe protection of the inept.

9. Formed organizations vary considerably on several dimensions. Several factors help account for this variation.
  9.1 Describe the role of the external environment for organizational structure.
  9.2 Contrast the adaptation model and the selection model.
  9.3 Summarize the five nonbureaucratic strategies used by many Japanese organizations to become more successful.
  9.4 Identify the lessons learned about organizational structure at the Volvo plant in Sweden.

CHAPTER SUMMARY

1. What is a social group?

A *social group* is a set of individuals who identify with one another and who interact in informally structured ways based on norms, goals, and values that they share implicitly. A *formal organization* is a set of people whose activities are precisely and intentionally designed for the rational achievement of explicitly stated goals. Social groups differ from formal organizations in several ways: social groups are usually smaller than formal organizations; statuses, roles, and responsibilities are more fluid and less precise in social groups than in formal organizations; and goals are explicit in formal organizations but are implicit (understood without being articulated precisely) in social groups.

Social groups influence the lives of members in several important ways. Through membership in various social groups, people's private lives are connected to others and to the wider society. Membership in social groups also provides us with security and support from people we can count on. Finally, social groups shape our values, attitudes, and behavior.

Not all collections of people are social groups. Shoppers in a grocery store do not constitute a social group: they do not interact frequently; their behavior is not structured in terms of statuses, roles, and shared norms; they do not agree on collective goals, values, or norms; and they do not consider this activity to be an important part of their social identity. The term *aggregate* is used to describe people who just happen to be in the same place at the same time.

By contrast, the boys marooned on an island in Golding's novel exhibit the following four characteristics of all social groups: the members interact with each other regularly; members' interactions are structured (or organized into patterns of expected behavior) through statuses, roles, and norms; the members agree (to some extent) on shared norms, goals, and values; and membership in the group becomes a part of each member's social identity.

2. What are group dynamics, and how are these affected by the size of a social group?

Group dynamics are the recurrent patterns of social interaction among members of a social group. Groups dynamics include patterns of conformity and control, emergence of leadership roles, and processes of group decision making. Each of these group dynamics is affected strongly by the size of the group.

The number of people in a social group has profound implications for its organization and for the behavior of its members. The consequences of group size for group dynamics are apparent even in the seemingly slight increase from a two-person group (a *dyad*) to a three-person group (a *triad*). For example, in a dyad both members must participate or the group ceases to exist; in a triad, the third member could quit and the group could continue as a dyad. For this reason, interactions in dyads often contain more tension than those in triads because each member of the pair knows that the group would not survive without him or her. In addition, members of a dyad cannot hide responsibilities for events, but in a triad one can never be certain *which* of the other two members is to be blamed or praised for something that happens. In a dyad there is no mediator or third party who might intercede in a dispute between the other two members, a situation that cannot occur in a dyad. Finally, two people can join in a coalition against the third in a triad, but this is obviously impossible in a dyad.

Other changes occur when a social group is enlarged from two or three members to one hundred or one thousand members. First, the increase in size encourages development of a specialized division of labor, as tasks are assigned to occupants of specific roles. Second, increased group size creates difficulties in communicating information among members (proportionately fewer members speak in large groups than in small ones). Third, large groups have more resources (money, expertise, personnel) to solve problems, but the proportional contribution of each member is reduced as the group increases in size. Fourth, because of greater amounts of differentiation among members, it is more difficult to reach consensus in large groups than in small groups.

3. How do patterns of conformity (to group norms), leadership, and decision making vary among social groups?

Social control in social groups takes two forms. First, members of the group may be committed to a set of norms and values, and their behavior conforms to these shared expectations. The acceptance of shared norms binds a group together. When such commitment and conformity break down, however, a second form of social control sometimes arises: the use--or the threatened use--of force.

According to Bales, social groups need two different kinds of leaders in order to accomplish two different goals. The *instrumental* leader directs group members to perform certain tasks, while the *expressive* leader maintains good spirits and relations within the group.

All groups are required to make decisions, a process that involves four stages: 1) orientation to the problem and collection of available information; 2) evaluation of the possibilities; 3) eliminating options and making the decision; and 4) restoring equilibrium or balance after the consequences of the decision become apparent. Sometimes *groupthink* prevents effective decision making: members become so concerned about agreement, consensus, and unanimity that they overlook or dismiss as unimportant some of the major problems that confront them. Groupthink often results when a group insulates itself from new ideas and helpful criticism from those outside the group. The pressures for conformity within the group make it impossible for insiders to question the value of the group's decision.

4. What are the major types of social groups?

Sociologists have identified several types of social groups, distinguished by their different effects on the members' attitudes, feelings, and behavior. For example, *in-groups* are those with which a person identifies and in which he or she feels at home. *Out-groups* are the opposite: groups with which a person does not identify and in which he or she does not feel at home. Almost any social characteristic shared by more than a few people can give rise to an in-group: ethnic heritage, family name, age, economic status, occupation, drug use, or leisure activities. In-groups develop a sense of "we"-ness--togetherness, common perceptions and evaluations, and a consciousness of kind.

An important step in the formation of an in-group--and in its separation from out-groups--is the creation of *group boundaries* that distinguish in-group members from the rest of society. These social boundaries are implicitly understood lines that demarcate who is in from who is out. Such boundaries have two consequences: they keep outsiders from interacting with the in-group, and they inhibit insiders from moving out to interact with nonmembers. Group boundaries are established and made visible in several ways: members of an in-group symbolize their membership visually by wearing distinctive items (a fraternity pin or a nun's habit) or by talking in distinctive slang; conflict with out-groups also draws members together in the confrontation with a common enemy, and makes clear the line between inside and out.

Cooley distinguished primary groups from secondary groups. *Primary groups* have a very close-knit nature; examples include families and small-town neighborhoods. Primary groups have five characteristics: continuous face-to-face interaction, strong personal identity with the group, strong ties of affection among group members, multifaceted relationships (that is, on many different levels), and long-lasting or enduring relationships within the group. Cooley chose the word "primary" for these kinds of groups because of the functions they perform: primary groups are the "first" agents of socialization in the life course; they are important agents of social control in that they are responsible for the enforcement of social norms; and they satisfy people's basic emotional and psychological needs.

Secondary groups are the opposite of primary groups. They have the following five characteristics: limited face-to-face interaction, modest or weak personal identity with the group, weak ties of affection among members, limited relationship (that is, on only one level), and temporary existence. Typically, students who attend a large lecture class for a semester constitute a secondary group. The dichotomy of primary and secondary is considered more accurately as a continuum or a scale: actual groups have primariness or secondariness to some degree rather than absolutely.

Reference groups are those to which we look when evaluating and shaping our behavior, but to which we do not necessarily belong. Reference groups have two functions: they provide standards for evaluating ourselves and our accomplishments, and they serve a normative function by furnishing guidelines for how to think or act. A high-school basketball player who aspires to a professional career might adopt the Boston Celtics as a reference group. He takes their values and performances as the standard for evaluating his own progress as a basketball player and for guiding his behavior, even though he is not (yet) a member of the Celtics.

5. Why is commitment from members important for group survival?

All social groups need some degree of commitment from members if they are to survive. That is, members must be willing to give needed resources--their time and money, their labor, or even their "hearts and minds"--so that the group can accomplish its objectives. Some groups, like the Old Order Amish described in the textbook, require very high levels of commitment from their members. The Amish are an example of a *greedy group*--those groups that make exclusive, all encompassing claims on members for their hearts, minds, and undivided loyalties. Most social groups want only *part* of their members' time, energy, and resources, but greedy groups want *all* of these things.

How can greedy groups succeed in obtaining undivided, all encompassing loyalties and commitment from their members? Kanter identifies six commitment mechanisms that are prevalent in successful greedy groups: 1) Sacrifice: group members are required to give up something of value in order to join the group, something that is readily available in the outside world; 2) Investment: members are required to contribute tangible resources such as money or labor to the group; 3) Renunciation: members of the group are expected to relinquish all personal relationships with those (usually outsiders) who could interfere with members' obligations to the group; 4) Communion: members come together as a group in rituals or other joint, symbolic activities; 5) Mortification: members of the group are expected to let the *private* self die; and 6) Transcendence: members feel a special power or virtue as members of the group.

6. Why are formal organizations so prominent in modern societies?

Formal organizations differ from social groups in that specialized tasks are assigned explicitly to designated jobs; people are organized into hierarchies of control and responsibility; and detailed rules govern organizational procedures. Why have formal organizations come to dominate modern societies (an especially curious phenomenon because they are often associated in the public mind with red tape and other inefficiencies)? The answer is that formal organizations provide a more rational and more efficient way for large numbers of people to channel their efforts effectively into a common goal by integrating diverse operations and (in some cases) by overcoming rivals or other opposing forces. Once certain bureaucratic innovations are tried and are proved effective, other organizations adopt them rapidly. The result is a society regulated largely by formal organizations that share many of the same bureaucratic arrangements.

This general point becomes clear when we examine the introduction and the subsequent spread of bureaucratic innovations in three spheres of life: the military, business, and government. The Prussian general von Moltke introduced two bureaucratic innovations--1) thoroughly trained and similarly skilled staff officers and 2) standardized divisions--that were copied quickly by other major armies after the Prussians defeated the French in 1870-71. Swift was the first to expand the scope of his meat packing company (for example, by building and operating a fleet of refrigerator railroad cars) and to organize these diverse operations with a hierarchical, centralized administrative structure. Swift and Company was so successful in its integration of diverse operations that other companies in the meat-packing business were forced to copy Swift's bureaucratic innovations in order to compete. Finally, the Tennessee Valley Authority successfully employed still another now-common feature of formal organizations: *co-optation*, the processes of defusing potential opponents by making them part of one's own organizational structure. Residents who opposed the federal government's plans to build dams throughout the Tennessee River Valley were invited to join TVA "citizens' advisory boards."

When these people realized that they were being given a voice in the TVA's plans, they relaxed their opposition and the Authority was successful.

7. What is bureaucracy, and what are the limitations of bureaucratic organization?

A *bureaucracy* is an organizational structure characterized by specialization of tasks, hierarchy of offices, explicit rules, impersonality in handling employees and clients, and rewards based on merit rather than on personal factors. Structuring collective efforts in bureaucratic fashion enabled organizations to maximize effectiveness in reaching collective goals, to accomplish these goals at the lowest cost, and to control uncertainty most effectively by regulating workers, supplies, and markets.

Sociological researchers have found that not all features of bureaucracies allow organizations to attain their goals more effectively and more efficiently. For example, Roethlisberger and Dixon found in the 1920s that life in an organization was not determined completely by its *formal structure* (that is, by the official positions, duties, rules, and regulations as set by the leaders of an organization). Alongside the formal structure is an *informal structure*--a collection of unofficial norms that develop among members of an organization for the purposes of solving problems not covered by the formal rules, eliminating unpleasant duties, and protecting members' interests. As suggested by the case of the Hawthorne Western Electric plant, workers whose behavior conforms to the informal structure are often less effective in helping the organization reach the official goals stated explicitly in its formal structure.

Three other limitations hamper the ability of bureaucracies to achieve their organizational goals. First, many workers in bureaucracies succumb to *ritualism*, in which they follow rules slavishly while losing sight of why those rules were instituted in the first place. Such employees are often unable to recognize changing circumstances or to deal with them effectively. Second, *Parkinson's Law* suggests that work loads in bureaucracies expand to fill the available time. In other words, there is considerable waste in many formal organizations because employees perform tasks *just* to fill time. Third, bureaucracies often protect inept workers (rather than getting rid of them) in order to reduce costs of personnel turnover and to maintain company morale. A related form of inefficiency has been identified as the *Peter Principle*: workers who are effective at a job are promoted again and again until inevitably they reach a level of incompetence (that is, they finally attain a job that they cannot handle).

8. What variations in bureaucratic organizations exist, and why?

Organizations vary in other structural features: size, complexity (in diversity of jobs), centralization or dispersion of control, and range (or variety) of organizational goals. Why do formal organizations vary in regard to these four characteristics?

Most sociologists agree that formal organizations vary in their structural arrangement as a response to differences in their external environment. The external environment can be considered as elements outside the organization that influence its effectiveness in reaching organizational goals. The availability of competent labor and of raw materials, demand for goods or services produced, and competition from other providers are all aspects of the external environment of a business organization.

Two models have been proposed to describe the relationship between the external environment and the structure or functioning of formal organizations. Each model is an attempt to explain why bureaucracies differ in their structural features. The *adaptation model* suggests that organizations structure themselves to increase the chances of their success in a particular environment--that is, they adapt to changing circumstances. The *selection model* suggests that organizations have too much inertia to respond swiftly to changing environments; instead, the external environment determines or selects which organizational structures will succeed and which will fail. For example, in unstable environments where conditions are changing quickly and are unpredictable (as with fickle restaurant patrons who move quickly from ethnic fad to ethnic fad), *generalist* organizations (restaurants that offer varied menus) are more likely to succeed than *specialist* organizations (restaurants offering only one kind of food). In this case, consumer demand--one element of the external environment--selects which kind of restaurant will succeed.

Many Japanese organizations are more successful than their American counterparts. Ouchi has identified five strategies contributing to this success: 1) lifetime employment, 2) promotion based on seniority, 3) emphasis on group achievements, 4) decentralized decision making, and 5) holistic concern for employees. To a large extent, such features are rooted in Japanese culture, which may make it difficult to simply transmit the features to another culture. To use another example, the Volvo plant in Sweden restructured the assembly line to include small teams of craftsmen to assemble an entire car. This restructuring was in part a response to aspects of Swedish culture, such as guaranteed full employment. Although workers at the plant are happier, absenteeism remains high and productivity has suffered.

REVIEW OF CONCEPTS

Match the concept with the definition.

Concepts

a. adaptation model	j. group dynamics	r. primary group
b. aggregate	k. groupthink	s. reference group
c. bureaucracy	l. informal structure	t. ritualism
d. co-optation	m. in-group	u. secondary group
e. dyad	n. instrumental leadership	x. selection model
f. expressive leadership	o. out-group	y. social model
g. formal organization	p. Parkinson's law	z. triad
h. formal structure	q. Peter principle	aa. vertical integration
i. greedy group		

Definitions

_____ 1. Individuals who happen to be in the same place at the same time.

_____ 2. The process of defusing potential opponents by making them part of one's organizational structure.

_____ 3. A group characterized by continuous face-to-face interaction, strong personal identity with the group, strong ties of affection among group members, multifaceted relationships, and a tendency to be very enduring.

_____ 4. Leadership for the purpose of directing group members to perform various tasks.

_____ 5. An organizational structure characterized by specialization and division of labor, a hierarchy of offices, explicit rules and regulations, impersonality in decision making, and rewards and promotions based on merit.

_____ 6. A chain of command or vertical line of authority that helps facilitate the movement of information and strategic decisions both from the bottom up and from the top down.

_____ 7. An attempt to account for the incompetence of many bureaucratic employees by arguing that "in a hierarchy, every employee tends to rise to his [or her] level of incompetence."

_____ 8. Leadership for the purpose of maintaining good spirits and relations within a group.

_____ 9. The theory that an organization adapts actively to its external environment by structuring itself so as to increase the chances of succeeding in that particular environment.

_____ 10. The tendency for members of small, highly cohesive groups with forceful, respected leaders to be so intent on maintaining unanimity that they overlook or dismiss as unimportant the flaws in their decisions.

_____ 11. The theory that the external environment determines which organizational structures will succeed and which will fail. Organizations will thrive if they have chosen structures well suited to the external environment; they will perish if they have chosen structures that are poorly suited.

_____ 12. A three-person group.

_____ 13. A group with which a person does not identify and toward which he or she feels like an outsider.

_____ 14. A group to which people refer when evaluating themselves and shaping their behavior, but to which they may not necessarily belong.

_____ 15. A set of individuals who identify with one another and who interact in informally structured ways based on norms, goals, and values that they share implicitly.

_____ 16. Merton's term for following rules and regulations without regard for original goals or the consequences of one's action.

_____ 17. A two-person group.

_____ 18. A group characterized by limited face-to-face interaction, modest or weak personal identity with the group, weak ties of affection among group members, limited relationships, and a tendency not to be very enduring.

_____ 19. A group with which a person identifies and feels at home.

_____ 20. An explanation of why bureaucratic employees often appear busier than they should be: "Work expands to fill the time available for its completion."

_____ 21. A set of individuals whose activities are designed consciously and precisely for the purposes of achieving explicitly stated goals.

_____ 22. The unofficial norms that develop among the members of an organization for the purposes of solving problems not covered by the formal rules, eliminating unpleasant duties, and protecting their own interests.

1.	b	9.	a	17.	e
2.	d	10.	k	18.	u
3.	r	11.	x	19.	m
4.	n	12.	z	20.	p
5.	c	13.	o	21.	g
6.	aa	14.	s	22.	l
7.	q	15.	y		
8.	f	16.	t		

REVIEW QUESTIONS

After studying Chapter 8, answer the following questions. Correct answers are listed after the questions; each is followed by a short explanation. You are also referred to pages in the textbook for relevant discussion.

1. Which of the following characteristics is typical of social groups but *not* of formal organizations?
   a. large size (that is, number of participants)
   b. formality of social structure
   c. status, roles, and responsibilities assigned explicitly
   d. activities designed consciously to achieve explicit goals
   e. values, norms, and goals shared implicitly

2. Which of the following is best defined as a social group, as understood by sociologists?
   a. fans at a football game
   b. passengers on a bus
   c. shoppers in a supermarket
   d. members of a Girl Scout troop
   e. women

3. Which statement does *not* describe how group experiences influence our lives?
   a. Social groups link our private lives to the larger society.
   b. Group membership determines our race.
   c. Groups provide security and support.
   d. Groups shape our values.
   e. Groups affect how we behave.

4. Which is the best example of an aggregate, as defined by sociologists?
   a. members of a college sorority
   b. members of a small church
   c. a nuclear family
   d. children at a day care center
   e. customers in a shopping mall

5. Which is likely to occur in a triad but *not* in a dyad?
   a. Members do not need to worry about giving a third party (from within the group) "air time".

b. Members cannot hide their responsibility for events that occur within the group.
c. No other insider is available to act as mediator between two group members.
d. If one member ceases to participate, the group dies.
e. Coalition can form.

6. Which is more likely to be found in small groups than in large groups?
   a. Each member's average contribution is smaller.
   b. Members are more inhibited from speaking during collective assemblies.
   c. Greater resources are available for problem solving.
   d. It is easier to reach consensus among group members.
   e. Division of labor is specialized.

7. Joe was the leader of a small group of men who hung around at the corner tavern. The other men respected Joe because he was able to resolve differences within the group; he was good at "smoothing ruffled feathers,' and he made everyone feel important and well-liked. One night a fire broke out in the tavern. Interestingly enough, it was not Joe but Peter who took decisive leadership to clear out the tavern in a safe manner. What might a sociologist conclude from this story?
   a. Joe had charisma.
   b. Peter had charisma.
   c. Peter was a task leader but Joe was a socio-emotional leader.
   d. Joe was a victim of groupthink.
   e. Both Peter and Joe had characteristics found in all group leaders.

8. Which one of the following is the *first* stage out of sequence in the stages groups go through in making choices? Or are they all in the correct order?
   a. orientation
   b. evaluating possibilities
   c. eliminating less desirable options and picking the best one
   d. restoring equilibrium
   e. the stages are in the correct order

9. A group of men and women who work together on a factory assembly line hold a meeting to discuss possible improvements in their working conditions. A number of workers had talked privately about various reorganizations of the shop floor, but once the meeting began, none of them offered their proposals because they feared that other members would disagree and argue against them. No one wanted to rock the boat, so no decision was reached. This story illustrates
   a. task leadership.
   b. socio-emotional leadership.
   c. groupthink.
   d. coalition formation.
   e. co-optation.

10. In the congregation of a Methodist church in small-town America, which of the following is most likely to be an out-group?
    a. member of the local YMCA
    b. participants in a summer softball league (with teams representing each church in town)
    c. shoppers at the local farmer's market on Saturday morning
    d. heroin addicts

e. organizers of the local Fourth of July parade

11. Which is a *false* statement about group boundaries?
    a. Conflict with outsiders weakens or destroys group boundaries.
    b. Boundaries prevent outsiders from entering spheres of interaction with insiders.
    c. Boundaries inhibit insiders from moving beyond the confines of the group.
    d. Members display symbols such as badges or uniforms to establish visible boundaries between insiders and outsiders.
    e. Forms of slang distinctive to a group establish its boundaries of membership.

12. Which is the best example of a primary group?
    a. all children between five and eight years old in New York City
    b. a hippie commune during the 1960s
    c. traveling salesmen
    d. farmers' daughters
    e. people in an elevator

13. Anna would like to be a ballet dancer. She hopes to join a major New York company and go on tour. She watches the American Ballet Theater on public television and uses that company as a model to shape and evaluate her own progress as a dancer. For Anna, the American Ballet Company is
    a. an in-group.
    b. an out-group.
    c. a reference group.
    d. a primary group.
    e. a secondary group.

14. All Amish men are required to wear black suits, collarless shirts, and wide brimmed hats; all Amish women are required to wear long dresses, black stockings, and traditional aprons and caps. These features of Amish life illustrate which of Kanter's commitment mechanisms?
    a. transcendence
    b. mortification
    c. investment
    d. renunciation
    e. communion

15. Which of the following is best described as a formal organization?
    a. members of a summer softball team
    b. the congregation of a Methodist church
    c. the McDonald's Corporation
    d. customers at a shopping mall
    e. participants in an anti-smoking rally

16. A local real estate developer plans to build a large complex of student condominiums in the middle of a neighborhood of detached single family homes. The neighborhood residents organize a protest. The developer invites them to join an "advisory board" on which they can voice their complaints and make suggestions. Eventually most residents give up the protest and come to see the development as an asset to the neighborhood. This process illustrates
    a. coalition.
    b. co-optation.

110

c. highly trained, interchangeable leaders.

d. hierarchy of personnel.

e. integration of diverse operations.

17. The local Japanese restaurant is not succeeding: customers are few and costs are rising. The operator notices that hot, spicy foods have become increasingly popular. He expands his menu so that it includes not only his Japanese dishes but Schezuan Chinese dishes as well. This action illustrates

a. collectivist organization.

b. degree of complexity in range of jobs.

c. stability in the external environment.

d. the selection model.

e. the adaptation model.

18. Jackie Whizkid was promoted up the ladder so quickly that by age 38 she found herself in a job she simply could not handle. This situation illustrates

a. ritualism.

b. mortification.

c. transcendence.

d. the Peter Principle

e. Parkinson's Law.

19. Harley the librarian becomes so devoted to keeping the books arranged *neatly* on the shelves that he discourages people from browsing and eventually from using the library. This pattern is an example of

a. the Peter Principle.

b. ritualism.

c. protection of the inept.

d. Parkinson's Law.

e. informal structure.

20. Workers on the shop floor decide that their employer's expectations for output per hour are unreasonable and impossible to satisfy. They agree among themselves that the rate of work on the assembly line should be slower in the afternoon than in the morning. This agreement illustrates

a. informal structure.

b. sacrifice.

c. co-optation.

d. transcendence.

e. aggregate interests.

21. The example of Mitsubishi in Japan and Volvo in Sweden illustrate which principle about organizations?

a. Organizational structure reflects a society's culture.

b. Generally, larger organizations are better than smaller ones.

c. Cultural values affect organizational members but not the organizations themselves.

d. Organizations in Europe and Japan are more effective than those in the United States.

e. The formal structure is more important than the informal structure in making organizations more effective.

1. *e.* A social group is a set of individuals who identify with one another and interact in informally structured ways based on norms, goals, and values that they share implicitly. See page 181.

2. *d.* Only the Girl Scout troop has the characteristics of a social group: regular face-to-face interaction, agreement on important norms and values, and shared identity. See page 181.

3. *b.* A person's race--Caucasian or black, for example--is a trait determined at birth by a combination of genetic factors (skin color) and social factors (how skin color is defined and interpreted in a given culture). One's race is not the result of group membership, but it may affect the kinds of groups one may join. See page 182.

4. *e.* Customers in a shopping mall are an aggregate of people who just happen to be in the same place at the same time. They do not interact regularly, nor do they necessarily share common values, norms, and goals. The other choices are examples of social groups. See page 182.

5. *e.* A dyad is a two person group; a triad is a three person group. The formation of coalitions--where two members line up against a third in some debate--can occur in triads but not dyads. See page 184.

6. *d.* Because the average contribution of each member decreases as the group increases in size, and because the diversity of opinions is likely to grow with increasing group size, sociologists expect that large groups would find it more difficult than small groups to reach consensus. See page 184.

7. *c.* The story illustrates the situational nature of leadership in groups. Joe is an expressive leader: he provided leadership for the purpose of maintaining good spirits and relations within a group. When circumstances changed, however, Peter took over as an instrumental leader: he provided leadership (appropriate in that emergency) for the purpose of directing group members to perform various tasks. See page 186.

8. *e.* Groups typically go through four steps in decision making. They are listed in the correct order. See page 186.

9. *c.* Groupthink is a tendency for members of a group to be concerned so strongly about maintaining group harmony and solidarity that they do not consider major issues or problems in the decision they are trying to make. See page 186.

10. *d.* Chances are good that the Methodists would not identify with heroin addicts, nor would they feel at home among them--both characteristics of out-groups. See page 187.

11. *a.* An effective way to create and maintain group boundaries is through conflict with outsiders. A common enemy draws insiders together and reaffirms the differences between them and outsiders (as when a key football game with an arch-rival tends to increase school spirit). See page 188.

12. *b.* Communes are usually surrogate or substitute nuclear families. They have the following characteristics of primary groups: continuous face-to-face interaction, strong personal identification with the group, strong ties of affection among members, multifaceted relationships, and long-lasting (enduring) relations in the group. See page 188.

13. *c.* Reference groups are those groups to which we refer consciously or unconsciously when we shape our behavior and evaluate our life situations. As the case of Anna shows, people do not necessarily belong to their reference groups. See page 189.

14. *d.* Renunciation means that members of a group are required to relinquish (or "renounce") all interpersonal relationships that could disrupt group cohesion by interfering with members' obligations or commitments. Development of close friendship ties with outsiders could cause Amish persons to question their beliefs and values; the wearing of distinctive Amish

dress--especially when among nonmembers--is one way to reduce the probability that such friendships will arise. Distinctive dress helps to establish a social boundary between the Amish and others. See page 191.

15. *c.* The McDonald's Corporation conforms to the definition of a formal organization: a set of individuals whose activities are designed consciously and precisely for the purpose of achieving explicitly stated goals. See page 192.

16. *b.* Co-optation is a process of diffusing potential opponents by making them part of one's own organizational structure. As suggested by the example of the Tennessee Valley Authority (in the textbook), co-optation can "cool out" the protestors, but often the organization's goals are altered in the process. Thus, in the example given in this question, it is likely that the details of the condominium plan were altered after the protesting residence were co-opted. See page 195.

17. *e.* The adaptation model is an attempt to explain bureaucratic variation (that is, why bureaucracies have different structural features). This model suggests that an organization (such as this restaurant) adapts actively to its external environments by restructuring itself so as to increase the chances of succeeding in a particular external environment. See page 199.

18. *d.* According to the Peter Principle (an example of one limitation of bureaucratic organization), workers rise to their own level of incompetence. Those who do well at the job are promoted until they reach a job that is beyond their competence. See page 199.

19. *b.* Ritualism describes another limitation of bureaucratic organization. It refers to the process of following rules and regulations slavishly without regard for original goals or the consequences of one's actions. The librarian is expected to keep books neat so that patrons can find what they need, but Harley's fastidiousness had the opposite effect. See page 198.

20. *a.* Informal structure refers to the informal norms that develop among the members of an organization for the purpose of solving problems not covered by the formal rules, eliminating unpleasant duties, and protecting their own interests. This example shows that the informal structure within a bureaucracy sometimes can work against the attainment of official organizational goals. See page 198.

21. *a.* Both examples show that organizational structures reflect the cultures in which they exist. Mitsubishi's structure reflects the Japanese emphasis on group achievement, and Volvo's structure reflects the Swedish guarantee of full employment. See pages 200-202.

EXERCISES

Exercise 1

Think about a job you hold now or held previously and describe the formal organization involved.

1. Describe your job and organization. Give examples of the features in Weber's ideal type: specialization, hierarchy of offices, rules, impersonality, and rewards based on merit.

2. Give examples of the informal structure and show how this structure both helped and hindered goal attainment.

3. Give examples of bureaucratic failure: ritualism, Parkinson's Law, and protection of the inept.

4. Discuss whether your organization's relationship with its environment can be explained more accurately with the adaptation model or the selection model.

5. What is the likelihood that your organization will adapt some of the features of the Japanese organizations that have made them so successful?

Exercise 2

A sociogram is a visual display (a map or picture) of links among people in a social group. Sociograms illustrate patterns of interaction; they also show which members are centrally located in the interaction network and which members are on the periphery.

1. Think about a small social group to which you belong. It might be a dormitory floor, a friendship group, an extended family, a work group, or even people attending a party. Draw a sociogram for this small group. Locate each member on the map; draw links among those people who seem tightly connected.

2. With the help of this sociogram, can you identify people who occupy certain roles in the group, such as instrumental leader or expressive leader?

3. Think about the people whom you have located in the center of the map. How do they differ sociologically from those you have located at the edges?

4. Are the boundaries of this group precise or ambiguous? That is, were you unsure whether a certain individual should or should not be included on the sociogram? What is the relationship between the precision or ambiguity of group boundaries and levels of commitment by individuals to the group?

Exercise 3

A social group is a set of individuals who identify with one another and who interact in informally structured ways based on norms, goals, and values that they share implicitly. Even though all social groups share these general characteristics, they vary dramatically in other ways. Think of three social groups to which you belong. Fill in the following chart; as you do so, try to gain a sense of how some characteristics of a group affect its other characteristics. For example, do you find that small groups have different leadership patterns from large groups?

Characteristic	Group #1	Group #2	Group #3
Name			
Goals			

Characteristic	Group #1	Group #2	Group #3
Size			
Leadership structure			
Important norms or rules			
Rituals			
Frequency of meetings			
Intimacy among members			
Formal offices			
Informal division of labor			

Characteristic	Group #1	Group #2	Group #3
Sources of conflict within group			
Conflicts with outsiders			
Criteria for membership			
Dues or membership fees			
Strength of group boundaries			
Commitment mechanisms			

Chapter 9

CLASS AND STRATIFICATION

OBJECTIVES

After reading Chapter 9, you should understand the following main points and be able to answer the objectives.

1. Stratification refers to the division of a society into layers (strata) of people who have unequal amounts of scarce but desirable resources.
   1.1 Define stratification.
   1.2 Differentiate closed stratification systems from open stratification systems.
   1.3 Describe the relevance of achieved statuses.
   1.4 Describe how stratification is a systematic arrangement.
   1.5 Define social class.

2. Stratification reflects the five key concepts.
   2.1 Regarding structure, summarize and assess Marx's views on stratification.
   2.2 Regarding functional integration, summarize and assess the views of Davis and Moore.
   2.3 Regarding power, summarize and assess the views of Weber.
   2.4 Regarding culture, define status group and prestige.
   2.5 Define caste system.
   2.6 Summarize the views of Bourdieu on cultural capital.
   2.7 Regarding social action, compare the views of Marx, Davis and Moore, and Weber.

3. Considerable differences exist among the various social classes; mobility from one class to another is limited.
   3.1 Differentiate wealth from income.
   3.2 Profile the five social classes.
   3.3 Summarize the data on the distribution of wealth and income.
   3.4 Determine if the gap between rich and poor has narrowed or widened.
   3.5 Define social mobility and indicate the relevance of mobility rates.
   3.6 Define structural mobility.
   3.7 Describe the role of immigration in social mobility.
   3.8 Assess the historical and current patterns and rates of mobility.
   3.9 Summarize the research on status attainment.

4. Poverty has a variety of effects.
   4.1 Explain how poverty is relative.
   4.2 Indicate the poverty line for a family of four.

4.3 Indicate the proportion currently living in poverty and state how this proportion has changed since 1960.

4.4 Construct a profile of the poor.

4.5 Give two reasons for the growing number of working poor.

4.6 Profile the ghetto poor.

4.7 Synopsize the views of Wilson regarding the underclass.

4.8 List the causes of the rise in homelessness.

4.9 Link poverty to various indicators of life chances.

CHAPTER SUMMARY

1. What is stratification and why are sociologists interested in stratification?

Sociologists are interested in explaining how social characteristics influence people's experiences and attitudes. Our society stresses equality of opportunity, but in reality, access to high-paying jobs and to other rewards is determined as much by race, sex, social class, and parents' occupation as by individual effort. *Stratification* refers to the division of a society into layers (strata) of people who have unequal amounts of scarce but desirable resources, unequal life chances, and unequal social influence. Stratification systems are generally institutionalized; inequalities are built into the social structure and may persist from generation to generation. In a *closed stratification system* it is difficult or virtually impossible to move up in the social hierarchy. In an *open stratification system*, on the other hand, no positions are officially denied to people because of their birth or other inherited characteristics. This open ideology reflects the belief that class positions are mostly achieved statuses, the result of individual effort. In reality, however, the class position of one's parents remains the most accurate predictor of one's own class position.

Social stratification does not occur by chance. It is a systematic arrangement that serves the interests of some people more than others. In fact, stratification has been found in all societies. In modern industrial societies, wealth and income are particularly salient in determining stratification. The term *social class* reflects this emphasis on economic differences.

2. What is the role of wealth and income in determining social class?

Karl Marx was one of the first to provide a structural analysis of inequality. He argued that the developing division between the rich and the poor in the nineteenth century was new in two ways. First, capitalism produced new sources of wealth, especially industrial production. Second, capitalism divided the rich from the poor in new ways. Marx believed that capitalists had to exploit workers in order to survive and make profits. Hence the interests of capitalists and of workers were fundamentally opposed, a situation that could lead only to economic crises and class conflict. Marx's major contribution lies in his emphasis on the role of structural inequality in social organization.

Marx's structural view was challenged by the functional integration view of Davis and Moore, who emphasized how opportunities to earn varying levels of income would motivate people. They argued that some jobs are more important than others to the functional integration of complex societies. As a result, higher wages are necessary to encourage the limited number of people who have the talents or are willing to invest in the education required to perform these jobs. Hence social inequality is functionally necessary. Davis and Moore also completely ignored the effects of power, influence, and inheritance on the labor market. Critics have noted that it is difficult to assess functional importance objectively.

Weber underscored the role of power in his analysis of economic stratification. He argued that modern societies contained other sources of power than ownership of the means of production. He also believed that power should be seen as a dimension of stratification in itself, not merely as a support for economic stratification. Weber highlighted the power of those who control the bureaucracies that have become so influential in modern societies.

Weber believed that cultural factors must be considered in addition to wealth and power to fully explain stratification systems. He used the term *status group* to describe groups of people whose prestige derives from cultural factors, such as race and ethnicity, rather than economic or political elements. *Prestige* is the social esteem, respect, or approval that is given to people because they possess attributes that their society considers admirable. The prestige attached to different attributes varies considerably across societies. For example, in India's traditional *caste system* (a closed stratification system), spiritual status is important; this status and one's position in the social hierarchy are determined at birth. Americans emphasize other factors as significant for prestige, such as how people earn their money, how they spend it, who they are, whom they know, and how successful they are.

Prestige is an important issue in stratification analysis. Sociologists measure the prestige of an occupation by asking representative samples of people to rate the social standing of various jobs. Bourdieu has suggested that people accumulate not only wealth or power, but also what he calls "cultural capital"--resources that benefit an individual because of the prestige they confer (a college degree, for example).

Social stratification directly affects social action. Marx showed that class inequality is not only the result of individual action but also a product of the class structure. He believed that workers could change their situation only by joining together to overthrow the capitalist system. Davis and Moore, taking a functional integration view, emphasized individual action. They felt that motivating society's members to work had to be a socially organized system. Weber was more concerned with individuals' efforts to change their own position, or that of their social group, within the class structure. Because these efforts involved competition, they reflected the differences in individuals' power.

3. Is America really the land of opportunity?

Our country was founded on the principle that "all men are created equal," although exceptions have existed since the very beginning. For example, women were denied the vote and were excluded from many economic privileges in American society until the twentieth century. Also, although American culture values equality, it accepts a very unequal class structure as legitimate.

It is difficult to determine how many classes exist in American society. Sociologists commonly define classes by looking at wealth, income, and occupational characteristics. *Wealth* refers to people's valuable property--what they own. *Income*, on the other hand, refers to how much people receive rather than to what they already possess. Wealth is the most important factor in distinguishing the persons at the top of the American class structure. Differences between middle- and working-class Americans are related more to occupational characteristics. Kerbo divided the class structure into five groups. The *upper class* includes families that own a great deal of property, especially major corporations and real estate, and who possess the great authority that results from such ownership. These are generally old, established families. The *corporate class* includes people who have great bureaucratic authority in major corporations and government, usually this authority is not based on ownership. Examples include top corporate executives and board members. The *middle class* includes people who own relatively little property but whose occupations give them medium to high income, prestige, and authority. The *working class* includes people who own little or no property and whose occupations give them low to medium income and prestige, with little or no authority. The *lower class* includes individuals with no property, who are often unemployed. They have no authority and no prestige.

The distribution of wealth in the United States is very lopsided. Most Americans possess very little wealth, only one-fifth own stocks or bonds, and only one-tenth own any real estate besides their homes. Oliver and Shapiro found that the median net worth of the wealthiest 1 percent of the population is 22 times the median for the remaining 99. This disparity is even greater when financial assets are examined. The distribution of income is also very uneven: the bottom one-fifth of American families receive only 4 percent of the nation's total income, while the top one-fifth receive 47 percent. The top 5 percent of households receive 17 percent of all income, more than three times the share they would receive if income were distributed equally. This gap between the rich and the poor widened significantly during the 1980s. The richest 1 percent of Americans receive almost as much income as the bottom 40 percent. The incomes of the middle class increased only slightly in the 1980s. The working class saw no increase in income, and the lower class actually lost ground. Finally, the proportion of income that poor households paid in taxes increased, while it decreased for the upper and the corporate classes. One of the main reasons for this widening gap was that a greater share of Americans' national income came from property-based income or capital gains rather than from wages.

4. How extensive is social mobility?

Social mobility refers to movement from one social position to another. *Mobility rates* are general patterns of movement up or down the social scale. Most upward mobility occurs in small incremental steps. Sociologists emphasize that social mobility in the United States generally results from structural change rather than from individual success. *Structural mobility* refers to changes in the number and kinds of occupations available in a society, relative to the number of workers available to fill them. Structural mobility occurs as a result of external changes in opportunities for stability or mobility.

The United States has long been an upwardly mobile society, primarily because of the dramatic rise in the labor market and in technological developments. Widespread immigration also has stimulated occupational advancement because immigrants actually may help to create more and better jobs. The fact that white-collar workers tend to have fewer children than workers in other categories also stimulates upward mobility. Today, however, this pattern is disintegrating. The auto and steel industries are in decline, and other industries have moved their production facilities overseas. Automation has eliminated many jobs. As a result, downward mobility has occurred. Although downward mobility has been particularly pronounced in the working class, it has also affected the middle class.

Sociologists have developed status achievement models to understand how status is transmitted and determined. Blau and Duncan concluded that social origin affects ultimate social status primarily by influencing the level of education one attains. Sewell and his colleagues concluded that educational and occupational attainment are the result of two processes: those which shape one's status aspirations and those which convert the aspirations into a new status. Once an individual finishes school, the impact of social class background becomes inconsequential.

5. How widespread is poverty? Who are the poor?

Poverty is relative: how poor a person feels is influenced strongly by the groups used for comparison. The *poverty line* is the minimum amount of money that families of different sizes and compositions need to purchase a nutritionally adequate diet, on the assumption that they spend one-third of their income for food. In 1990 the poverty line for a family of four was $13,359 per year. The poverty line is somewhat controversial because it does not take into account such noncash benefits as food stamps, does not reflect regional differences in the cost of living, and does not consider changing patterns of family expenses. In 1960, 20 percent the country's population lived in poverty. It reached a low of 9.5 percent in 1969 and remained below 10 percent until 1980. In 1991, 14.2 percent lived in poverty. It is hard to generalize about America's poor. Neither the homeless nor inner-city unwed teenage mothers account for the majority of poor people. A wide variety of people are represented, such as farmers, recently unemployed persons, and individuals who have suffered crises such as divorce or death. Although most poor Americans are white, African-Americans and Hispanic-Americans are more likely to be poor. One of the major changes in the poor population is the rapid increase in the number of poor children and the simultaneous reduction in poverty among the elderly. Nearly half of those living below the poverty line are employed. Changing family structure, particularly the increase in female-headed households, has accounted for nearly half of the rise in child poverty rates since 1980.

Many of those who are poor are employed as well. In fact, the number of Americans who worked full-time but remained in poverty increased by 37 percent in the 1980s. Two factors help to explain the growing number of the working poor. First, the occupational structure of the economy shifted from manufacturing to services in the 1970s and 1980s. Plant closings and new technologies reduced the need for manual labor. Second, the value of the minimum wage declined steadily in the 1980s. Most minimum-wage workers are adult, not teenaged. In 1979 the minimum wage was worth about half the average wage in terms of purchasing power, but by 1987 it was worth only one-third of the average wage. The working poor live especially in rural America.

Many of the poor are concentrated in the ghettos. Residents of a ghetto are often known as the "underclass," people at the very bottom of the class structure. William Julius Wilson, the leading authority on this subject, disagrees with the popular notion that the rise of ghetto poverty reflects the development of a "welfare mentality" or a "culture of poverty" among urban black people. He underscores the role of social structure rather than of culture or voluntary action and argues that nonconforming and deviant behavior among the ghetto poor is the result, not the cause, of their living conditions and of the restricted opportunities available to them. Changes in the economy and the migration of higher-income African-Americans out of the inner cities have contributed to the rise of ghetto poverty.

The homeless population exploded in the 1980s for several reasons. First, economic changes increased the number of poor people. Second, the availability of low-cost housing diminished rapidly. Third, government assistance for poor people was cut back. Fourth, thousands of mentally ill people became homeless when they were released from hospitals without adequate community facilities to help them. In short, the rise in the homeless population occurred because the poverty rate increased at the same time as social supports were cut back.

Poverty affects the life chances of the poor. The term *life chances* refers to the distribution, within a social system, of opportunities that affect people's health, survival, and happiness. For example, nonwhite babies are twice as likely as white babies to die in infancy. They are also twice as likely to be born to poor mothers. The availability of medical care also varies by social class. For example, the proportion of the poor covered by Medicaid declined from about 65 percent in 1976 to 38 percent in 1986. This differential access to medical care continues throughout the life cycle. The poor also spend a much greater proportion of their incomes on food than do other Americans, and often pay more for less. In addition, they pay proportionately more for housing. As a result, the poor experience more hunger.

REVIEW OF CONCEPTS

Match the concept with the definition.

Concepts

a. achieved statuses
b. caste system
c. closed stratification system
d. corporate class
e. income
f. life chances

g. lower class
h. middle class
i. open stratification system
j. prestige
k. social class
l. social mobility

m. stratification
n. structural mobility
o. upper class
p. wealth
q. working class

Definitions

____ 1. A social class system in which it is difficult or impossible to move up the social hierarchy.

____ 2. A stratification system in which there are few obstacles to social mobility; positions are awarded on the basis of merit, and rank is tied to individual achievement.

____ 3. The social class that is composed of people who own little or no property, whose jobs give them middle-to-low income, and who have little or no prestige.

____ 4. The opportunities to realize health, long life, and happiness in a social system.

____ 5. The movement of people from one social position to another, either upward or downward.

____ 6. The division of a society into layers of people who have unequal amounts of any given scarce reward or resource.

____ 7. What people own and draw upon in time of need and pass to future generations.

____ 8. The social class that is made up of families who own large amounts of property, from which they derive a great deal of authority.

____ 9. Social esteem resulting from the possession of attributes that are regarded as admirable and perhaps enviable by people in a specific social setting.

____ 10. Changes in the number and kinds of occupations available in a society, relative to the number of workers available to fill them.

____ 11. People who occupy the same layer of a system of social stratification.

____ 12. The social class that comprises people who own relatively little property but whose occupations provide them with high-to-middle incomes, prestige, and authority.

____ 13. The social class consisting of people who have a great deal of bureaucratic authority in major corporations and in government not based on ownership of these corporations.

Answers

1.	c	6.	m	11.	k
2.	i	7.	p	12.	h
3.	q	8.	o	13.	d
4.	f	9.	j		
5.	l	10.	n		

REVIEW QUESTIONS

After studying Chapter 9, answer the following questions. The correct answers are listed after the questions; each is followed by a short explanation. You are also referred to pages in the textbook for relevant discussion.

1. A college professor has considerable prestige but a relatively low income. This situation reflects
   a. Marx's distinction between the bourgeoisie and the proletariat.
   b. Weber's distinction between the economic, political, and social dimensions of stratification.
   c. the disproportionate distribution of wealth in our country.
   d. the centrality of educational attainment in stratification.
   e. the weaknesses of stratification as an analytical concept.

2. Marx's view of stratification emphasized
   a. the role of religion.
   b. the sharp political division between the haves and the have-nots.
   c. the interconnectedness of economic status, political status, and social status.
   d. the role of overpopulation.
   e. the sharp economic division between those who own the means of production and those who work for wages.

3. Which of the following statements supports a functionalist theory of stratification?
   a. Psychiatrists are given more prestige because their work is enjoyable.
   b. Psychiatrists have high incomes because their job is important and difficult.
   c. Psychiatrists have high incomes because of their social class background, which helped them to decide to become psychiatrists.
   d. Psychiatrists have a great deal of personal and institutional power because of the prestige their job affords.
   e. Psychiatrists have power and prestige because they control who and how many people enter the field.

4. Which of the following statements supports a power perspective on stratification?
   a. Physicians are scarce because medical schools turn down many qualified applicants.
   b. Physicians are scarce because few people are willing to sacrifice time and social activities to obtain medical training.
   c. Lawyers have high incomes because they do the work that others do not have the patience to do.
   d. Lawyers have high incomes because they have struggled through many years of law school when others would not consider it worth the effort.
   e. b and d.

5. What did Weber mean by "status group?"
   a. A group that derives its status from economic power.
   b. A group that collectively seeks status.
   c. A group that derives its status from an occupation.
   d. A group that derives its status from its wealth.
   e. A group that derives its status from cultural factors like race and ethnicity.

6. Bourdieu argued that
   a. People accumulate wealth and power, which generates prestige.
   b. Social class is a product of economic struggle.
   c. People accumulate cultural capital resources that benefit an individual due to the prestige they confer.
   d. Prestige is an overworked term in stratification analysis and should be discarded.
   e. Cultural capital is equally distributed.

7. If the population is divided into fifths, the top and bottom fifths received approximately what percentages of the total national income?
   a. 20 percent and 20 percent
   b. 10 percent and 34 percent
   c. 10 percent and 44 percent
   d. 47 percent and 4 percent
   e. 65 percent and 5 percent

8. Available data shows that in the 1980s
   a. most Americans continued to have wealth greater than $20,000 per person.
   b. Americans' wealth increased substantially.
   c. the income gap between the top and the bottom segments of the population narrowed.
   d. the income gap between the top and the bottom segments of the population widened.
   e. cultural capital is equally distributed.

9. The main general determinant of prestige in American society is
   a. how people earn their money (occupation).
   b. how they spend their money (mode of consumption).
   c. who they are (ancestry).
   d. whom they know.
   e. how successful they are.

10. Which one of the following is correct?
    a. Open systems emphasize ascribed status and closed systems emphasize achieved status.
    b. Open systems and closed systems both emphasize ascribed status.
    c. Open systems emphasize achieved status and closed systems emphasize ascribed status.
    d. Open systems and closed systems both emphasize achieved status.
    e. Open systems and closed systems emphasize ascribed and achieved status, but the emphasis depends on the major societal values at a given time.

11. The American system could be classified as
    a. a closed class system emphasizing equality of results.
    b. a closed class system emphasizing equality of opportunity.
    c. an open class system emphasizing both equality of opportunity and equality of results.
    d. a class system between open and closed, emphasizing equality of opportunity.
    e. an open class system emphasizing equality of opportunity.

12. Mobility in America has historically been upward, primarily because of
    a. growth in the labor market.
    b. growth in technology.
    c. large-scale immigration.
    d. the lower birth rate among white-collar workers.
    e. all these factors.

13. The status attainment research has found that
    a. once someone has finished school, social class background becomes unimportant.
    b. once someone has finished school, social class background still has a major effect.
    c. the effect of schooling is much greater for men than for women.
    d. social class background has become much less important over the past few decades.
    e. we can conclude very little about the status attainment process.

14. In 1990, the poverty line for a family of four was
    a. about $9,500 per year.
    b. about $4,500 per year.
    c. about $13,500 per year.
    d. about $17,500 per year.
    e. about $20,500 per year.

15. Which one of the following statements regarding poverty is *false*?
    a. Poverty has increased among the young.
    b. Poverty has decreased among the old.
    c. The rate of poverty among blacks is higher than among whites.
    d. The majority of poor people are black.
    e. All are true.

16. Between 1960 and 1991, the poverty rate
    a. steadily declined.
    b. steadily increased.
    c. declined considerably and then increased.
    d. increased considerably and then declined.
    e. remained fairly constant.

17. Two factors stand out in explaining the growing number of working poor:
    a. the work ethic has declined and the occupational structure has changed.
    b. the occupational structure has changed and the value of the minimum wage has declined.
    c. the value of the minimum wage has declined and the definition of working poor has changed.
    d. the definition of working poor has changed and welfare benefits have declined.
    e. welfare benefits have declined and the work ethic has declined.

18. Wilson argues that ghetto residents are poor because
    a. they do not want to work.
    b. they develop a welfare mentality.
    c. they experience a culture of poverty.
    d. of changes in the social structure.
    e. they have large families.

19. Data on nutrition in America suggests that
    a. families earning less than $5,000 per year spend 40 percent of their incomes for food.
    b. the poor earn less but also pay less because they buy inferior products.
    c. poor children suffer from protein, iron, and vitamin deficiencies.
    d. none of the above.
    e. both a and c.

Answers

1. *b.* A noticeable discrepancy between prestige and income reflects Weber's distinction among the economic, political, and social aspects of stratification. See page 213.
2. *e.* Marx rejected the multilayered view of society. He saw a simple, sharp economic division between those who own the means of production in capitalist societies and those who must work for wages in order to survive. See pages 211-212.

3. *b.* The functionalist view states that societies must motivate people to seek important positions. They also must reward such people with income and prestige. See page 212.

4. *a.* Those stressing a power perspective maintain that stratification is the result of the struggle for scarce resources and that it persists because those in power preserve their positions. Weber highlighted the power of those who run the bureaucracies that have become more influential. See page 213.

5. *e.* Weber used the term "status group" to describe groups of people whose prestige derives from such cultural factors as race and ethnicity, as opposed to wealth and power. See page 214.

6. *c.* Bourdieu felt that people accumulate not just wealth or power, but also what he calls "cultural capital," resources that benefit an individual because of the prestige they confer. See page 215.

7. *d.* If the population is divided into fifths, in 1985 the top fifth received 46.6 percent and the bottom fifth received 3.9 percent of all income. See page 220.

8. *d.* Between 1980 and 1990, income in the lowest fifth dropped by 4 percent while income in the highest fifth increased by about 30 percent. See page 220.

9. *a.* The main general determinant of prestige is one's occupation. See page 214.

10. *c.* An open class system offers few impediments to social mobility and assigns status on the basis of achievement. A closed, or caste, system contains many obstacles to social mobility and assigns status on the basis of inherited characteristics. See page 210.

11. *d.* The American system falls somewhere between open and closed class systems, with emphasis on equality of opportunity. The class position of a person's parents remains the best predictor of the class position that person will occupy. See pages 210-211.

12. *e.* An expanding labor market, improved technology, immigration, and lower birth rates among white-collar workers all have contributed to upward mobility in the United States. See page 222.

13. *a.* The status attainment research has shown that social class background clearly affects level of education received, but social class background has little independent effect on occupational attainment beyond its effect on schooling. See pages 224-225.

14. *c.* In 1990, the poverty line for a family of four was $13,359 per year. See page 225.

15. *d.* Poverty has increased among the young and has decreased among the old. Although the rate of poverty among blacks is higher than among whites, the majority of poor people are white. See pages 226-227.

16. *c.* The poverty rate was more than 20 percent in 1960, 9.5 percent in 1969, and 14.2 percent in 1991.

17. *b.* Two major factors that help explain the growing number of working poor are the change in the occupational structure of the economy and the decline in the value of the minimum wage. See page 227.

18. *d.* Wilson argues that social structure, not culture or voluntary action, explains poverty in the ghetto. Two major structural factors include changes in the economy and migration of higher-income African-Americans out of the inner cities. See page 219.

19. *e.* Families earning less than $5,000 a year spend 40 percent of their incomes for food; yet a high portion of poor children suffer from protein, iron and vitamin deficiencies. The poor often pay more for inferior products. See page 232.

EXERCISES

Exercise 1

The text notes that in 1990 the official poverty threshold for a family of four was $13,359 ($1,113 per month). Develop a monthly budget for a poverty family. Be sure to cover all categories of expenses, including the two children. You may wish to review the classified ads for rent, call the utility companies for rates, and talk to people to determine car costs, medical costs, and the like.

Expense Category   *Monthly Amount*

1. If you "ran short," which categories did you reduce? Why?

2. Compare your budget with those of three other students. Describe and explain any differences. Discuss the proposed budgets and arrive at a common budget.

Exercise 2

Listed below are ten occupations with their prestige scores. Interview five people according to the sampling instructions provided by your instructor. Determine their ratings of these occupations. Use this interview guide:

"I will list ten occupations. For each, please rate the prestige of that occupation on a scale of one to 100."

After completing the ratings, ask:

Chapter 10
RACE AND ETHNICITY

OBJECTIVES

After reading Chapter 10, you should understand the following main points and be able to answer the objectives.

1. Sociologists are interested in cultural diversity and its sources.
   1.1 Resolve the apparent disparity between describing American society as both culturally unified and culturally diverse.
   1.2 Define ethnocentrism.
   1.3 List the four factors contributing to the tension between cultural diversity and cultural unity.
   1.4 Describe the role of immigration for cultural diversity.
   1.5 List the three factors that help maintain cultural and racial biases in immigration policies.
   1.6 List the three ways in which the changes in the international situation have contributed to the rise in immigration.
   1.7 Define minority group.
   1.8 Differentiate race from ethnicity.

2. Several generalizations can be made about the various forms of intergroup conflict.
   2.1 State the relationship between ethnocentrism and intergroup competition.
   2.2 Contrast the major patterns of conflict and domination. Colonialism, displacement, and slavery and segregation.
   2.3 Differentiate prejudice from discrimination.
   2.4 Define racism.
   2.5 Describe the flow patterns of resistance to domination.
   2.6 Assess the degree to which the image of the melting pot applies to the United States today.
   2.7 Differentiate assimilation from pluralism.

3. American society contains many minority groups.
   3.1 Describe the past and present experiences of African-Americans.
   3.2 Describe the past and present experiences of Hispanic-Americans.
   3.3 Describe the past and present experiences of Native Americans.
   3.4 Describe the past and present experiences of Asian-Americans.

CHAPTER SUMMARY

1. How can American society be characterized by both cultural unity and cultural diversity?

The Pledge of Allegiance and other cultural symbols reflect our belief in cultural unity. Yet cultural diversity also prevails: Americans have cultural roots in all the other countries on earth and still identify with their ancestral heritage. In most modern nations, the ideal of cultural unity frequently clashes with the reality of cultural diversity. Cultural unity often generates *ethnocentrism*, the belief that one's own culture is superior to all others. The Holocaust is perhaps the most notorious example. Four factors have contributed to the tension between cultural unity and cultural diversity: 1) most modern states have joined together populations that formerly considered themselves separate and distinct; 2) although colonialism brought Europeans into contact with other cultures and Europeans learned much from the peoples they conquered, this period tended to reinforce ethnocentrism; 3) modern states have attracted large numbers of immigrants; and 4) international relations and international business keep goods, ideas, and people flowing across national borders and cultural boundaries.

The United States is one of the most culturally diverse nations in the world. Widespread immigration has contributed to this situation, although immigration regulations are still highly selective. Cultural and racial biases in immigration patterns are maintained in several ways. First, a system of regional quotas still operates. Second, people with close relatives in the United States are given preference. Third, the American government uses immigration as a tool in foreign policy.

Despite immigration policies, immigration to the United States has climbed in recent decades for two reasons. First, immigration laws have been relaxed somewhat. Second, the international situation has changed in several ways: 1) the lives of millions of people around the world have been disrupted by political crises and transformations, civil wars, and natural catastrophes; 2) the gap between the rich and the poor countries has widened; and 3) the increasing interconnections of the global economy and global culture are drawing people from different cultures into closer relationships with one another.

A racial or ethnic group is an example of a *minority group*: a category of people who, because of their physical appearance or cultural characteristics, are singled out from others in their society, held in low esteem, and subjected to unequal treatment. The size of a group does not make it a minority; rather, the degree of social power it possesses contributes to its minority-group status. In fact, numerical majorities can be social minorities.

Race denotes a category of people who perceive themselves and are perceived by others as distinctive on the basis of certain biologically inherited traits. Race is a social and cultural category, not simply a biological classification. An *ethnic group* consists of people who perceive themselves and are perceived by others as sharing distinctive cultural traits such as language, religion, family customs, and food preferences. In short, race is based on the perception of physical differences whereas ethnicity is based on the perception of cultural differences. However, the distinction between racial and ethnic groups is not always clear-cut. For example, are Hispanics a race or an ethnic group?

2. What patterns of intergroup relations have occurred over time?

Ethnocentrism, combined with competition for territory and other scarce resources, generates explosive results. One pattern of conflict and domination is *colonialism*: the takeover of a territory or population by a foreign government or nation, and the subsequent political and social domination of the native population. The most notable example of is fifteenth century European colonialism. A second pattern of conflict and domination is displacement of native populations, in which an invading group actually displaces the native people. Displacement occurs most often in areas that are rich in natural resources and that possess a geography and climate similar to those of the invading group's homeland. Forms include attrition (in which the native group gradually moves on or dies out), forced population transfers, or genocide. All three occurred in the displacement of Native Americans.

A third pattern of conflict and domination is slavery and segregation. Both occur frequently when minority labor is essential to the economy. Once slavery was abolished in the United States, patterns of *segregation* developed: that is, enforced separation of racial or ethnic groups. In a segregated society, only certain types of contact between the dominant group and the minority group are allowed. Segregation applies to all aspects of life: residence, schools, work, public facilities, and marriage.

Both prejudice and discrimination continue to this day. *Prejudice* is a rigid positive or negative opinion about a category of people, such as a racial or ethnic group, based on its members' real or imagined characteristics. People make prejudgments independent of factual confirmation. Prejudices become woven into the cultural normative fabric and are maintained through stereotypes and avoidance. One of the most common forms of prejudice is *racism*: the view that certain physical attributes are related to inferiority or superiority in moral, intellectual, and other nonphysical attributes. Prejudice results in *discrimination*: significant social decisions about, and actions toward, people that are based on their presumed racial or ethnic identities. In summary, prejudice is a set of culturally based beliefs, while discrimination is the social act based on those beliefs.

Victims of prejudice and discrimination employ several response mechanisms. One is to avoid confrontation and unpleasant interaction by "self-segregation." That is, members of the minority group choose to stick together. Covert resistance is another response. A third is nonviolent resistance, personified by Ghandi and Martin Luther King, Jr. Nonviolent protest is basically a method of the weak. A fourth response is open revolt, which occurs when minority group members are strong enough to actually revolt. This response is most likely to occur when the social minority group is actually a numerical majority of the population.

Although conflict between racial and ethnic groups is common, intergroup relations can also be characterized by tolerance and respect. When different groups join together in a common, socially interconnected population, the result is *integration*; it exists insofar as interaction between different racial and ethnic groups is frequent and social relationships are open and common. The concept of the melting pot was coined to describe a situation in which members of different ethnic and racial groups mix freely and allow their customs and values to blend; intermarriage also occurs. One could argue that the melting pot concept applies to American culture because a new culture has been created from the many separate cultures reflected in various immigrant groups. Yet racial, ethnic, and cultural differences continue to exist. Many immigrant groups blended in very easily, particularly those which migrated earliest, occupied more or less equal positions in the power structure, had the most similar cultures initially, and were most alike in physical traits labeled as racial. However, African-Americans and other groups have not blended in.

The melting pot may not be the most accurate image for contemporary intergroup relations. Some sociologists favor the concept of *assimilation*: the incorporation of a minority group into the culture and social life of the dominant group so that the minority eventually disappears as a separate, identifiable unit. According to the melting pot concept, all groups will be changed equally into something new; assimilation suggests that minorities must conform to the existing majority culture. A pattern of intergroup relations in contrast to assimilation is *pluralism,* in which different racial and ethnic groups within a society maintain their own cultural identities and social networks but participate in shared political and economic systems. In such societies, each group has its own language, religion, and the like, and members interact socially among themselves. *Multiculturalism* exists when different racial and ethnic groups within a society maintain their distinctive cultures but live together in mutual harmony, tolerance, and respect. Proponents of multiculturalism view cultural diversity as a source of strength. The increasingly multicultural nature of social relations in a more international, globally integrated world will enhance multiculturalism.

3. What are the most important minority groups in the United States? What have been their experiences?

132

The racial and ethnic composition of the United States changed more in the 1980s than at any other time in the twentieth century. Minority populations increased twice as fast as in the preceding decade; immigration was a major factor. Higher-than-average birth rates among minorities also contributed to the rise; today almost one Americans in four is of African, Asian, Hispanic, or Native American ancestry. In recent years, hostility between minority groups and the rest of the population has increased. These tensions are the product of several factors: different ethnic groups have had very different experiences, they live in very different conditions, and often they feel that they are in competition with one another.

African-Americans constitute the largest racial minority, representing more than 12 percent of the United States population. Many of the first Africans to come to America were imported as slaves so that the economy in the south might prosper. They were forbidden to bring their native traditions to this country; hence they were deprived of much of their cultural heritage and of preexisting social networks. Yet they developed a unique subculture, which provided a framework for struggle. This struggle found life in black churches and communities, and gathered momentum with the civil rights movement. Although the many African-Americans have higher socioeconomic status than did that of their parents, as a group they still not have achieved full equality. Black students generally earn lower grades and score below the national average on standardized achievement tests because low-income black children are at a disadvantage from the beginning of their educational careers. The percentage of African-Americans attending and graduating from college has declined. The median income for all blacks is only 60 percent of the median income for whites, and the poverty rate among blacks has remained about three times that of whites. The unemployment rate for blacks is twice the rate for whites. The number of black elected officials has risen dramatically, however.

The least progress towards integration has occurred in housing, where the level of segregation has remained virtually unchanged since 1970. About 30 percent of African-Americans live in almost complete racial isolation, primarily in our inner cities, but racial segregation also exists in the suburbs. Although the public generally supports equal opportunity for blacks, they are less likely to support the practice of equality. Support among whites for programs to implement equal opportunity has declined.

Hispanic-Americans, the second largest minority group in the United States, come from very different backgrounds. Mexican-Americans began entering the United States as seasonal agricultural workers. Population growth, high unemployment, and severe poverty in Mexico have contributed to the high levels of legal and illegal immigration. Puerto Ricans began immigrating en masse after World War II. Because the island is part of the United States, Puerto Ricans visit their homeland frequently. Cuban-Americans arrived in this country in three main ways: 1) in the early 1960s, after Castro seized control of the Cuban government; 2) in the late 1960s and early 1970s, when Castro permitted freedom flights; and 3) in 1980, as part of the boat lift. Most Cuban-Americans live in southern Florida and in New York City; they are the most politically organized and economically successful group of Hispanics. These different Hispanic-American groups have retained their distinct identities, although they share such cultural features as religion (Roman Catholicism) and strong commitment to the family. Hispanics have made modest social and economic gains, but few have achieved equality with Anglo-Americans. They still tend to be employed in low-level occupations and to experience a higher unemployment rate.

Native Americans settled in America more than 20,000 years ago. Considerable diversity has always existed among the different Native American groups. Beginning with the arrival of Europeans, they have experienced a long history of displacement and persecution. About half of today's Native Americans live on reservations, which has helped to preserve their traditional way of life and social structures. Regrettably, the U.S. government historically has refused to honor its treaties with various Indian nations, and the services provided by the Bureau of Indian Affairs have been substandard. In recent years Native Americans have been increasingly militant; Indian tribes have begun to take social policy into their own hands. Native Americans are among the poorest minority groups in the country;

those who live on reservations are worse off than those who do not. The unemployment rate for Native Americans is twice the rate for the population as a whole; one-fourth of Native Americans live below the poverty line as compared with one-tenth of the general population. They have the shortest life expectancy of all American racial and ethnic groups.

Asian-Americans have become the fastest-growing ethnic group in the United States; they are also one of the most diverse in terms of national origins, social class, income, education, and skills; they display greater economic stratification. The Chinese and Japanese, who have been in the United States the longest, have encountered more prejudice and discrimination than any other group of immigrants. Both the Chinese and the Japanese began immigrating to the United States in the middle of the eighteenth century. Asian-Americans have equaled and often surpassed other groups of Americans in occupational success; this success has resulted in the stereotype of a "model minority." Several facts suggest that the stereotype is exaggerated: 1) the Asians send more family members into the work force, thereby contributing to higher family incomes; 2) they earn less than others with equivalent education; and 3) the apparent stability of Asian families may reflect their tradition of "saving face," or avoiding shame, by keeping their troubles to themselves. The stereotype of a model minority has led to their exclusion from minority programs, has been used against other groups as proof that the United States is racially tolerant, and has generated resentment among other ethnic groups. The explanations of achievements by Asian immigrants reflect both culture and functional integration. Their culture includes such values as a devotion to education, strong family ties, self-denial and hard work, self-employment, and a tradition of pooling funds and hiring family members. The functional integration of family and community also has played an important role: Asians have been very successful in reuniting families and in developing strong communities.

REVIEW OF CONCEPTS

Match the concept with the definition.

Concepts

a. affirmative action
b. assimilation
c. colonialism
d. de facto segregation
e. de jure segregation

f. discrimination
g. ethnic group
h. integration
i. minority groups
j. multiculturalism

k. pluralism
l. prejudice
m. race
n. racism
o. segregation

Definitions

_____ 1. The legal or customary restriction or prohibition of contact between groups according to such criteria as race, ethnicity, sex, and age.

_____ 2. A group of people who believe themselves and who are believed by others to be genetically distinct.

_____ 3. Segregation imposed by law.

_____ 4. An approach to life in a pluralistic society which calls for finding ways for people to understand and interact with one another that do not depend on their sameness but rather on respect for their difference.

_____ 5. Expulsion or exploitation based on group membership.

_____ 6. The coexistence of different racial or ethnic groups, each of which retains its own cultural identity and social structural networks while participating equally in the economic and political systems.

_____ 7. Special consideration and preferential treatment accorded to members of minority groups to remedy past discrimination.

_____ 8. The unimpeded interaction and contact between different racial and ethnic groups.

_____ 9. A categorical predisposition to like or dislike people for their real or imagined social characteristics.

_____ 10. Racial separation that results from unofficial social patterns.

_____ 11. A category of people who perceive themselves and are perceived by others as possessing shared cultural traits.

_____ 12. People who are singled out for unequal treatment in the society in which they live, and who consider themselves to be victims of collective discrimination.

_____ 13. The incorporation of a minority into the culture and social life of the majority such that the minority eventually disappears as a separate, identifiable unit.

_____ 14. The economic takeover of one nation by another, more powerful nation, and the subsequent political and social domination of the native population.

_____ 15. The doctrine that some races are inherently inferior and some are inherently superior to others.

Answers

1.	o	6.	k	11.	g
2.	m	7.	a	12.	i
3.	e	8.	h	13.	b
4.	j	9.	l	14.	c
5.	f	10.	d	15.	n

REVIEW QUESTIONS

After studying Chapter 10, answer the following questions. The correct answers are listed after the questions; each is followed by a short explanation. You are also referred to pages in the textbook for relevant discussion.

1. American culture can be characterized most accurately as
   a. culturally unified but minimally culturally diverse.
   b. culturally diverse but minimally culturally unified.
   c. both culturally diverse and unified.

d. neither culturally diverse nor unified.
e. impossible to categorize on cultural unity and diversity.

2. Which one of the following is *not* one of the factors contributing to the tension between cultural unity and cultural diversity?
   a. Modern states have mixed populations that were once considered separate.
   b. European colonialism reinforced ethnocentrism.
   c. Modern states have attracted many immigrants.
   d. International relations keep foods, ideas, and people flowing across boundaries.
   e. The educational level has risen in most modern states.

3. Current immigration policies
   a. discriminate against people from specific nations.
   b. maintain cultural and racial biases.
   c. have tightened immigration laws considerably.
   d. fail to respond to changes in the international situation.
   e. have contributed to the dramatic decline in immigration.

4. Which of the following is a minority group?
   a. blacks
   b. children
   c. women
   d. the aged
   e. all are members of minority groups

5. Which of the following statements is *not* true?
   a. Celebrating Easter is an aspect of ethnicity.
   b. White skin and round eyes are aspects of race.
   c. Speaking Spanish is an aspect of race.
   d. Having black skin is an aspect of race.
   e. being Jewish is an aspect of ethnicity.

6. Although Saul Barnum lives in a racially mixed town, he avoids selling his home, which is in a predominately white neighborhood, to a black because he feels that the neighbors would not like it. Barnum is practicing
   a. discrimination.
   b. prejudice.
   c. segregation.
   d. immigration.
   e. assimilation.

7. In South Africa, blacks are not allowed to live where whites live and they are not allowed to use the same public facilities. This situation reflects
   a. segregation.
   b. integration.
   c. amalgamation.
   d. assimilation.
   e. ethnicity.

8. "Americans should have first option on available world oil reserves; our needs and projects are

of vital importance." This statement is an example of
a. racism.
b. ethnocentrism.
c. colonialism.
d. displacement.
e. accommodation.

9. When the British settled in South Africa they repealed old Dutch laws, abolished slavery, established a civil service, populated the cities, and dominated the indigenous peoples. This process reflects
   a. segregation.
   b. displacement.
   c. amalgamation.
   d. colonialism.
   e. integration.

10. Placing Native Americans on reservations best reflects
    a. segregation.
    b. integration.
    c. colonialism.
    d. displacement.
    e. racial and ethnic myths.

11. Revolt as a form of resistance to domination is most likely to occur when
    a. a minority group is first colonized.
    b. members of a minority group try to become accepted by the majority.
    c. members of a minority group is actually a numerical majority of the population.
    d. members of a minority group believe that there is little hope of improving their lot by working within the system.
    e. a minority group is displaced.

12. The basic difference between the melting-pot concept and assimilation is that the melting-pot concept
    a. applied to earlier immigration, while assimilation applies to recent immigration.
    b. refers to immigration, while assimilation refers to subcultures within a country.
    c. reflects a new cultural hybrid, while assimilation reflects the incorporation of the minority into the majority culture.
    d. is characterized more by ethnocentrism than by assimilation.
    e. reflects a pattern of accommodation, while assimilation reflects a pattern of conflict and domination.

13. Most major cities include sections like Chinatown or Little Italy. These sections represent what aspect of immigration?
    a. assimilation
    b. ambivalence
    c. pluralism
    d. acculturation
    e. homogeneity

14. African-Americans constitute about what proportion of the United States population?

14. African-Americans constitute about what proportion of the United States population?
   a. 4 percent
   b. 8 percent
   c. 12 percent
   d. 16 percent
   e. 20 percent

15. Which one of the following is *false* regarding African-Americans?
   a. They have a much lower high school graduation rate than whites.
   b. They have lower grades than whites.
   c. Their median income is only about 60 percent of that for whites.
   d. Their political participation has risen dramatically.
   e. They experience as much residential segregation as they did in 1970.

16. The second-largest minority group in the United States is
   a. African-Americans.
   b. Hispanic-Americans.
   c. Native Americans
   d. Chinese.
   e. Japanese.

17. The poorest minority group in the United States is
   a. African-Americans.
   b. Hispanic-Americans.
   c. Native Americans.
   d. Chinese.
   e. Japanese.

18. The relatively high performance of many Asian-Americans on science and other academic tests is due primarily to
   a. the educational values and cohesiveness of the family.
   b. the training in science that they receive before immigrating to the United States.
   c. the special schools for highly talented science students in areas populated by Asian-Americans.
   d. their greater degree of assimilation compared to other minority groups.
   e. genetic differences.

19. The minority group with several major subgroups due to immigration in recent decades is
   a. African-Americans.
   b. Hispanic-Americans.
   c. Native Americans.
   d. Asian-Americans.
   e. Chinese Americans.

Answers

1. *b.* Cultural unity is more of an ideal and cultural diversity more of a reality in describing American culture. See page 239.
2. *e.* Although the first four answers have contributed to the tension between cultural unity and diversity, the role of education is less salient. See page 239.

3. *b.* Current immigration policies maintain cultural and racial biases by enforcing regional quotas, favoring those with close relatives in the United States, and using immigration as a tool in foreign policy. See page 239.

4. *e.* Minority groups are people whose physical appearance or cultural characteristics mark them as different from the dominant group and subject them to unequal treatment. Blacks, children, women, and the aged all fit this description. See page 241.

5. *c.* Speaking Spanish is a cultural, not a physical difference. See page 241.

6. *a.* Discrimination is an *act* of mistreating people on grounds rationally irrelevant to the situation. See page 246.

7. *a.* When people from different racial and ethnic groups are separated physically and socially by custom or law, they are said to be segregated. See page 244.

8. *b.* Believing that our country is superior to any other and therefore needs the resources exemplifies ethnocentrism. See page 238.

9. *d.* Colonialism occurs with the economic takeover of one nation by another, more powerful nation, and with the subsequent political and social domination of the native population. See page 242.

10. *d.* Throughout the history of the United States, Native Americans have been displaced because whites wanted their land and needed a strategy to reduce intergroup conflict.

11. *c.* Members of a minority group are sometimes strong enough to revolt, and this is most likely to occur when the minority group is actually a numerical majority of the population. See page 247.

12. *c.* The melting-pot concept reflects the blending of majority and minority cultures into a new cultural hybrid; assimilation reflects the incorporation and disappearance of the minority culture into the majority culture. See ages 248-250.

13. *c.* When each group retains its own language, customs, and religion while participating in the economic and political systems of the larger group, pluralism exists. See page 251.

14. *c.* African-Americans constitute about 12 percent of the U.S. population. See page 252.

15. *a.* High school graduation rates for black students nearly equal those of whites. See page 253.

16. *b.* Hispanic-Americans are the second-largest minority group; about nine percent of the population are Hispanic-Americans. See page 255.

17. *c.* Twenty-five percent of Native Americans live below the poverty level compared to 10 percent of the general population; thus Native Americans are among the poorest of American ethnic groups. See page 260.

18. *a.* Asian immigrants tend to come from an affluent, educated stratum of society that emphasizes educational values and family cohesiveness. See page 264.

19. *b.* Hispanic-Americans are comprised of several major subgroups due to immigration in recent decades: Mexican-Americans, Puerto Ricans, and Cuban-Americans. See pages 256-257.

EXERCISES

Exercise 1

The table on the next page compares the racial or ethnic groups described in the chapter with respect to several variables. Within each group, the data are presented for members of that group who are in the lower, middle, and upper classes.

1. Identify three variables related to conclusions made in the text about the various racial or ethnic groups. Compare them with the data in the table.

Variables Related to Race/Ethnicity by Social Class in a Random Sample of 28,240 Seniors in Public and Private High Schools in the United States in 1980*

Variables	White (Lo/Mid/Up)	Black (Lo/Mid/Up)	Hispanic (Lo/Mid/Up)	Native Am. (Lo/Mid/Up)	Chinese (Lo/Mid/Up)	Japanese (Lo/Mid/Up)
1. % working more than 21 hours per week on job	41/40/37	38/39/35	41/42/41	41/46/48	35/24/55	36/38/39
2. % earning $3.10 per hour or more on job	55/61/63	45/53/59	53/57/56	48/55/65	54/47/45	60/59/58
3. % who say they will accept $3.50 or less as minimum hourly wage after graduation	43/40/38	33/27/32	39/37/30	45/41/39	38/49/45	46/57/28
4. % expecting a professional occupation at age 30	27/37/57	37/46/58	32/40/56	29/31/39	44/45/66	27/53/75
5. % expecting college degree or higher	23/43/78	43/61/80	36/48/73	28/34/59	82/80/95	63/71/89
6. % with mother in household	88/92/93	86/87/94	88/91/91	82/91/94	91/94/83	100/91/97
7. % with father in household	70/82/88	44/56/71	68/80/81	58/73/90	83/79/89	73/85/94
8. % stating mother monitors schoolwork	78/85/88	82/90/91	82/85/89	80/84/87	65/79/83	64/76/92
9. % stating father monitors schoolwork	57/72/83	40/60/74	58/72/84	55/64/80	53/53/72	55/64/86
10. % watching 5 or more hours TV per day	21/16/9	31/27/22	18/18/16	28/20/16	9/18/6	9/13/19
11. % who like working hard in school	47/49/55	71/66/67	64/56/60	58/49/59	82/68/67	55/69/51
12. % strongly agree "I take a positive attitude toward myself"	23/29/36	54/58/52	32/38/40	30/38/26	30/27/28	46/28/28
13. % agree "People who accept their condition in life are happier than those who try to change things"	44/36/25	44/39/30	49/41/36	43/39/40	59/35/34	27/23/25

* These data are part of the "High School and Beyond" study sponsored by the National Center for Education Statistics. Percentages are rounded.

140

2. Select four other variables and compare the racial or ethnic groups. For each variable, rank the groups and indicate of the rankings are similar or different. Explain the results.

3. Examine social class differences in the same four variables. Determine how social class differences compare with racial or ethnic group differences. Explain the results.

Exercise 2

An increasing number of states are instituting minimum competency testing, whereby high school seniors must obtain a specified score on a standardized test before being eligible to graduate. Minority group students fail these exams at a much higher rate than do whites, due in part to "social promotions." Such promotions occur in the lower grades because teachers do not want the responsibility of holding students back, and school districts to not have the resources to provide the required remedial education. Reactions among minority groups have generally been negative, although some districts have seen growing minority group acceptance of competency testing following initial resistance, due to the improved job success such a program often brings.

1. Identify four concepts or theories that this situation illustrates.

2. What is your reaction to competency testing? Why?

Exercise 3

This chapter has focused on racial and ethnic minority groups. Many other minority groups exist. Examples might include women, the aged, ex-convicts, the disabled, midgets, veterans, the Amish, and the like. Select one of these groups or some other minority group.

1. Describe why this group can be defined as a minority group.

2. Apply the patterns of conflict and domination discussed in the text to this group.

3. Apply the patterns of accommodation discussed in the text to this group.

4. Give specific examples of the prejudice and discrimination experienced by this group.

Chapter 11

SEX AND GENDER

OBJECTIVES

After reading Chapter 11, you should understand the following main points and be able to answer the objectives.

1. Gender is a socially constructed phenomenon.
   1.1 Differentiate gender from sex.
   1.2 Determine if gender inequality is universal.
   1.3 Describe the role of biology in differentiating men and women.
   1.4 Summarize the psychological evidence on the difference between men and women.
   1.5 Summarize the cross-cultural evidence on the differences between men and women.
   1.6 Relate gender to the five key concepts.

2. Gender roles and gender stereotypes influence each other.
   2.1 Define gender roles.
   2.2 Define and give examples of gender stereotypes.
   2.3 Show how gender roles and gender stereotypes influence one another in both directions.
   2.4 Define sexual orientation.
   2.5 Define essentialism and show how it is a source of homophobia and gay-rights activism.
   2.6 Determine the role of biology in influencing sexual orientation.

3. Several agents of socialization affect gender socialization.
   3.1 Describe the role of parents in gender socialization.
   3.2 Describe the role of peers in gender socialization.
   3.3 Describe the role of schools in gender socialization.
   3.4 Describe the role of the media in gender socialization.

4. Gender inequality is particularly evident in the workplace.
   4.1 Assess the degree of progress in reducing gender inequality in the workplace.
   4.2 State the increase in the proportion of women working outside the home between 1950 and 1991.
   4.3 List four factors accounting for the steadily increasing flow of middle-class women into the labor force.
   4.4 Explain the concept of occupational segregation.
   4.5 Describe and assess the comparable worth debate.
   4.6 Describe and assess the role of discrimination in hiring and promotion in explaining gender inequalities on the job.

4.7   Describe and assess the comparable worth debate.
4.8   Present a few statistics portraying the role of women in politics.

CHAPTER SUMMARY

1. How is gender socially constructed?

At birth, babies are classified as girls or boys on the basis of physical appearance. This biological difference is basic to the distinction between male and female. Also beginning at birth, people are subjected to a set of cultural expectations, a different set for each gender. Gender socialization begins at birth.

The term *gender* refers to nonbiological culturally and socially produced distinctions between men and women and between masculinity and femininity. *Sex* refers to the biological differences that are relevant to reproduction. Sex differences are the products of heredity and biology; gender differences result from socialization. All societies employ gender as a basic organizing principle to establish appropriate male and female roles.

Sociologists acknowledge that biology shapes our behavior and potential, although it does not rigidly determine what kind of people we will be. Humans have a much greater capacity to learn and to change than do members of other species.

Many people assume that clear differences exist between women and men, but in reality, there is more similarity than dissimilarity. The psychological evidence was summarized by Maccoby and Jacklin in their 1974 review of more than 2,000 books and articles on sex differences in a variety of traits. They concluded that males and females do not differ significantly in sociability, suggestibility, self-esteem, achievement motivation, rote learning, analytical skills, or responses to auditory and visual stimulation. They found differences in only a few areas, and these differences were small. Males tended to be more aggressive and to perform better in visual-spatial tasks and in mathematics, whereas females performed better in verbal skills. Differences between males and females are particularly small before puberty. Subsequently, cultural norms and sexual maturation begin to produce a new differentiation of behavior and experience. In short, we must be careful in drawing conclusions from evidence of biological differences; a wide range of individual variation exists in the expression of any given trait. Even for physiological differences, it is not clear that the explanations are purely biological.

The cross-cultural evidence shows wide variation across cultures; this finding argues against the simplest biological explanation for gender roles. Margaret Mead identified several cultures in which women's and men's roles were substantially different from those in American society, as well as from each other. In short, there is a wide range of variation in what different cultures consider to be male or female. In almost all cultures, the skills and traits considered masculine are valued more highly than those considered feminine.

2. How do gender roles and gender stereotypes influence each other?

Gender roles are the expected obligations, privileges, and expected behaviors and attitudes that a society assigns to each sex. *Gender stereotypes* are oversimplified but strongly held ideas about the characteristics of males and females. They help to maintain gender roles by shaping ideas about the tasks to which men and women are "naturally" suited.

Gender roles and stereotypes influence one another in both directions. Stereotypes help to create our expectations about the tasks men and women should perform, while seeing people in traditional roles every day reinforces our belief that gender stereotypes are valid. Gender stereotypes sometimes result in *role conflict*, clashes between the demands associated with different roles. The conflicting expectations between motherhood and career may pose special problems for women. One thing is clear, however: gender roles tend to persist.

Cultural factors and social learning also affect *sexual orientation*, the development of a characteristic pattern of choice of sexual partners. The term sexual orientation is most common in discussions of homosexuality. However, there are many ways to be heterosexual or homosexual, and some people do not regard themselves as exclusively one or the other.

The most common distinction in American culture is between heterosexual and homosexual. Many people believe that being a homosexual is such an important identity that other aspects of the person's life do not matter; this a way of thinking is called *essentialism*. Essentialist thinking leads many Americans to treat the choice of partners as an either/or matter basic to both sexual orientation and personal identity. Essentialism produces *homophobia*, the irrational fear and hatred of homosexuals; it is also a source of gay rights activism. Essentialists also have pushed for biological explanations of homosexuality. Such explanations typically ignore the wide variation in what is labeled as homosexuality. Regardless of the role of biology, social learning and cultural factors again are paramount.

3. Which agents of socialization contribute to gender role socialization?

Gender role socialization is influenced by parents, peers, schools, and the media. Recent research shows that parents treat boys and girls equally in many respects; differences are slight in verbal interaction, physical play, warmth and responsiveness, encouragement of achievement, and strictness in discipline. Parents, however, perceive their children in gender-related ways and encourage gender-appropriate activities. They see their newborn daughters as weak, soft, and delicate, while they view their newborn sons as strong, firm, and well-coordinated. Fathers are particular gender-conscious in their treatment of sons. For example, they tend to be more strict with a son than with a daughter. Gender stereotyping persists throughout childhood through the assignment of traditional domestic chores and their differential expectations regarding intellectual achievements. For example, parents tend to attribute a girl's success in mathematics to effort and a boy's success to talent. Many gender differences simply reflect the traditional division of family labor.

From an early age, they promote and reinforce ideas about what is acceptable behavior. In adolescence, peers shape attitudes about dating and sexuality. Peers also influence career aspirations and choices.

Schools also reinforce traditional gender roles. In nursery school, girls most often receive attention and praise for being obedient and helpful, whereas boys more often receive attention and reprimands for misbehavior. In elementary school, girls are more likely to be praised for neatness, and boys for the quality of their work. The social structure of schools reinforces gender socialization: although the great majority of elementary school teachers are women, the great majority of principals are male. Home economics classes and school sports programs remain largely segregated.

The media also are involved. All types of media--TV, radio, magazines, books--are filled with illustrations of traditional gender roles. Some progress has been made in the representation of male and female characters in books, but even recent studies show that females are portrayed as more visible, while males still have more adventures, more responsibilities, and more fun. Children's TV shows contain more than twice as many male as female characters, and the males are portrayed more favorably. Although the number of women on adult TV programs has increased significantly, men still outnumber women by almost three to one in prime time. Female characters are still less likely than male characters to be seen working outside the home, and physical appearance still plays a primary role for women on TV. Newspapers still portray more photos of men than of women, while magazine ads remain very gender-stereotypical.

4. What patterns of gender inequality exist in the workplace?

The proportion of female lawyers, physicians, and other professionals has risen substantially over the last decade or two, but women still hold second-class status in these and other occupations. The best jobs, the highest salaries, and the positions with the most power generally fall to males.

Between 1950 and 1988, the proportion of women employed outside the home increased from 30 percent to 57 percent. The greatest change has occurred among white middle-class women. Four factors account for this dramatic increase. First, the number of service jobs traditionally filled by women increased rapidly. Second, the real value of men's wages declined. Third, the divorce rate doubled between 1960 and 1990. Fourth, attitudes about working wives changed considerably.

Even today, women tend to be segregated in jobs that society considers appropriate for women. They experience not only occupational segregation but also the lower pay, lower prestige, and lesser power that accompany such segregation. Even when lower-status male jobs are compared with typical female jobs, men still earn more money. The average woman's annual pay is 65 percent of the average man's, an improvement of only 5 percent since 1950. Because women are less likely to work full-time, they receive fewer employee benefits. The occupational status and incomes of black women improved; by 1985, black women earned almost 90 percent as much as white women. These gains, however, were offset by a sharp decline in employment opportunities and pay for black men.

The 1964 Civil Rights Act prohibits discrimination because of sex or race. The law requires employers to provide equal pay for equal work, which is usually interpreted as meaning identical work. Yet enforcing equal pay statutes does little to close the gender gap in earnings because most women and most men do not work in gender-integrated or gender-neutral jobs. In response to this situation, the idea of *comparable worth* has been introduced--that is, basing wages for a job category on the amount of skill, effort, responsibility, and risk the job entails, plus the amount of income the job produces, rather than on other criteria. Proponents believe that comparable worth complies with the antidiscrimination statutes. Under comparable worth programs, jobs are rated in terms of educational requirements, working hours and conditions, and other concrete measures. Equal salaries are paid for jobs with equal ratings; seniority, merit, and productivity are taken into account. Opponents of this argument believe that equal pay provisions alone are insufficient to eliminate gender discrimination, and opponents also think that comparable pay would be too costly. Even so, studies of employers who have implemented comparable pay policies here and abroad suggest that the cost has been greatly exaggerated. Opponents also do not take into consideration the hidden costs of unequal pay to society as a whole and to taxpayers.

Women experience gender bias on the job. Women in unconventional roles may be the butt of jokes of sexual harassment. They are offered valuable business contacts and mentoring relationships less often than are men. Although cultural stereotypes have weakened and women continue their progress in entering nontraditional fields, the numbers are still quite small. Women still encounter a "glass ceiling"--unofficial and often invisible barriers to the upper levels of management. Gender discrimination occurs in two ways: by deciding in advance that women are not temperamentally suited to certain positions and by devaluing certain jobs because they are traditionally performed by women. Both types of discrimination occur regularly. Gender bias is at its strongest when women choose traditionally masculine occupations.

The women's movement gathered momentum in the 1970s, when women's role in American politics began to change. The proportion of women who voted equaled and even surpassed the number of male voters. In fact, the 1992 elections were referred to as "the year of the woman." The number of women elected to office has increased considerably, although the percentage remains quite small. For example, the 53 female members of Congress represent only 10 percent of the total. This under-representation of women among elected and appointed officials prevails around the world.

REVIEW OF CONCEPTS

Match the concept with the definition.

Concepts

a. comparable worth
b. date rape
c. essentialism
d. gender

e. gender roles
f. gender stereotypes
g. gender stratification
h. homophobia

i. machismo
j. sexism
k. sexual harassment
l. sexual orientation

Definitions

_____ 1. Refers to all the socially constructed, nonbiological traits assigned to men and to women.

_____ 2. Thinking about a complex phenomenon as though it were an either/or issue and treating one dimension of identity as overriding all others.

_____ 3. A person's basic approach to sexual relationships, including choice of partners and activities, and the meaning attached to these.

_____ 4. Oversimplified but strongly held ideas about the characteristics of males and of females.

_____ 5. The distinct tasks and activities that society assigns to each sex and defines as masculine or feminine.

_____ 6. The demand that someone respond to or tolerate unwanted sexual advances from a person who has power over the victim.

_____ 7. The unequal treatment of men and women on grounds of sex or gender; usually refers to prejudice and discrimination against women.

_____ 8. The assigning of men and women to unequal positions in the social hierarchy.

_____ 9. The irrational fear and hatred of homosexuals.

_____ 10. The practice of basing wages for a job category on the amount of skill, effort, responsibility, and risk the job entails, to offset inequalities based on the sex or race of incumbents.

Answers

1.	d	5.	e	9.	h
2.	c	6.	k	10.	a
3.	l	7.	j		
4.	f	8.	g		

REVIEW QUESTIONS

After studying Chapter 11, answer the following questions. The correct answers are listed after the questions; each is followed by a short explanation. You are also referred to pages in the textbook for relevant discussion.

1. Many people believe that women are better suited for "caring" occupations such as teaching and nursing. This view reflects
   a. gender stratification.
   b. gender roles.
   c. gender stereotypes.
   d. gender inequalities.
   e. gender differential socialization.

2. In their extensive review of the psychological evidence on the differences between men and women, Maccoby and Jacklin found all but one of the following statements to be true. Which statement is *false*?
   a. Men are more aggressive than women.
   b. Men perform better on visual-spatial tasks than do women.
   c. Women perform better on verbal tasks than do men.
   d. Women have higher self-esteem than do men.
   e. Men perform better on mathematical tasks than do women.

3. The most accurate summary of the biological evidence on gender differences is that
   a. biology plays the predominant role.
   b. biology affects only the determination of whether an embryo becomes male or female.
   c. biology does have certain effects, but they are much less pervasive than socialization.
   d. biology affects only aggressiveness.
   e. biology affects females more than males.

4. The cross-cultural evidence on gender differences shows that
   a. what people consider masculine or feminine varies widely.
   b. gender differences are primarily characteristic of western societies.
   c. the effects of biology differ by culture.
   d. the effects of culture differ by biology.
   e. gender differences are linked closely to the religious values in a culture.

5. The terms used for biological differences and cultural differences respectively between men and women are
   a. gender and sex.
   b. sex and gender.
   c. gender socialization and gender stereotyping.
   d. gender stereotyping and gender socialization.
   e. biological determinism and cultural determinism.

6. Which statement most accurately reflects the connection between gender roles and gender stereotypes?
   a. Roles influence stereotypes.
   b. Stereotypes influence roles.
   c. Roles influence stereotypes only for men.
   d. Stereotypes influence roles only for women.
   e. They each influence each other in both directions.

7. Which type of thinking underlies the tendency to treat the choice of partners as an either/or matter basic to both sexual orientation and personal identity?
   a. deconstructionist
   b. human capital
   c. homophobia
   d. sexism
   e. essentialism

8. Gender typing and gender-role socialization begin
   a. at birth.
   b. at about 6 months of age.
   c. at about 1 year of age.
   d. at about 1 1/2 years of age.
   e. at about 2 years of age.

9. What parents teach their children may not be as important as
   a. what they do (e.g., mother work outside the home).
   b. how they relate to each other at home (e.g., share housework).
   c. the structure of the family (e.g., single parent).
   d. a, b, and c.
   e. a and b only.

10. The influence of peers on gender socialization
    a. is widespread.
    b. is more salient for men than women.
    c. is more salient for women than men.
    d. is much greater than the influence of parents.
    e. dissipates between the ages of 10 to 18.

11. Regarding the influence of schools on gender socialization,
    a. schools reinforce the effects of parents and peers.
    b. gender-specific behavior is encouraged at all grade levels.
    c. even the social structure of schools reflects gender stratification.
    d. home economics classes and school sports programs remain largely segregated.
    e. all of the above are true.

12. Between 1950 and 1988 the proportion of women who worked outside the home rose from about
    a. 10 percent to 77 percent.
    b. 15 percent to 60 percent.
    c. 20 percent to 55 percent.
    d. 25 percent to 50 percent.
    e. 30 percent to 57 percent.

13. The research on the influence of television on gender-role socialization shows that
    a. programs are only minimally gender-role stereotyped today.
    b. heavy TV watchers hold more traditional ideas about gender.
    c. educational TV has had no effect on gender-role perceptions.
    d. people do not watch enough TV to feel an impact.
    e. the effect depends on parental values and socialization patterns.

14. The major theme regarding the involvement of women in the work force is that
    a. women have been entering in record numbers but still have second-class status.
    b. only more educated women have entered the work force in record numbers, but they still have second-class status.
    c. women have been entering in record numbers and finally have attained nearly equal status.
    d. the number of women entering has been overstated because most women leave the work force again.
    e. women's greater involvement has led to increased conflict between males and females.

15. Women receive about what percentage of men's average earnings?
    a. 45 percent
    b. 55 percent
    c. 65 percent
    d. 75 percent
    e. 85 percent

16. All **but** which one of the following factors contributed to the rise in women's participation in the labor force in the 1970s?
    a. The birth rate increased.
    b. The number of service jobs traditionally filled by women increased.
    c. The real value of men's wages declined.
    d. The divorce rate increased.
    e. Attitudes about working wives changed.

17. Regarding changes in the occupational status and incomes of African-American men and women,
    a. they improved for both males and females.
    b. they improved for females, with little change for men.
    c. they improved for females, with a decline for men.
    d. they declined for both men and women.
    e. they declined for females but improved for males.

18. The comparable worth approach to gender inequalities on the job shows that
    a. women select crowded occupations.
    b. when the qualifications required for different jobs are analyzed, women's work pays less than men's work.
    c. socialization has so deeply instilled in women the concept that they are secondary wage earners that most women are not motivated to pursue higher-paying jobs.
    d. substantial discrimination exists in hiring and promotion.
    e. It is extremely difficult to make any valid comparisons between men's and women's work.

19. Keri Anne works at Continental Can Corporation as a mid-level executive and wants to become a senior executive. She is told she has insufficient experience, she does not receive the same mentoring contacts as men do, and she is not given the same access to information as the men. What phenomenon is she experiencing?
    a. a glass ceiling
    b. a semipermeable membrane
    c. reverse discrimination
    d. exploitation
    e. a glass slipper

20. What percentage of Members of Congress are female?
    a. 2 percent
    b. 10 percent
    c. 20 percent
    d. 37 percent
    e. 55 percent

Answers

1. *c.* Gender stereotypes are oversimplified but strongly held ideas about the characteristics of males and of females. See page 272.
2. *d.* Maccoby and Jacklin saw no differences in sociability, self-esteem, achievement motivation, analytical skills, and other characteristics. Men are somewhat more aggressive and perform better on visual-spatial tasks, as well as in mathematics. Women perform better on verbal tasks. See page 270.
3. *c.* Biology does play a role in gender differences, particularly through the role of hormones, but the biological contribution is far less pervasive than the role of socialization. See page 269.
4. *a.* The cross-cultural evidence shows that what people consider masculine or feminine is quite variable. See pages 270-271.
5. *b.* Sex refers to the biological differences that are relevant to reproduction and gender refers to nonbiological, culturally and socially produced distinctions between women and men. See page 269.
6. *e.* Gender roles and stereotypes influence one another in both directions. Stereotypes help set up expectations about appropriate tasks for women and men; seeing people in traditional roles reinforces our belief that stereotypes are valid. See page 272.
7. *e.* Underlying this tendency is essentialism: the idea that being a homosexual is such an important identity that other aspects of the person's life do not matter. See page 274.
8. *a.* Gender typing and gender-role socialization begin at birth. See page 275.
9. *d.* The structure of the family, the social relations in the family, and the social actions in the family are more important in fostering gender socialization than what parents say to their children. See pages 275-276.
10. *a.* Peers exert a powerful influence on the development of gender roles in such areas as acceptable behavior, dating and sexuality, and career aspirations and choices. See page 276.
11. *e.* Schools remain a powerful agent of socialization regarding gender roles. See page 277.
12. *e.* Between 1950 and 1988 the proportion of women who worked outside the home rose from 30 percent to 57 percent. See page 278.
13. *b.* There is evidence that heavy TV watchers hold more traditional ideas about gender than do those with little exposure to TV. See page 278.
14. *a.* Women are entering the work force at many levels in record numbers, but they still have largely second-class status in the working world. See page 280.
15. *c.* Women receive only about 65 percent of men's average earnings. See page 280.
16. *a.* The birth rate actually declined, but has not been linked to increased participation in the labor force by women. The other factors listed all played a role. See page 280.
17. *c.* By 1985, black women earned almost 90 percent as much as white women. But these gains were offset by the sharp decline in employment opportunities and pay for black men. See page 281.
18. *b.* The comparable worth approach involves analyzing the levels of training, skill, and other qualifications needed for different jobs. An examination of men's and women's jobs with the relatively equal levels of these qualifications shows that women's work pays much less

than comparable men's work. See page 282.

19. *a.* These and similar experience are part of the "glass ceiling," unofficial and often invisible barriers to the upper levels of management. See page 284.
20. *b.* Ten percent of the Members of Congress are female. See page 287.

EXERCISES

Exercise 1

Obtain a current issue of *Newsweek, Time,* or *U.S. News & World Report.* Then find an issue from the same month five years ago and an issue from the same month ten years ago. Review each of the three issues in terms of the advertisements, the sex of authors of letters to the editor, the sex ratio of the editorial board, the male or female focus of the articles, and the use of pronouns. Then analyze each of the following topics for each of the three issues.

1. The roles of women.

   Current:

   Five years ago:

   Ten years ago:

2. The roles of men.

   Current:

   Five years ago:

   Ten years ago:

3. The relationships between women and men.

Current:

Five years ago:

Ten years ago:

4. Extent of gender role stratification and sexism:

Current:

Five years ago:

Ten years ago:

Exercise 2

Select either print or television advertisements to examine for evidence of sexism. Find five advertisements that include women and/or men. Describe the appearance and actions of the men and women and access the level of sexism reflected. If you use television advertisements, briefly describe each. If you use print advertisements, number and attach them.

1. Advertisement 1:

2. Advertisement 2:

3. Advertisement 3:

4. Advertisement 4:

5. Advertisement 5:

Exercise 3

Describe your own gender role socialization. Discuss the specific contributions of the various agents of socialization (family, peers, schools, media, religion). Describe specific aspects of each agent of socialization which contributed to your own gender role socialization.

1. Family:

2. Peers:

3. Schools:

4. Media:

5. Religion:

Describe any other factors that have contributed to your gender role socialization, such as the books you read, the games you played, and your heroes/heroines.

Chapter 12

THE FAMILY

OBJECTIVES

After reading Chapter 12, you should understand the following main points and be able to answer the objectives.

1. A family consists of two or more people united by ties of marriage, ancestry, or adoption, and having the responsibility for rearing children.
   1.1 Define family.
   1.2 List five basic needs fulfilled by the family.
   1.3 Show how family life is structured in different societies.
   1.4 Differentiate monogamy from polygamy, polygyny, and polyandry.
   1.5 Define nuclear family and differentiate family of orientation from family of procreation.
   1.6 Define extended family and differentiate patrilocal residence from matrilocal residence.
   1.7 Differentiate bilateral descent from patrilineal descent and matrilineal descent.
   1.8 Differentiate patriarchy from matriarchy and egalitarian authority.
   1.9 Show how the five key concepts help in understanding the family.

2. Marriage is a socially recognized union between two or more people that involves sexual and economic rights and duties.
   2.1 Define marriage.
   2.2 Differentiate endogamy from exogamy.
   2.3 Explain why arranged marriages are desirable in some societies.
   2.4 Compare the advantages and disadvantages of romantic love as a basis of marriage.
   2.5 Profile the changes in age at first marriage.

3. Divorce has become more common over the last few decades.
   3.1 Profile the changes in the divorce rate.
   3.2 Note the percentage of new marriages that will end in divorce.
   3.3 List the major reasons cited for divorce.
   3.4 Show how structural and cultural developments have contributed to the divorce rate.
   3.5 Profile the situations in which the likelihood of divorce is highest.

4. The American family is changing dramatically in its basic structure and in the roles assigned to husbands and wives.
   4.1 Differentiate the nontraditional family from the traditional family.
   4.2 Describe the problems and prospects for dual-career families.
   4.3 Describe how the role of grandparents in the family has changed.

4.4 Describe the problems and prospects for blended nuclear families.
4.5 Give two reasons for the rise in families without children.
4.6 Describe the following family forms: singlehood, cohabitation, and single-parent families.

5. Changes in the social structure and culture have contributed to family problems.
   5.1 Compare the teenage pregnancy rate in the United States with that in other countries.
   5.2 List the factors associated with teenage parenthood.
   5.3 Describe the social consequences of teenage parenthood.
   5.4 Assess efforts to reduce teenage pregnancy.
   5.5 Explain why violence exists among family members.
   5.6 Compare child abuse, wife abuse, and elder abuse.
   5.7 Use the chapter's content to predict the future of American families.

CHAPTER SUMMARY

1. What is the family?

Because of significant variation from society to society, it seems almost impossible to define family in a way that would make the definition applicable to all societies. Family structures vary dramatically within a society as diverse as our own, and they have changed considerably through history. Despite the wide variation, however, most sociologists agree that a *family* is any group of people who are united by ties of marriage, ancestry, or adoption, and who have the responsibility for rearing children.

Some form of family structure is found in all human societies. This basic social institution fulfills five basic needs: 1) the need for love and emotional security, 2) the need to regulate sexual behavior, 3) the need to produce new generations, 4) the need to protect the young and the disabled, and 5) the need to place people in the social order.

2. How and why does the social organization of families vary widely from society to society?

Although families everywhere satisfy the five basic needs noted above, the social organization of family units differs significantly among societies. Social scientists have categorized these variations in family structure along several dimensions. One is the number of partners involved in a marriage. Our society advocates *monogamy*, marriage between one man and one woman. Other societies permit *polygamy*, marriage involving more than two partners at the same time. *Polygyny* is a form a form of polygamy in which a man has more than one wife at the same time; in *polyandry*, a woman has more than one husband at the same time. Another structural dimension is the degree of importance given to marital ties as opposed to blood ties. We speak of a *nuclear family* when marital ties are the most important--that is, when a husband, wife, and their immature children form a core unit. This arrangement is the preferred family structure in the United States and in most other modern Western countries. Two forms of the nuclear family exist: the *family of orientation* includes oneself and one's parents and siblings; the other, called *the family of procreation*, includes oneself and one's spouse and children. In contrast to the nuclear family, the *extended family* gives priority to blood ties, and includes blood relatives who live together in a single household. A common form is a three-generation extended family, in which some of a couple's married adult children live with their parents, along with their own spouses and children. Three-generation extended families can be classified as either patrilocal or matrilocal in their pattern of residence. In the case of *patrilocal* residence, a newly married couple live with or near the husband's family. In *matrilocal* residence, a son leaves his family and sets up housekeeping with or near his wife's family. In societies that favor the nuclear family, *neolocal* residence is preferred, in which the newlyweds establish a home of their own.

Family structure also can be categorized according to rules of descent. *Bilateral descent* exists when children are regarded as descended from both their mother's and their father's kin group. Other societies practice *patrilineal descent*, in which people are considered members of their father's kin group, or *matrilineal descent*, in which kinship is traced through the female line only. The person who wields authority in the home may also be used for categorizing family structure. *Patriarchy* exists when power is vested in the males; *matriarchy* exists when power is vested in females, an *egalitarian authority* system exists when power is distributed relatively equally between the two.

3. Which sociological factors help us to understand marriage?

Marriage may be defined as a socially recognized union between two or more people that involves sexual and economic rights and duties. All societies retain some control over the selection of a marital partner; cultural norms define the range of acceptable mates from whom a person can choose. Rules of *endogamy* require that people marry within their own social group; rules of *exogamy* require that people marry outside a group to which they belong. Many societies practice arranged marriages because they believe that this decision is too important to leave to the young. Arranged marriages make sense in societies where newlyweds become part of an extended family because the family has a stake in the type of spouse chosen. Families also want to choose someone who will share their values. In many of these societies a substantial amount of wealth is exchanged when a couple marries, so both families have a financial interest in making sure the marriage lasts. Arranged marriages occur most frequently in societies where elders control land or other resources on which future generations depend for their livelihood. Although arranged marriages are not practiced in the United States, parents still influence their children's selection of spouses in many informal ways. Examples include the neighborhood and the schools selected for the children.

American society still formally believes romantic love to be an important basis for marriage. This belief has its advantages. Couples become relatively independent of other kin when they set up a new household, thereby avoiding tensions and jealousies among other household members. In addition, romantic love is a more reliable motivation for mutual support than a sense of duty would be in a living arrangement that requires the spouses to depend heavily on each other. Romantic love also helps to weaken the strong emotional ties that bind young people to their families of orientation. Romance also has its limitations, however: it conflicts with the daily demands of married life and may create unrealistic expectations.

Norms also regulate the appropriate age for first marriage. The median age of first marriage remained stable during the 1950s, 1960s, and 1970s; men married at about age 23 and women at 20 or 21. In 1991, however, the median age was 26.3 for men and 24.1 for women. The reasons for the increase are not clear. Perhaps marriage plans are delayed by greater involvement in postsecondary education or by higher rates of cohabitation. Women may be postponing marriage until they have finished their education and established a career. Also, the high divorce rate may make some people more cautious.

4. Which sociological factors help to explain divorce?

Although 90 percent of Americans marry at least once, almost two-thirds of marriages will end in divorce. Divorce rates climbed in the 1970s, reached a peak in the 1980s, and since have leveled off and even declined slightly. However, divorce rate in the the United States today remains higher than in previous times and in other societies.

Which changes in the social structure may help to explain the increase in divorce rates? No-fault divorce laws have eliminated much of the acrimony of earlier divorce proceedings. Because of wom-en's increased involvement in the labor force, women are less likely to remain in a troubled marriage

157

if they can support themselves. A shift to such cultural values as self-fulfillment, autonomy, personal happiness, and personal growth also may be relevant. As a result, marriage has become deinstitution-alized; today it is more a matter of personal preference than a lifetime obligation.

Sociologists have uncovered several factors associated with divorce: 1) the husband and wife live in an urban area; 2) both spouses work, but their incomes are not high; 3) they married early; 4) they have not been married long; 5) the wife has egalitarian attitudes about the division of labor in the home and the husband does not; 6) neither husband nor wife has strong religious convictions; 7) both husband and wife have liberal attitudes; 8) both husband and wife are rather pessimistic about life; and 9) one or both have parents who are divorced. Having children has mixed effects on a marriage.

5. How does the modern-day reality of the nuclear family compare with the "ideal"?

The "ideal" family structure includes a competent working father and a devoted homemaking mother, both preferably young, white, and middle-class, and their two or more well-adjusted children. To-day's nuclear families, however, tend to be more inclusive and more open to role variations. Dual-career families are the product of the dramatic rise in the proportion of married women who work outside the home; currently nearly two-thirds do so. In *dual-career families* both husband and wife hold jobs that offer opportunities for professional advancement. Child care, division of household chores, and competing opportunities for career advancement become issues in these families.

Blended families occur with the marriage of two people, one or both of whom also have children. Blended families account for more than 17 percent of all nuclear families with children; about one-fourth of American children will live with a stepparent before reaching their sixteenth birthday. Blended families present adjustment difficulties for both the parents and the children.

American nuclear families also have been shrinking. In 1990 the number of childless married couples outnumbered those with children under age 18 living at home. Today's longer life span has contributed to this increase. Also, many women are marrying later and having fewer children. Ameri-cans seem to prefer smaller families now than in the past. Women who voluntarily remain childless tend to be white, to live in an urban area, and to be employed, highly educated, fairly well-off finan-cially, and not devoutly religious. Education plays a particularly important role in childbearing deci-sions.

6. What are the alternatives to the nuclear family?

Singlehood is viewed increasingly as an acceptable alternative to the nuclear family. The rise in the number of single males and females has been greater than the change in most other household ar-rangements. Most singles have never married; most live alone. Several social and economic trends account for the increase in the number of single Americans: the postponement of marriage, the rise in the divorce rate, career developments for women, the easing of credit discrimination against women, and young people's growing independence from their parents. The proportion of African-American women who never marry is particularly high, almost three times as great as the proportion of never-married white women. Social structural explanations for this difference include the higher rates of early death and imprisonment for young African-American men and the shortage of black men with steady jobs. Cultural reasons include the decline in stigma attached to bearing children out of wedlock among African-Americans.

Cohabitation (living together without being formally married) has increased fivefold since 1960. The high divorce rate has increased fivefold since 1960 and the changes in the norms governing sexual relationships may account for this increase.

Nearly three-fourths of single-parent families are formed by divorce or nonmarriage; 22 percent are caused by marital separation and 6 percent by the death of a spouse. The great majority of single parents are mothers; this family pattern is far more common among African-Americans than in other groups. The proportion of single-parent families doubled between 1970 and 1990. Births outside marriage are also on the rise, from 4 percent in 1950 to 26 percent in 1989. More than half of all children and more than 80 percent of African-American children will spend time in a single-parent family. Significant differences exist between single-parent families and two-parent families in economic well-being, levels of stress, and parent-child relationships. Growing up in a single-mother family is associated with numerous problems such as lower educational goals, lower levels of educational attainment, lower income, higher divorce rates, and greater involvement in delinquency. It is difficult, however, to separate the effects of living in a single-parent family from the effects of the poverty often associated with such families.

7. What is known about teenage pregnancy and parenthood?

The United States has the highest teenage pregnancy rate of any industrialized democratic nation, even though American teenagers are no more sexually active than those in other countries. Only about one-third of pregnant teenagers marry today, compared with almost 90 percent in 1960. Unmarried motherhood no longer carries the same social stigma as in the past. Few economic incentives exist for pregnant teens.

Four risk factors are associated with teenage pregnancy: 1) becoming sexually active at an early age; 2) being African-American or Hispanic; 3) living in a poor neighborhood with segregated schools; and 4) having low school achievement and aspirations. Although the rate of teenage pregnancy is highest among low-income African-Americans and Hispanics, the number of births to teenagers is highest among white, nonpoor young women who live in small cities or towns. Also, the birth rate for white teenagers is increasing, whereas that for minority youths has declined recently. The difference in birth rates between minority and white teenagers disappears when differences in income and academic skills are controlled.

About half of teenage mothers and nearly one-third of teenage fathers drop out of school. Early parenthood is not an inevitable result, or even the usual result of being born to a teenage mother. Still, a substantial proportion of teenagers' children are not doing well.

Many people believe that teenagers deliberately become pregnant to collect welfare and that they have additional children in order to increase their benefits. However, little evidence exists to support this belief. Early sex education programs may help to reduce the rate of teenage pregnancy. Some people believe that sex education programs encourage teens to become sexually active, but an exhaustive review of the literature found no evidence to support this view.

8. What are the causes of family violence?

More people are assaulted, beaten, and killed in their own homes at the hands of a loved one than anywhere else, or by anyone else. Several factors cause family violence: 1) people make a large emotional investment in family relationships, and hence take family members' words and actions very seriously; 2) substantial power differences exist within the family; 3) our culture tends to approve of physical aggression; 4) many people still believe that physical aggression in the family is normal; and 5) the isolation of nuclear families makes violence in the home less visible and therefore less subject to social control.

The number of reports of suspected child abuse filed in 1990 was double the number filed 10 years earlier. We do not know whether this increase is due to a real rise in the incidence of child abuse or to a greater willingness to report it. The most reliable estimate is that 2.5 percent of American children are neglected or abused each year. The typical child abuser is a young single parent who was married less than 10 years (or not at all) and had a child before age 18. Economic difficulties, other stresses such as divorce or death of a family member, and few friends or relatives in the community also contribute to child abuse. Child abuse victims suffer a decline in intelligence and an

159

increased risk of depression and suicide. As young children they tend to be hyperactive, easily distracted, and unpopular. As adolescents and adults, they are more likely than others to abuse drugs or alcohol and to become involved in juvenile delinquency and violent crime. Some sociologists argue that child abuse can end only when the social conditions that cause it are alleviated. This would involve identifying families at risk for abuse and providing them with the various forms of support and assistance they need, such as child-rearing classes, rent supplements, and drug treatment.

Each year about 30 women in 1,000 are assaulted by their husbands. A typical wife beater is young, has been married less than 10 years, and is employed part-time or not at all. He feels a need to play the role of male provider and to dominate his wife and children, but lacks the social and economic resources to do so without physical force. Some researchers have linked wife battering to status inconsistency, a gap between the role the man thinks he ought to play in relation to others and the actual position in which he finds himself. The roots of wife abuse lie in our cultural beliefs in violence and male superiority. The most effective way to reduce wife abuse is to combine criminal sanctions for abusers with counseling and shelter for victims.

About one elderly person in 20 is abused each year; this rate is on the rise. Elder abuse is particularly likely to go unreported, so the actual numbers may be higher. Forms of elder abuse include physical assaults, neglect, financial abuse, or psychological abuse. In one study, the key difference between abused and nonabused elders was that the abusers depended on the elders for housing, help with household repairs, financial assistance, and transportation. Two-thirds of the abusers had mental or emotional problems or were alcoholics. There was no evidence that the abusers had been victims of family violence themselves.

REVIEW OF CONCEPTS

Match the concept with the definition.

Concepts

a. bilateral descent	i. family	q. neolocal residence
b. blended families	j. family of orientation	r. nuclear family
c. cohabitation	k. family of procreation	s patriarchy
d. dual-career family	l. marriage	t. patrilineal descent
e. egalitarian authority	m. matriarchy	u. patrilocal residence
f. endogamy	n. matrilineal descent	v. polyandry
g. exogamy	o. matrilocal residence	w. polygamy
h. extended family	p. monogamy	x. polygyny

Definitions

_____ 1. A group of people who are united by ties of marriage, ancestry or adoption, having responsibility for rearing children.

_____ 2. A socially recognized union between two or more individuals that typically involves sexual and economic rights and duties.

_____ 3. A nuclear family consisting of oneself and one's mother, father, and siblings.

_____ 4. A household consisting of married couples from different generations, their children, and other relatives; the core family consists of blood relatives, and spouses are functionally marginal and peripheral.

___ 5. A marriage arrangement consisting of a husband or wife and more than one spouse.

___ 6. An arrangement in which a couple lives together without being formally married.

___ 7. A nuclear family consisting of oneself and one's spouse and children.

___ 8. A pattern in which power within the family is vested equally in males and females.

___ 9. A marriage in which both partners pursue careers outside the home.

___ 10. A household consisting of spouses and their offspring; other blood relatives are functionally marginal and peripheral.

___ 11. Marriage consisting of one husband and one wife.

___ 12. The reckoning of descent through both the father's and mother's families.

___ 13. A pattern in which power within the family is vested in males.

___ 14. Marriage consisting of one wife and two or more husbands.

___ 15. Families formed by the marriage of two people one or both of whom also have children.

___ 16. A rule that requires a person to marry someone from within his or her own group-- tribe, nationality, religion, race, community, or other social grouping.

___ 17. An arrangement in which the married couple, upon marriage, sets up a new residence.

Answers

1.	i	7.	k	13.	s
2.	l	8.	e	14.	v
3.	j	9.	d	15.	b
4.	h	10.	r	16.	f
5.	w	11.	p	17.	q
6.	c	12.	a		

REVIEW QUESTIONS

After studying Chapter 12, answer the following questions. The correct answers are listed after the questions; each is followed by a short explanation. You are also referred to pages in the textbook for relevant discussion.

1. Which is *not* a part of the explanation for recent increases in the number of single fathers?
   a. Sex roles have become less rigid.
   b. Unemployment rates among men are increasing.
   c. Career opportunities for women are increasing.

d. Men are becoming more involved in child-rearing activities.

e. Changes in divorce laws are causing courts to view men and women as equally responsible parents.

2. According to Geoffrey Greif, what is the most difficult problem for single fathers?
   a. learning how to shop for food
   b. doing the laundry and dressing the children
   c. balancing demands of child care and work
   d. developing a satisfying relationship with children
   e. feelings of incompetence

3. Which is *not* one of the basic human and social needs satisfied by the family?
   a. the regulation of sexual behavior
   b. providing love and emotional security
   c. production and distribution of essential goods and services
   d. care and protection of dependent offspring
   e. reproduction of a new generation

4. From the moment you are born into a particular family, characteristics of your parents such as race, ethnicity, nationality, religion, and social class are ascribed automatically to you. These characteristics will significantly affect your life chances and achievements. This process describes which one of the following basic needs satisfied by families?
   a. providing love and emotional security
   b. regulation of sexual behavior
   c. reproduction of a new generation
   d. social placement
   e. care and protection of dependent offspring

5. In comparing the wide variations in family organization in various cultures, the most important sociological conclusion is that
   a. people do not need regular sexual intercourse.
   b. social fatherhood always coincides with biological fatherhood.
   c. communal child rearing will be the dominant pattern in the future.
   d. unrelated people can share a household with little disruption.
   e. a wide variety of family organizations can produce healthy, well-socialized children.

6. Some societies permit marriage involving more than two partners at the same time, a practice known as
   a. bilateral descent.
   b. endogamy.
   c. patriarchy.
   d. exogamy.
   e. polygamy.

7. The nuclear family is a household made up of
   a. a mother, a father, and their dependent children.
   b. a mother, a father, their dependent children, and one or both of the mother's parents.
   c. a mother, a father, their dependent children, and their dependent children's children.
   d. a mother, a father, their dependent children, and at least one of the father's brothers or sisters.

162

e. a mother, a father, their dependent children, and at least one of the mother's brothers or sisters.

8. Which of the following family forms is most likely to result when priority is given to blood ties over marital ties?
   a. dual-career marriage
   b. extended family
   c. serial monogamy
   d. nuclear family
   e. egalitarian family

9. The family into which you are born, and which consists only of you, your parents, and your siblings, is precisely called
   a. an extended family.
   b. a matrilocal family.
   c. the family of orientation.
   d. a composite family.
   e. the family of procreation.

10. Murdock found that in 40 percent of the societies he studied people are considered members of their father's kin group, a practice known as
    a. patrilineal descent.
    b. matrilineal descent.
    c. patriarchy.
    d. matriarchy.
    e. patrilocal residence.

11. Which is the least likely pattern in the selection of marriage partners?
    a. Marriage partners are arranged by other kin, such as the bride's or the groom's parents.
    b. Marriage partners are chosen freely with no explicit or implicit social pressures.
    c. Powerful social pressures push people to select "appropriate" marriage partners.
    d. The choice of a marriage partner is backed by strong social sanctions.
    e. People choose marriage partners from among their "own kind."

12. One of the disadvantages of romantic love as a basis for marriage is that
    a. romantic love between marriage partners provides a basis for emotional and physical support.
    b. romantic love prevents the formation of tensions, jealousies, and competition among family members.
    c. romantic love weakens the strong emotional bonds between young people and their parents.
    d. romantic love ensures that the marriage will not be guided by strictly defined rights and obligations.
    e. romance thrives on mystery and does not prepare a couple for the businesslike nature of enduring relationships.

13. Since 1960, the median age at first marriage
    a. has increased steadily for both men and women.
    b. has declined steadily for both men and women.
    c. has increased for women but declined for men.
    d. has increased for men but declined for women.

e. has remained relatively constant.

14. Which factor has **not** contributed to the apparent rise in divorce rates in American society.
    a. It is easier for unmarried women to adjust and to be accepted socially.
    b. Values have shifted to an emphasis on self-sacrifice and commitment.
    c. Divorce is perceived as a sign of psychoemotional health and of personal growth.
    d. The legal apparatus for obtaining divorce has been made less complex.
    e. Women now are less economically dependent on men than in the past.

15. Which of the following couples is most likely to get a divorce?
    a. Carol and Bob go to church twice each week; neither set of their parents was divorced.
    b. Janet and Peter were married in their early thirties.
    c. Max and Susan are politically conservative and are optimistic that the country soon will solve its economic problems.
    d. Greg and Linda live on a farm with two teenage daughters.
    e. Ken and Barbara live in New York City; though both have jobs outside the home, Barbara does the housework.

16. What percentage of children under the age of five were regularly cared for by someone other than a parent in 1988?
    a. 20 percent
    b. 35 percent
    c. 50 percent
    d. 60 percent
    e. 75 percent

17. About what percentage of all nuclear families with children do stepfamilies represent?
    a. 2 percent
    b. 10 percent
    c. 17 percent
    d. 30 percent
    e. 45 percent

18. The two basic reasons for the increase in families without children at home are
    a. declining economic standards and the lesser value placed on having children.
    b. the lesser value placed on having children and the increased divorce rate.
    c. the increased divorce rate and today's longer life span.
    d. today's longer life span and the later age at marriage for women.
    e. the late age at marriage for women and declining economic standards.

19. Singlehood is particularly high among
    a. males.
    b. females.
    c. African-American females.
    d. Hispanic-American males.
    e. Native Americans of both sexes.

20. Two approaches noted in the text to discourage teenage pregnancy are
    a. increasing welfare benefits and encouraging pregnant teens to stay in school.
    b. encouraging pregnant teens to stay in school and making abortion more widely available.

c. making abortion more widely available and reducing welfare benefits.

d. reducing welfare benefits and providing teens with sex education and early access to contraceptives.

e. providing teens with sex education and early access to contraceptives and providing better vocational training.

21. The presence of violence within the American family
   a. results in part from the deep emotions that we invest in family relationships.
   b. is encouraged by our acceptance of violence in our culture.
   c. reflects power differentials in the family.
   d. is widespread, and includes children, wives, and the elderly among its victims.
   e. all of the above.

Answers

1. *b.* Male unemployment rates have no connection with the increasing rate of single fathers. Those increases are due instead to less rigid sex roles, fathers' increasing desires and opportunities to spend time with their children, and changes in divorce laws that make it more likely for fathers to assume custody over the children. See page 293.

2. *c.* Greif reports that men discovered that they had to choose between success at home and success at work. Most single fathers had to cut back on the amount of time spent on their careers; in some cases, this decision cost them pay increases or promotions. See page 293.

3. *c.* Production and distribution of essential goods and services is a function generally served by economic institutions, not by family institutions. The family serves five functions: regulation of sexual behavior, socialization, reproduction, care and protection of infants, and social placement. See page 294.

4. *d.* Families are responsible for assigning new members of society to a variety of consequential statuses and roles. In doing so, the family plays a critical role in facilitating or limiting social mobility. See page 294.

5. *e.* These societies have very different family arrangements, but each perpetuates itself successfully by giving birth and socializing new generations of members. See pages 294-295.

6. *e.* Some societies permit marriage involving more than two partners at the same time, a practice known as polygamy. See page 295.

7. *a.* The nuclear family household consists *only* of a mother, a father, and their dependent children. If any additional kin live in the household, it becomes an extended family. See page 295.

8. *b.* When blood ties assume priority over marital ties, connections across multiple generations are more important than connections between husband and wife. This situation results in extended family arrangements. See page 295.

9. *c.* The family of orientation is defined as a nuclear family consisting of you, your parents, and your siblings. It is the family into which you are born. See page 295.

10. *a.* Societies differ in terms of whose kin group defines descent. In patrilineal descent people are considered members of their father's kin group. See page 296.

11. *b.* The choice of a marriage partner is rarely a private matter left up to the bride and the groom. In every society, laws and customs define the appropriate pool of candidates from which one can choose a mate. See page 297.

12. *e.* When the romance fades, often the marriage fades along with it. If people are drawn together for love alone, they may be ill prepared for the compromises, division of labor, and financial debates that are the part of any stable, long-lasting union. See page 299.

13. *a.* Since 1960, the median age at first marriage has increased from 22.8 to 26.3 for men and

from 20.3 to 24.1 for women. See page 299.

14. *b.* One cause of the rise in divorce rates is a shift *from* values emphasizing self-sacrifice and commitment *to* values emphasizing individual happiness and personal satisfaction. Couples today are less willing to stick together "for the children's sake" if they are not achieving marital fulfillment as individuals. See pages 300-301.

15. *e.* Divorce rates are higher for couples in urban areas, for couples in which both partners work, and for couples in which the husband does not share his wife's egalitarian attitudes toward housework. See page 302.

16. *d.* In 1988, 60 percent of children under the age of five were regularly cared for by someone other than a parent. See page 304.

17. *c.* In 1987, stepfamilies accounted for 17.4 percent of all nuclear families with children. See page 305.

18. *d.* Today's longer life span means that a much smaller proportion of married life needs to be devoted to child-rearing. Many women marry late in life and hence have fewer or no children due to fertility problems or as a matter of choice. See page 305.

19. *c.* The proportion of African-American women who never marry is particularly high, reaching 25 percent for those born in the early 1950s (compared to only 9 percent of white women). Reasons include high rates of early death and imprisonment for young African-American men and a shortage of black men in secure jobs. See page 306.

20. *d.* One approach to discouraging teenage pregnancy involves reducing welfare benefits, although little evidence exists to support the belief that teens deliberately become pregnant to collect welfare and that they bear more children to increase their benefits. The other approach involves providing teens with sex education and easy access to contraceptives. See page 310.

21. *e.* The family is expected to be a haven from the aggressiveness and competitiveness of the public world, but frequently it becomes the scene for violence. The emotional or even passionate relationships within the family sometimes can turn minor squabbles into physical confrontations. See pages 310-311.

EXERCISES

Exercise 1

Select a few comics in the daily paper or select a few TV programs that feature family life.

1. Describe family life in each comic or TV program.

2. Describe the sociological characteristics in each: race and ethnicity, class, age, presence of children, and the like.

3. Which two of the five key concepts best help you understand the comics or programs?

4. How typical do you consider the family portrayed in each comic or program?

5. Discuss any evidence of gender roles.

Exercise 2

Imagine that you are eavesdropping on the following families as they sit down to dinner together. Describe the dominant topics of conversation and the typical patterns of interaction in each family. Who talks and who listens? What do they argue about? How do these things vary depending on the makeup of the family?

Family 1: White, upper-middle-class, nuclear family. Father is a 40-year-old business executive; mother works at home; 18-year-old daughter is home on vacation from prestigious East Coast university; 16-year-old son is a senior in high school and a basketball star.

Family 2: A cohabiting, unmarried couple, recent college graduates, who go to the woman's parents' house for dinner.

Family 3: Black, working-class family. Father is a 38-year-old assembly-line worker; mother is 35 and works at McDonald's restaurant; 15-year-old son has just dropped out of high school; 13-year-old daughter is an honor student.

Family 4: Poor, white extended family. Father is deceased; mother works as a schoolteacher; mother's sister (who lives in the household) was just fired from her job at a canning factory; 15-year-old son was just arrested for burglary; 14-year-old daughter is five months pregnant.

Family 5: Dual-career marriage. Husband works as professor at large university; wife is manager of a bank; they have no children, but their dinner tonight was prepared by a hired domestic.

Family 6: Single-mother family. The mother has recently divorced the father; father has left the household; mother works as part-time secretary; she lives with her three teenage sons, all of whom have after-school jobs.

Exercise 3

In *Women's Work* (Pantheon Books, 1974, page 101), Ann Oakley presents the table below.

1. Summarize in your own words the main message from this table.

Percent Experiencing

	Boredom/Monotony	Fragmentation	"Never Having Enough Time"
Housewives	75	90	50
Factory workers	41	70	31
Assembly/line workers	67	86	36

2. Explain *why* housewives do not seem happy with their jobs.

3. Discuss the implications of these statistics for future changes in the structure of the traditional nuclear family.

4. Evaluate the following prediction: "The housewife role will be extinct by the year 2000."

5. Describe alternative arrangements for assigning the chores typically performed by housewives.

Chapter 13
EDUCATION

OBJECTIVES

After reading Chapter 13, you should understand the following main points and be able to answer the objectives.

1. Schools perform several functions.
   1.1 Define education and differentiate it from other forms of socialization.
   1.2 Show how the five key concepts are related to education.
   1.3 Describe how the hidden curriculum functions to instill self-discipline.
   1.4 Describe how schools contribute to cultural transmission.
   1.5 Describe how schools help to perpetuate the socioeconomic power structure.
   1.6 Describe how schools function to select talent.
   1.7 Define self-fulfilling prophecies.
   1.8 Describe how schools teach skills.

2. Several social forces determine amount and quality of education children receive.
   2.1 Demonstrate the connection between socioeconomic status as well as ethnicity and various educational outcomes.
   2.2 Explain the role of tracking.
   2.3 List two problems with using intelligence tests as a basis for tracking.
   2.4 Explain why differences in tracking exist.
   2.5 Identify the reasons for class-related differences in parents' involvement in their children's school.
   2.6 Define creeping credentialism.
   2.7 Develop a profile of the typical dropout.

3. Education has a substantial effect on opportunities and attainment.
   3.1 Summarize the results of the Coleman Study.
   3.2 Define compensatory education.
   3.3 Indicate the findings of Jencks.
   3.4 Indicate the findings of Rutter.
   3.5 Indicate the findings of Kozol.
   3.6 Indicate the results and popularity of busing.
   3.7 Define white flight.

4. Public schools in the United States are in crisis.
   4.1 Summarize the results of the Gallup Poll.

4.2 Explain the superior performance of private schools.
4.3 Determine the prevalence of functional illiteracy.
4.4 List several causes for the rise in functional illiteracy.
4.5 List other indicators of the crisis in public education.
4.6 Describe and assess some of the proposed solutions to our educational problems.
4.7 Define magnet schools.

5. Higher education plays a key role in American society.
   5.1 Profile today's college student.
   5.2 Describe the contribution of community colleges.

CHAPTER SUMMARY

1. What are the social functions of schools?

Sociologists define *education* as a structured form of socialization in which a culture's knowledge, skills, and values are formally transmitted from one generation to the next. Schools are the formal and specialized institutions in which education is carried out in complex societies. Education is not limited to schooling; just as education is a specialized form of socialization, so school is a more specialized form of education. In preindustrial societies, children are educated by their elders and peers in the course of daily activities. In modern complex societies, most education is conducted in formal, specialized institutions, mainly schools.

Schools perform several social functions. First, they instill self-discipline, primarily through the *hidden curriculum*. This is the set of unwritten rules of behavior taught in a school to prepare the children for life outside the small, informally structured world of the family--that is, to prepare them for the world of large, formally structured organizations. Public opinion polls support the importance of teaching discipline. Second, schools transmit culture--the values, beliefs, language, and knowledge of a society. Schools respond to shifts in cultural values and emphases by revising their curricula. However, they teach less about various subcultures than about the mainstream culture. Cultural transmission occurs directly through the formalized curriculum and indirectly through the hidden curriculum. Third, schools perpetuate the socioeconomic power structure by emphasizing capitalism at the expense of other ideologies. Schools socialize students from different social backgrounds very differently, thereby contributing to the perpetuation of the stratification system. Fourth, schools serve to select talent. Again, they provide very different educational experiences and opportunities for development of talent to children from different social classes. The labeling processes that occur often result in *self-fulfilling prophecies*: expectations which themselves evoke behavior that helps to make those expectations come true. Fifth, schools teach skills, including such basic skills as reading, writing, and arithmetic, the ability to reason and solve problems, and general and specific knowledge to be used in the workplace. Recent evidence suggests that public schools are failing in this last task.

2. Who receives what kind of education?

Social class background is connected closely to educational opportunities and attainment. Social class and ethnicity remain strong predictors of attending college and receiving high SAT scores. This pattern is perpetuated by *tracking*, a practice in which students are grouped in school according to their perceived interests and abilities. The underlying assumption is that some students have less academic ability than others. School officials use IQ tests to assign students to tracks. However, IQ tests assess only a small range of mental abilities and are biased against students with certain experiences and backgrounds. Tracking also is practiced because of the belief that students learn better in homogeneous groups. Recent research suggests that homogeneous groups benefit only the students at the very top of the performance ladder. Because of inequalities in the social system, however, middle- and upper-class parents will have more to say about the structure and functioning of schools than other parents.

Parental involvement in schools also affects educational achievement. Once again, middle- and upper-class parents are more involved in their children's education. Although most working-class parents value education, their feelings of academic incompetence and passivity prevent them from becoming more involved. In addition, middle- and upper-class parents have many more social connections that keep them informed about educational matters. Finally, the degree of connection between work and home tends to influence family-school relationships. Because middle- and upper-class parents bring their work home, they see their children's education as work and something that should not be confined to the classroom. Working-class parents see a much sharper division between home and school. Even when working-class children attain the minimum credentials needed to enter the work force, they often experience *creeping credentialism*, a steady rise in the credential requirements in the job market. As a result, the jobs they want often remain beyond their reach, even when they receive a better education.

Minority students from low-income families are more likely than others to drop out of high school. Although the black dropout rate is slightly higher than that of whites (about 14% versus 12%), one Hispanic in three drops out. Students from single-parent families and large families and those from big cities and from the South are also more likely than others to drop out. Dropouts experience many problems with school: they are often tardy or absent; they often are suspended; they are more likely to become pregnant and to engage in delinquent behavior; and they feel alienated from school and have low self-esteem. They also have low achievement test scores and no plans for education beyond high school. Few are in academic tracks. Some observers such as Jackson Toby believe that we should simply admit that American education would be better off if some students dropped out. Others, such as Charles Finn, think that Americans should be required to stay in school until they have achieved a certain level of basic skills and knowledge.

3. What can schools do to foster equal opportunity?

Efforts to reduce racial segregation began in 1954 with the Supreme Court's *Brown v. Board of Education* ruling, which declared unconstitutional the traditional separation of black and white children into different schools. The ruling had little effect on desegregation, however. Desegregation efforts were promoted by the 1964 Civil Rights Act and by the 1985 enactment of a program of federal aid to public schools. A major study conducted by James Coleman in 1966 found only minimal effects of school characteristics such as expenditure per pupil, building age, library facilities, number of textbooks, teachers' characteristics, and class size. Far more critical for academic success was the child's social environment, especially the attitudes and behaviors of family members and peers. Coleman also found that the students' social environment was the main factor related to their achievement. His report provided a strong rationale for *compensatory education*, enrichment programs that help students from disadvantaged backgrounds to catch up with more privileged students.

Christopher Jencks also found that social inequality outside the classroom is the major determinate of inequality within, but argued that schools could do nothing about this situation. In England, Michael Rutter performed an in-depth analysis of 10-year-olds in inner-city London schools. He found that some schools were superior to others regarding students' performance and behavior. Good schools emphasized academic achievement and set clear standards for discipline. Jonathan Kozol has documented extensively the "savage inequalities" that distinguish schools in rich districts from those in inner-city and rural areas.

Courts have mandated busing to redress the racial imbalances in schools. Although busing has proved very effective, public support has been low. Busing also has resulted in *white flight*: white parents remove their children from public schools by sending them to private schools or moving to a predominantly white suburb to avoid busing.

4. Why are our public schools in crisis? What can be done about it?

Today's students are no less capable than those of the past, as suggested by the fact that some schools (particularly private schools) are able to produce higher levels of performance. The academic advantage of private schools exists even with controls for academic track, ability, educational aspirations, and social class. The success of private schools is probably due to the higher levels of order and discipline they demand from students, the extra encouragement that private school teachers can offer, the heavy emphasis on college attendance, and the greater commitment to their children's education among parents who choose private schools.

Perhaps the most dramatic evidence for the crisis in public education is the increasing illiteracy rate. One young adult in three now is barely literate, and 75 percent of those who are unemployed are functionally illiterate. American students score near the bottom in international comparisons of performance in mathematics and science. Several changes have been proposed to remedy this situation. First, the quality of teachers should be improved. Second, we need to provide alternatives to schools of education as the route to teacher certification. Third, individual schools should be given more power to make important decisions about budgets, staffing, and curricula. Fourth, parents should have more freedom about which schools their children attend. Possible means include vouchers (a "check" that parents can spend at any school) and *magnet schools*, public schools with high academic standards and curricula that are specialized in a particular field.

5. What is the role of higher education in American society?

In 1991 more than one-fifth of the adult population had completed four years of college or more, and that proportion was growing. Today's college student is older than in the past; the average age is now almost 22. Slightly more than half of all college students are women, and the majority are white. The desire to obtain a better job is the leading reason why students decide to go to college. Nearly one-third of full-time students and more than four-fifths of part-time students work 21 hours or more each week. Regarding goals, college students today give high priority to their personal ambitions and desires. Although business remains the most popular major, its popularity is leveling off.

Enrollments in two-year schools have risen while enrollments in four-year schools have declined, perhaps because today's average student is older and wishes to receive more more practical, vocationally oriented training. The lower tuitions at two-year colleges may also be relevant. Community colleges usually offer three types of programs: vocational training, transfer programs (which enable students to transfer to four-year schools), and community education. Most community colleges emphasize vocational training. Students who take these courses probably will enter jobs with limited upward mobility.

REVIEW OF CONCEPTS

Match the concept with the definition.

Concepts

a. compensatory education
b. creeping credentialism
c. education
d. hidden curriculum
e. magnet schools
f. tracking
g. white flight

Definitions

_____ 1. The formal, systematic transmission of a culture's skills, knowledge, and values from one generation to the next.

_____ 2. The tendency of some white parents to remove their children from desegregated urban public schools, either sending them to private schools or moving to a distant suburb not affected by busing.

_____ 3. Enrichment programs to help disadvantaged students to compete more equally with privileged students.

_____ 4. The tendency for employees to require ever-higher levels of education and other formal qualifications as a condition of employment.

_____ 5. Grouping children according to their perceived interests and abilities.

_____ 6. A set of unwritten rules of behavior taught in school that prepare children for academic success and social relations in the world outside school.

Answers

1.	c	3.	a	5.	f
2.	g	4.	b	6.	d

REVIEW QUESTIONS

After studying Chapter 13, answer the following questions. The correct answers are listed at the end of the questions; each is followed by a short explanation. You are also referred to pages in the textbook for relevant discussion.

1. Which one of the following statements is correct?
   a. Socialization is a specialized form of education and schooling is a specialized form of education.
   b. Education is a specialized form of socialization and schooling is a specialized form of education.
   c. Education is a specialized form of socialization and education is a specialized form of schooling.
   d. Socialization is a specialized form of education and education is a specialized form of schooling.
   e. Both education and schooling are part of the institution of socialization.

2. The self-fulfilling prophecy is most likely to occur in which of the following situations?
   a. James is labeled as "dumb."
   b. Susie is labeled as "cooperative."
   c. Marty is labeled as "smart."
   d. a and c only.
   e. a, b, and c.

3. The hidden curriculum best reflects which one of the following functions of schools?
   a. perpetuating the socioeconomic power structure
   b. talent selection
   c. cultural transmission
   d. teaching skills
   e. instilling self-discipline

4. Teachers in middle- and upper-class schools stress proper English, whereas teachers in working-class and slum schools may permit ethnic slang and street grammar. This example reflects which one of the following functions of education?
   a. perpetuating the socioeconomic power structure
   b. talent selection
   c. cultural transmission
   d. teaching skills
   e. instilling self-discipline

5. Which one of the following functions of schools is illustrated when teachers ask students to pledge allegiance to the flag each morning?
   a. perpetuating the socioeconomic power structure
   b. talent selection
   c. cultural transmission
   d. teaching skills
   e. instilling self-discipline

6. Tracking refers to
   a. organizing schools into various academic units.
   b. placing better teachers in lower-class schools.
   c. more clearly differentiating public and private schools.
   d. placing males and females into different curricula.
   e. grouping students according to their perceived interests and abilities.

7. Two major drawbacks to using IQ tests as the criterion for tracking are
   a. they measure only a small range of mental abilities and are biased against some students.
   b. they are biased against some students and are too expensive.
   c. they are too expensive and are overused.
   d. they are overused and discriminate against females.
   e. they discriminate against females and measure only a small range of mental abilities.

8. Verbal and mathematics scores, college attendance, and other indicators of educational outcomes are linked most closely to
   a. students' socioeconomic status.
   b. the quality of teachers.
   c. the level of school discipline.
   d. the amount of money spent per pupil.
   e. the educational climate of schools.

9. Which one of the following is *not* one of the social forces keeping working-class parents uninvolved with their children's education?
   a. a low level of respect for teachers
   b. a feeling of academic incompetence.

c. passivity.
d. lack of social connections.
e. less connection between work and home.

10. Dropouts have all but one of the following characteristics. Which one?
   a. They tend to be low-income minority students.
   b. They tend to be from single-parent homes.
   c. They tend to be from small families.
   d. They tend to be from urban areas.
   e. Their families are less likely to have books at home.

11. Which one of the following statements is *false* regarding Coleman's conclusions about equality of educational opportunity?
   a. Expenditures per pupil have no clear effect on achievement.
   b. Mostly black and mostly white schools differ considerably in expenditures per pupil, age of building, and class size.
   c. The difference noted in b had a substantial effect on learning.
   d. Low-income blacks in ghetto schools performed more poorly than did low-income blacks in largely middle-class schools.
   e. All are true.

12. Rutter's study of school quality found which of the following to be the most critical influence on school quality?
   a. how teachers teach
   b. teachers' training and experience
   c. the students' social class
   d. the school's socioeconomic status
   e. total expenditures per pupil

13. Busing to reduce segregation has been
   a. effective and popular.
   b. effective but unpopular
   c. ineffective but popular
   d. ineffective and unpopular
   e. never implemented fully enough to determine its effectiveness

14. The major conclusion of Coleman's study of private schools was that
   a. private schools are inferior to public schools.
   b. private schools are superior to public schools.
   c. there is no difference in quality between private and public schools.
   d. private schools contribute to the decline of public schools.
   e. private schools lack sufficient funds and should be subsidized by the government.

15. Approximately what proportion of adults is functionally illiterate?
   a. 10 percent
   b. 25 percent
   c. 33 percent
   d. 45 percent
   e. 56 percent

16. Changes needed to reform American education include all *but* which one of the following?
    a. improve the quality of teachers
    b. increase the federal role in education
    c. provide alternative routes to teacher certification
    d. empower individual schools
    e. provide parents with greater choice

17. The major reason students go to college is
    a. to learn more.
    b. to get better jobs.
    c. to get a general education.
    d. to meet new and interesting people.
    e. to become more well-rounded individuals.

18. The value of a college degree has declined in recent years primarily because of
    a. increased minority enrollments.
    b. more people earning college degrees.
    c. more females attending college as a result of the women's movement.
    d. competition by two-year colleges.
    e. reduced federal spending on higher education.

19. Regarding enrollment in four-year and two-year colleges,
    a. enrollment is up in both.
    b. enrollment is up in four-year colleges but down in two-year colleges.
    c. enrollment is down in four-year colleges but up in two-year colleges.
    d. enrollment is down in both.
    e. enrollment in both is down for men but up for women.

Answers

1. *b.* Education is a specific structured form of socialization that encompasses but is not limited to schooling. See page 318.
2. *e.* The self-fulfilling prophecy reflects an initial false definition that encourages new behavior consistent with this definition. All three examples reflect the self-fulfilling prophecy. See page 323.
3. *e.* The hidden curriculum includes the unwritten rules of behavior that prepare children for the adult world. Thus, it reflects the function of instilling self-discipline and to socialize children into public, adult life. See page 320.
4. *a.* This example shows how schools socialize students from different social backgrounds differently, in ways that are consistent with their future places in society. See page 322.
5. *c.* Pledging allegiance to the flag helps to transmit the American cultural emphasis on the virtues of democracy. See pages 320-321.
6. *e.* Tracking involves grouping students according to their perceived interests and abilities. It places lower-income students into lower-quality and lower-status courses. See page 325.
7. *a.* Using IQ tests as the basis for tracking is flawed because they measure only a small range of abilities and are biased against students with certain experiences and backgrounds. See pages 325-326.
8. *a.* Students' socioeconomic status is the best predictor of educational outcomes. See page 325.
9. *a.* Working-class parents look up to teachers and defer to them. The other four factors help keep working-class parents uninvolved with the children's education. See pages 328-329.

10. *c.* Dropouts are more likely to come from large families. See page 330.
11. *c.* Coleman found large differences between mostly black and mostly white schools in expenditures per pupil, age of building, library facilities, number of textbooks, teachers' characteristics, and class size. However, these factors had little effect on learning. See page 331.
12. *a.* Rutter found that a school was good primarily because of how teachers taught. For example, teachers in good schools emphasized academic achievement, assigned regular homework, set clear standards of discipline, and rewarded good work. See page 332.
13. *b.* Busing has been effective in reducing segregation but has never been popular. (see page 333).
14. *b.* Coleman found that the average private school is superior to the average public school in many ways. See page 334.
15. *c.* About one-third of young adults in America are functionally illiterate. See page 335.
16. *b.* Increasing the federal role in education is not one of the changes the text noted are necessary to reform American education. See pages 338-339.
17. *b.* Over three-fourths of students say that they want to go to college to get better jobs. See page 339.
18. *b.* The major reason for the decline in the value of a college degree is the dramatic increase in the number of degree holders. Too many degrees have been granted for the number of jobs that require a college education. See page 340.
19. *c.* Enrollment in four-year colleges has fallen while enrollment in two-year colleges has increased. This increase may reflect the greater age of today's average student as well as the concern of today's students with receiving more practical and more vocational training. See page 341.

EXERCISES

Exercise 1

Find an article in a newspaper or newsweekly that describes an educational reform or innovation.

1. Describe the reform or innovation.

2. Compare the reform or innovation with the educational reforms proposed in the text.

3. Link the reform or innovation with two of the five key concepts.

4. Assess the likelihood that the reform or innovation will succeed.

Exercise 2

A major theme in this chapter has been the effects of social class and race-ethnicity on the school experiences of students. Unfortunately, researchers frequently fail to control for one when studying the effects of the other, particularly when examining the effects of race-ethnicity. The table below describes several aspects of students' school experiences by social class and by race-ethnicity.

Educational Variables Related to Race and Social Class in a Random Sample of 28,240 Seniors in Public and Private High Schools in the United States in 1980.

	Lower Class			Middle Class			Upper Class		
	White	Black	Hispanic	White	Black	Hispanic	White	Black	Hispanic
1. Mean aptitude score (vocabulary, math, reading), range = 21-80	48	43	43	52	45	46	56	49	50
2. % receiving mostly As or half As and Bs	28%	23%	23%	36%	21%	24%	47%	25%	30%
3. % completing 3 years or more of math courses	21%	36%	26%	32%	41%	36%	50%	50%	46%
4. % doing 5 or more hours of homework per week	18%	25%	19%	23%	28%	23%	38%	39%	36%
5. % absent 1 or more days for reasons other than illness	77%	69%	73%	73%	69%	73%	73%	66%	73%
6. % with specific place to study in home	34%	42%	40%	46%	62%	52%	63%	70%	70%
7. % who think they will get college degree or higher	23%	43%	33%	42%	61%	47%	77%	81%	72%
8. % accepted by any college	35%	32%	27%	46%	38%	32%	62%	47%	43%
9. % interested in school	67%	86%	83%	72%	86%	79%	79%	89%	79%
10. % satisfied with education	67%	60%	66%	70%	60%	67%	75%	64%	68%
11. % in academic track	21%	29%	24%	38%	43%	35%	65%	61%	59%
12. % in vocational track	35%	34%	33%	24%	25%	24%	9%	15%	11%
13. Mean number of extra-curricular activities	2.1	2.7	2.2	2.7	3.1	2.6	3.1	3.6	2.7
14. % who were read to daily as a child before starting school	12%	13%	7%	17%	21%	14%	23%	33%	16%
15. % rating academic instruction as good or excellent	54%	47%	50%	62%	58%	60%	72%	65%	69%
16. % rating condition of building as good or excellent	60%	47%	57%	65%	49%	62%	73%	55%	73%
17. % stating they don't feel safe at their school	9%	14%	8%	7%	14%	11%	5%	13%	8%

Source: These data are part of the "High School and Beyond" study sponsored by the National Center for Education Statistics. Percentages are rounded.

1. Select five variables that interest you and describe the differences by race-ethnicity.

2. Describe the differences by social class for the same variables.

3. Compare the social-class differences with the race-ethnicity differences. Which of the two, if any, is greater? Explain the results.

4. Examine three other variables to determine if your general conclusions apply to them as well. Describe your results.

Exercise 3

Write a brief analysis of your own educational career using the concepts and perspectives in the chapter and relevant issues from other chapters. You may wish to examine:

--some classrooms you have been in
--the relationships between teachers and students
--the nature of the schools you attended
--the self-fulfilling prophecy as experienced by yourself or peers
--the role of the schools you have attended in attaining the functions of education
--your experiences with the hidden curriculum

--your experiences with tracking
--the effectiveness of your schools in teaching the basic skills
--the experiences of minority students in the schools you attended
--the extent to which the schools you attended incorporated some of the elements of quality schools
--your experiences with private schools in relation to the description of private schools in the text
--what you have gained or hope to gain from a college education
--the type of peer group with which you identify
--your reasons for attending college compared to those noted in the text
--the relevance of the five key concepts for your own experiences

Chapter 14
RELIGION

OBJECTIVES

After reading Chapter 14, you should understand the following main points and be able to answer the objectives.

1. Religion involves several basic elements.
   - 1.1 Define religion.
   - 1.2 List the three elements of religion, as described by Durkheim.
   - 1.3 Define animism and theism.
   - 1.4 Differentiate monotheists from polytheists.
   - 1.5 Distinguish the sacred from the profane.
   - 1.6 Explain the origins of religion, as described by Durkheim.
   - 1.7 Define and give an example of a totem.
   - 1.8 Give three examples of symbols of sacredness.
   - 1.9 Show how religion affects religious practices.
   - 1.10 Define and give examples of rituals.
   - 1.11 Define and give examples of moral communities.
   - 1.12 Show how religious communities vary according to the type of society.
   - 1.13 Show how religion affects religious experiences.

2. Religion is a crucial part of social life and serves several purposes both for individuals and for society.
   - 2.1 Identify three functions of religion.
   - 2.2 Provide examples for each of these functions.
   - 2.3 Define civil religion; note its relevance.
   - 2.4 Explain the role of power in religious communities.

3. From a sociological point of view, religious institutions can be studied in the same way as other institutions.
   - 3.1 Differentiate church, sect, and cult by definition and example.
   - 3.2 Present Stark and Bainbridge's critique of the church-sect typology; outline their alternative approach.
   - 3.3 Differentiate the three types of cults by definition and by example.

4. Religion and religious institutions may bring about social change and may be influenced in turn by such change.

4.1 Trace the effects of the Protestant Reformation on the modernization of western society.
4.2 Explain the conditions under which secularization is likely to occur.
4.3 Summarize the research on the importance of religion to individuals.
4.4 Describe religious revival and religious innovation as responses to secularization.
4.5 Use the creation of the Mormon faith to show how religious innovation occurs.
4.6 Use Islamic and Hindu fundamentalism to show how religious revival occurs.

5. As modern society becomes more complex, religious expression takes on more forms.
5.1 Define invisible or private religion; give reasons why it is apt to remain an important feature of American religious life.
5.2 Explain the overall decline in denominationalism.
5.3 Describe the changes taking place among American Catholics.
5.4 Describe the changes taking place among American Protestants.
5.5 List three beliefs of evangelical movements.
5.6 Describe the changes taking place among American Jews.
5.7 Summarize recent developments in American fundamentalism.
5.8 Define the New Christian Right; discuss the implications of this movement.
5.9 Develop a profile of television evangelism audiences.

CHAPTER SUMMARY

1. Why are sociologists interested in religion? What basic elements do they examine?

Religious attitudes and behaviors are social products. As such, they are subject to and shaped by the same social forces that influence other types of attitudes and behaviors. Religious beliefs and practices clearly affect people's lives, and reflect the social structure and culture in which they occur. In short, religion is not the highly personal and individualistic phenomenon that many people think it is, but a sociological phenomenon. According to Durkheim, *religion* refers to a set of beliefs and practices involving sacred things that unite people into a moral community. The key element is the notion of the *sacred*--that which is set apart from everyday experience and which inspires awe and reverence. In contrast, the *profane* is that which is mundane and ordinary.

Some of the elements found in most religions are religious beliefs, symbols, practices, a community of followers, and a variety of religious experiences. Religion is partly a system of beliefs about what is sacred. Different cultures hold different things sacred. Some believe that things in the world (such as a forest or a tree) are imbued with active, animate spirits; this belief is called *animism*. More common in western societies is *theism*--the idea that powerful, supernatural beings are involved with events and conditions on earth. *Monotheists* believe in a single supernatural being; *polytheists* believe in more than one deity.

Durkheim discovered that Australian aboriginal clans worshiped a *totem*, an object (usually an animal or plant) that symbolizes both the clan itself and that which the clan considers sacred. Durkheim noted that in worshiping a totem, the aborigines were revering their own society. This conclusion led him to note that religious beliefs stem from people's experiences with the social forces that shape their lives.

In addition to beliefs, most religions also incorporate moral principles--beliefs about what is right and wrong, good and bad, proper and improper. These principles provide prescriptions for behavior. Virtually all religions are expressed through *symbols*, objects that stand for something other than themselves. People assign symbolic meanings and agree among themselves as to what those meanings are. Words and actions as well as objects can be religious symbols.

Religion also shapes activities. Religious practices are activities in which believers engage to express their faith, to communicate it to others, to seek supernatural guidance or intervention, to honor their deities, to affirm their sacred beliefs, or simply to produce religious experiences. Such practices may be shared or solitary, compulsory or optional, rigidly structured or open to creative innovations. Some religious practices can be classified as *rituals*--standardized sets of actions used in particular ceremonies or on other specific occasions. Symbols play a central role in rituals. Followers of a particular religion do not always observe all of that religion's rituals or other practices.

Religion also has a social character. A *moral community* includes those whose shared beliefs, symbols, practices, and experiences bind them together into a larger social whole. A sense of community is critical for most religions, although the scope of a religious community varies from society to society.

Religious experiences are an important reflection of people's faith. Such experiences may involve intensified awareness of a supernatural being or power, such as being a born-again fundamentalist Christian. Religious experiences also may include ecstatic states that transcend the here and now. Sociologists have discovered that religious experiences are very much social phenomena; they are shaped by the expectations of the group to which the people having the experiences belong.

2. What is the relationship between religion and the social order?

Religion serves several important purposes for societies and for individuals. First, religion promotes social solidarity by providing norms that reduce conflict in the community. Second, religions link local communities together through national and international organizations. Third, it helps to legitimize the established social order by sanctioning the social arrangements that exist within that order. Such legitimization can be seen in *civil religion*, a sanctifying of the nation by associating its history, values, and institutions with God's special favor. Civil religion involves a very general seeking of blessings from God. Thus it creates links between the sacred and the secular and encourages a willingness to care about and sacrifice for the public good.

Power relations exist in religious organizations. Most religions reflect a power imbalance between leaders and followers. Religious leaders play a crucial role in defining religions and giving them their distinctive cultures. Religions themselves compete for authority.

3. What types of religious institutions have been identified by sociologists?

Sociologists identify three major forms of religious organizations: sect, church, and cult. A *sect* is a small, exclusive, uncompromising fellowship of people seeking spiritual perfection. Members are voluntary converts; their lives are controlled strongly by the sect. Most sects practice asceticism: austere, disciplined lifestyles.

As a sect grows, it evolves into a *church*--a large, conservative, universalist religious institution. At this stage growth comes more from those born into the group than from conversions. A church is more tolerant of other religious groups than is a sect. Its size also enables it to acquire a certain amount of social and political power.

Some sociologists believe that this distinction leads to classification difficulties, and thus prefer to classify religious institutions according to a single criterion: the degree to which the institution accepts or rejects its social environment. At one end of the continuum is the church, which is connected closely with its social environment. At the other end is the sect, which exists in a constant state of tension with the larger society. Stark and Bainbridge note that religious institutions experiencing tension with their environment can have very different origins. Some are formed by breaking away from an established church and forming what Stark and Bainbridge label a sect. Others are imported from other cultures or are formed when people create entirely new religious beliefs and practices; Stark and Bainbridge call such institutions *cults*. They distinguish three types of cults, based on how tightly they are organized. *Audience cults* have no formal organization; members are consumers via books, magazines, or the airwaves. In *client cults*, the religious leaders offer specific services to those who follow them. Although the leaders are well organized, the clients are not. *Cult movements* emerge as some client cults become larger and more tightly organized.

4. What is the relationship between religion and modernization?

The Protestant Reformation played a key role in the modernization of western societies. Calvin's objections to Catholicism helped to lay the groundwork for the Protestant Reformation. At the heart of Calvinist doctrine is the notion of predestination, the belief that one's fate after death is determined at birth. Because eternal life is bestowed by God's grace instead of by individual merit, Calvinists could not hope to learn of God's particular intentions for them. These beliefs left them with a profound uncertainty about their future. Many responded by trying to prove that they had a place among God's chosen few by achieving success in life through hard work, frugality, self-denial, and astute investment for future gain. This Protestant ethic included ideas and attitudes that encouraged the growth of privately owned businesses, particularly by encouraging the owners of the means of production to reinvest the profits.

Once capitalism and other parts of modern society were established, the new social order started to become secularized; it became more concerned with worldly matters and less concerned with spiritual affairs. This process occurred for several reasons. First, modernization involves the creation and growth of science, which emphasizes reason and systematic observation as the supreme authorities in our knowledge of the world. Second, modern societies are much more heterogeneous than traditional societies; this heterogeneity includes religious diversity. Finally, the nature of modern life is not always compatible with spirituality. Some people have predicted that continuing secularization may bring about the end of religion. Religious faith is not disappearing in the modern world, however; it remains pervasive and strong.

5. How does religion stay so vital when secularization is a fact of modern life?

The answer lies in the two opposing trends that secularization encourages: religious revival and religious innovation. *Religious revival* is an effort to restore more traditional and more spiritual features to established religions. *Religious innovation* is an effort to create new religions or to change existing religions to meet people's current needs more completely. Both these trends counteract the influence of secularization so that the importance of religion remains relatively constant. Religious innovation can be seen in the creation of the Mormon faith; religious revival is evident in Islamic and Hindu fundamentalism.

6. What characterizes religion in the United States today?

Religious pluralism characterizes religion in the United States; dozens of religious denominations exist. Recent years have seen a decline in denominationalism. Many people choose no denomination but practice *invisible religion*: they think of religion as a subjective personalistic experience, not as a group doctrine.

Most Americans have not abandoned traditional religion. Instead, there has been an attempt to make churches more responsive. The Catholic Church has experienced substantial changes in recent decades, primarily in the control exerted by the Church over the forms of worship and over individual behavior. Many Catholics reject the Church's teachings on such matters as birth control and divorce. The role of women in the Catholic Church remains a source of tension.

Although the mainline Protestant denominations have experienced a drop in membership, evangelical Protestant churches have grown substantially. Evangelical movements share three beliefs: 1) the Bible is the highest authority on the word of God; 2) eternal salvation comes only through acceptance of Jesus Christ as a personal savior; and 3) believers should share the gospel.

Orthodox Jews are the most traditional in their beliefs, ethnic loyalties, and religious practices. Reform Jews are the least traditional; Conservative Jews are intermediate. All three groups share a concern about the Holocaust, fear for Israel's survival, and a concern for survival of Jews and Judaism in America.

Fundamentalism has become a major voice in American religion. Fundamentalists oppose moderate liberal theologies, especially secular humanism (which emphasizes cultural and religious relativity). American fundamentalism has grown, especially among the well-educated. Fundamentalists have become more politically involved in recent years (what has become known as the new Christian right), and have developed new organizations.

Televangelism has played a major role in the increased visibility of fundamentalism. At least 60 million Americans tune in weekly to at least one of the evangelical programs. Audiences are socially and religiously diverse. They tend to be older and less educated.

REVIEW OF CONCEPTS

Match the concept with the definition.

Concepts

a. animism
b. church
c. civil religion
d. cult
e. evangelicals
f. fundamentalism
g. invisible religion
h. moral community
i. religion
j. religious innovation
k. religious revival
l. ritual
m. sect
n. secularization
o. theism
p. totem

Definitions

_____ 1. A set of beliefs and practices pertaining to sacred things that unite people into a moral community (Durkheim).

_____ 2. A standardized set of actions used in a particular ceremony or on some other specific occasion.

_____ 3. The process by which people and their social institutions become more concerned with worldly matters and less concerned with spiritual ones. It is often associated with modernization.

_____ 4. A religious group that tends to exist in a state of tension with the surrounding culture and that has no prior ties to any established religious body in the larger society.

_____ 5. A large, conservative, universalist religious institution that makes few demands on its members and accommodates itself to the larger society.

_____ 6. The idea that powerful supernatural beings are involved with events and conditions on earth.

_____ 7. Christians who feel a calling to emphasize the teachings of the Scriptures and to bear witness to God's influence on earth.

____ 8. An effort to create new religions or to change existing ones to meet people's needs more completely.

____ 9. The idea that things in the world are imbued with active, animate spirits.

____ 10. A small, exclusive, uncompromising fellowship that makes heavy demands on its members and sets them apart from the larger society (Troeltsch). A religious group formed by breaking away from an established religious body (Stark and Bainbridge).

____ 11. Bellah's term for sanctifying the nation by associating its history, values, and institutions with God's special favor.

____ 12. An object, plant, or animal that is worshiped as the mystical ancestor of a society or other social group.

____ 13. The view that religion is a subjective, personal experience, not a matter of group doctrine.

____ 14. A group of people who share religious beliefs, symbols, and practices that bind them together into a social whole.

Answers

1.	i	6.	o	11.	c
2.	l	7.	e	12.	p
3.	n	8.	j	13.	g
4.	d	9.	a	14.	h
5.	b	10.	m		

REVIEW QUESTIONS

After studying Chapter 14, answer the following questions. The correct answers are listed after the questions; each is followed by a short explanation. You are also referred to pages in the textbook for relevant discussion.

1. Durkheim emphasized which three elements of religion?
   a. symbols, beliefs, and theism
   b. beliefs, the sacred, and the profane
   c. beliefs, social practices, and moral community
   d. moral community, fundamentalism, and symbols
   e. animism, the profane, and polytheism

2. A tribe worships the river that flows through its territory. They believe that it is imbued with an active spirit. This is an example of
   a. theism.
   b. polytheism.
   c. a totem.
   d. monotheism.
   e. animism.

3. A clan worships the corn plant, which symbolizes both the clan itself and that which the clan considers sacred. This is an example of
   a. theism.
   b. polytheism.
   c. a totem.
   d. monotheism.
   e. animism.

4. The wine and bread in the Christian communion ceremony are religious
   a. beliefs.
   b. symbols.
   c. rites.
   d. experiences.
   e. communities.

5. Praying and singing are examples of
   a. rituals.
   b. religious communities.
   c. religious symbols.
   d. totems.
   e. a moral community.

6. Churches often sponsor social groups, which hold potluck suppers, bazaars, and similar events to raise money for the church. These church-related activities reflect which basic element of religion?
   a. religious experiences
   b. religious practices
   c. religious symbols
   d. religious beliefs
   e. religious community

7. Sociologically, religious commandments such as "Thou shalt not kill" perform which of the following functions?
   a. They promote stability in the community.
   b. They relieve personal anxiety and uncertainty.
   c. They promote social change.
   d. They discourage fundamentalism.
   e. They legitimate social groups.

8. The new president is sworn into office with a Bible. Our coins read, "In God we Trust." What do these examples reflect?
   a. private religion
   b. animism
   c. a sect
   d. civil religion
   e. religious beliefs

9. A small communal group organized around a religious doctrine of salvation through physical punishment of self would be classified as
   a. a church.

b. a sect.
c. fundamentalist.
d. a civil religion.
e. ritualistic.

10. Stark and Bainbridge believe that the traditionally defined church-sect dichotomy has too many dimensions. They prefer to rank religious organizations along a single continuum based on
   a. the degree to which the organization accepts its social environment.
   b. the size of the organization.
   c. the stability of the organization.
   d. tolerance.
   e. wealth.

11. Reverend Moon's Unification Church reflects most closely which type of cult?
   a. deviant cult
   b. cult movement
   c. client cult
   d. specialized cult
   e. audience cult

12. The Protestant ethic fostered the spirit of capitalism primarily through an emphasis on
   a. investment.
   b. predestination.
   c. building churches.
   d. anti-Marxism.
   e. debunking papal authority.

13. The growth of science, which endorses reason and systematic observation as the supreme authorities in our knowledge of the world, promoted
   a. civil religion.
   b. secularization.
   c. private religion.
   d. capitalism.
   e. fundamentalism.

14. The creation of the Mormon faith reflects which trend that keeps religion vital in the face of secularization?
   a. religious subjugation
   b. religious intervention
   c. religious innovation
   d. religious promulgation
   e. religious revival

15. Almost all Americans say that they believe in God, but fewer than half attend religious services regularly. This fact reflects
   a. civil religion.
   b. invisible religion.
   c. mainline religion.
   d. theism.
   e. fundamentalism.

189

16. Which one of the following is *not* one of the factors contributing to the politicization of fundamentalism?
    a. a born-again Christian president
    b. the emergence of a new set of social issues that were connected to moral questions
    c. an extensive infrastructure to mobilize political conservatives
    d. a and b only
    e. a, b, and c

17. Which one of the following is *false* regarding audiences of televangelism? Or are they all true?
    a. They don't watch much conventional TV.
    b. They are older.
    c. They are less educated.
    d. They feel they have been left behind.
    e. All are true.

18. Which of the following is the most traditional denomination in American Judaism?
    a. Contrarian Judaism
    b. Conservative Judaism.
    c. Reform Judaism.
    d. Orthodox Judaism.
    e. Modern Judaism.

19. The major change in Roman Catholicism in the past thirty years has been
    a. a decline in membership.
    b. an increase in membership.
    c. a power struggle between those who wanted to keep priestly powers versus those who wanted greater involvement by parishioners.
    d. an internal dispute over the role of fundamentalism.
    e. a complete rejection of the concept of papal infallibility.

Answers

1. *c.* Durkheim's definition of religion included beliefs, social practices, and moral community. See page 348.
2. *e.* Animism is the belief that things in the world, such as a river, are imbued with active, animate spirits. See page 348.
3. *c.* A totem is an object (usually an animal or a plant) that symbolizes both the clan itself and that which the clan considers sacred. See page 349.
4. *b.* Religious symbols are things that stand for something other than themselves. The Christian communion ceremony includes both symbolic things (wine and bread) and symbolic acts (drinking and eating). See page 349.
5. *a.* Rituals are activities in which adherents of a religion engage to express their faith, to communicate it to others, to seek supernatural guidance, to affirm their beliefs, or to produce religious experiences. See page 350.
6. *e.* The moral community is composed of those whose shared beliefs, symbols, practices, and experiences bind them together into a larger social whole. See page 351.
7. *a.* Religion enhances security in the community by providing a context in which relationships develop and by establishing norms of right behavior. See page 352.
8. *d.* Civil religion is a sanctifying of the nation by associating its history, values, and institutions with God's special favor. See pages 352-353.

9. *b.* A sect is a small, exclusive fellowship of individuals seeking spiritual perfection. Often they are characterized by asceticism and strong control over members. See page 355.

10. *a.* Stark and Bainbridge suggest a continuum reflecting the degree to which religious organizations accept their social environment, ranging from complete harmony to complete rejection. See page 356.

11. *b.* Stark and Bainbridge suggest that three types of cults exist. Audience cults have no formal organization; client cults offer specific services through a leader; cult movements are large and tightly organized. See page 356.

12. *a.* The Protestant ethic fostered the spirit of capitalism by promoting ideas that encouraged the growth of privately owned businesses, particularly through the reinvestment of profit. See page 357.

13. *b.* Once capitalism and other aspects of modern societies were established, the new social order started to become secularized. This secularization was promoted by a belief in science as an authoritative source of knowledge. See page 357.

14. *c.* The creation of the Mormon faith reflects religious innovation, namely an effort to create new religions or to change existing religions to meet people's current needs more fully. See page 359.

15. *b.* Invisible (or private) religion refers to the practice of regarding religion as a subjective, personal experience, not as group doctrine. The discrepancy between religious ceremonies reflects widespread practice of invisible religion. See page 363.

16. *e.* Several factors contributed to the politicization of fundamentalism: 1) the presidency of born-again Christian Jimmy Carter, 2) a new set of social issues (such as abortion rights) that were connected with moral questions, and 3) an extensive infrastructure that enabled fundamentalists to mobilize political conservatives and religious traditionalists, who usually avoided politics. See page 369.

17. *a.* Televangelism audiences are heavy consumers of conventional TV. See page 369.

18. *d.* Orthodox Judaism is the most traditional denomination in its beliefs, ethnic loyalties, and religious practices. See page 367.

19. *c.* Vatican II (1962-1965) was a turning point for Roman Catholicism in the U.S. It eliminated many previous restrictions on Catholics' behaviors and was the result of a long power struggle between those who wanted to maintain priestly powers versus those who wanted to personalize Catholicism. See page 365.

EXERCISES

Exercise 1

Review the table in Chapter 16 of this book showing the levels of confidence people have in various institutions since 1973 (see page 215).

1. Describe the changes over time for the confidence people have in organized religion. Explain any differences.

2. Compare the confidence level for religion with the confidence levels for other institutions. Explain any differences.

Exercise 2

Describe your religious socialization. Into which denomination were you socialized? What informal religious socialization did you experience? How would you describe your current religious affiliation? What factors accounted for your choice? If you were not socialized into a denomination, explain how your socialization experiences helped produce this identity.

Exercise 3

Watch two of the Sunday morning "television evangelism" programs. Develop comparisons while watching the programs.

1. Compare the two programs on whatever criteria seem relevant. Identify your criteria. You may wish to look at the type of religious message, the emphasis on monetary contributions, the possible differences in audiences, and the content of each program.

2. Compare this form of religion with traditional forms of religion on the basic elements of religion discussed in the text: beliefs, symbols, practices, community, and experiences.

3. Compare this form of religion with traditional forms of religion on the basic functions of religion. Provide examples.

4. Which of the two programs is more popular? Why?

Chapter 15

HEALTH AND HEALTH CARE

OBJECTIVES

After reading Chapter 15, you should understand the following main points and be able to answer the objectives.

1. Sociologists distinguish among disease, illness, and sickness.
   1.1 Differentiate disease from illness and sickness.
   1.2 Describe the historical changes in the leading causes of death.
   1.3 Define compression of morbidity.
   1.4 Describe how health and illness vary depending on sex, race and ethnicity, poverty, and unemployment.
   1.5 Show how the five key concepts relate to health issues.

2. The perception and experience of health and illness vary among social groups, as illustrated by three major health problems: hunger, smoking, and AIDS.
   2.1 Explain the increase in the number of Americans who go hungry.
   2.2 Discuss the relationship between cigarette advertising and patterns of smoking among men and women.
   2.3 Assess the success of the antismoking movement.
   2.4 Indicate the incidence of AIDS in the United States.
   2.5 Explain how the social structure influences the spread of AIDS.
   2.6 Describe the social pattern of transmission that most epidemics of infectious diseases have taken.
   2.7 Describe the linkage between cultural values and the spread of AIDS.
   2.8 Describe current efforts to stem the AIDS crisis.

3. The health care system in the United States is huge and still growing.
   3.1 Describe how medicalization has redefined illness.
   3.2 Describe how doctors attained the political and social power they now have.
   3.3 Give evidence of physicians' dominance of the health-care system.
   3.4 Identify the consequences of corporatization for health care.

4. The U.S. health care system remains plagued by several major problems.
   4.1 Identify the implications of our health care system emphasizing intervention instead of prevention.
   4.2 Describe the three tiers in the health care system.
   4.3 Identify the factors contributing to spiraling costs.

4.4   Describe developments in health insurance.

4.5   Describe some possible solutions to the high cost of health care.

4.6   Define health maintenance organizations and preferred provider organizations.

CHAPTER SUMMARY

1. Which social factors affect disease and its treatment?

Sociologists distinguish among disease, illness, and sickness. *Disease* is a medically diagnosed pathology; *illness* is a person's own subjective sense of not feeling well; *sickness* is the social acceptance of a person as ill. Sociological factors are associated with all three.

Acute infectious diseases took a heavy toll at the turn of the century; today most people die of chronic diseases. The primary reason for the change is that we now have antibiotics and other drugs which can cure infectious diseases. Standards of living and public health have also improved. *Compression of morbidity* is increasingly likely: suffering from disease is confined to the very end of life for most people. Our ability to reduce the factors that give rise to chronic diseases will affect the extent of compression of morbidity.

The incidence of disease differs significantly by sex, race and ethnic background, and socioeconomic status. Women experience more minor illness than men but outlive men by an average of more than seven years. Some sociologists cite differences in lifestyle as causes for this difference; others point to genetic factors that make women physiologically hardier than men. African-Americans and Hispanic-Americans have higher *mortality rates* (death rates) than do white Americans. The United States is not the world's healthiest nation because of the high poverty rate and the lack of a national health care system. For example, the overall infant mortality rate has been falling, but it is edging upward again in states with high levels of poverty which have suffered cutbacks in government aid for prenatal, maternal, and preventive health services. Life expectancy tends to be highest in countries that have the most nearly equal distribution of income. Poverty and illness frequently go hand in hand; this connection between poverty and poor health is worldwide. Infectious, parasitic, and respiratory diseases cause more than 40 percent of the deaths in underdeveloped countries, but only 10 percent of deaths in industrialized countries. Four-fifths of the world's population has no access to any permanent form of health care. Unemployment exacerbates the effect of poverty on health care and illness.

2. How do the three major health problems show how the perception and experience of health vary among social groups?

As many as 20 million people in this country go hungry much of the time; 5.5 million are children. Various government programs were enacted in the 1960s to make sure that food was available to the poor. In 1981, however, the federal government started to withdraw funds from these programs. Two factors account for the increase in hunger: a surge in unemployment in 1982-1984 and a tightening of eligibility requirements for virtually every federal assistance program. Worldwide, hunger and malnutrition are widespread.

Smoking accounts for about one-sixth of this country's death toll; each year 350,000 Americans die from smoking-related diseases. Advertising plays a heavy role in people's decision to smoke. Advertisers especially target the groups that smoke most or have shown little inclination to quit smoking: women, blue-collar workers, blacks and Hispanics, and members of the military. Large advertising budgets give tobacco companies something close to veto power over the editorial content of magazines that accept their advertising. Some evidence, however, suggests that the antismoking campaign is changing people's ideas about smoking. Smoking has declined much more sharply among men than among women because more teenage girls and young adult women are taking up smoking. Some observers believe that women smoke more because cigarette advertising aimed at women encourages them to do so.

Acquired immune deficiency syndrome (*AIDS*) is a devastating disease that has profoundly affected individuals and communities worldwide. It is caused by the human immunodeficiency virus (HIV) which destroys the body's ability to fight off infections and cancers. The virus is spread through contact with the blood, semen, vaginal secretions, or breast milk of an infected person. In the United States an estimated 1 to 1.5 million people tested positive for HIV in 1992. Sociologists have shown how a high degree of interconnectedness among members of the population segments that engage in risky behavior allows the virus to spread quickly in those segments. Examples include gay men and intravenous drug users. AIDS spreads because the groups initially most affected by AIDS are not isolated from other groups. The transmission of AIDS varies by country. In Africa, for example, 80 percent of the HIV-positive adults acquired the virus through heterosexual contact, whereas only 7 percent of AIDS cases in the United States were contracted in this way.

AIDS now spreads from one group to another primarily through unprotected sexual intercourse. Bisexual men may serve as a bridge between the strongly bounded populations of gay men and of heterosexuals. Intravenous drug users also serve as a bridge. Hence the nondrug-using heterosexual population may be on the verge of a sudden, rapid increase in the incidence of AIDS. The AIDS epidemic has influenced cultural values and behaviors: risky sexual activity has declined, and the use of condoms has increased.

The rapid spread of AIDS has made sex a topic for national discussion and the disease has posed interesting challenges to civil liberties. Some people have even suggested that all Americans should be tested for HIV and that those who test positive should be quarantined. Both the government and the health care community have been slow in responding to the AIDS crisis. National concern about prevention and treatment seemed to grow only when AIDS was perceived as a threat to the nondrug-using, heterosexual population. Homosexual communities have taken up some of the slack in AIDS treatment and prevention. Gay advocacy groups also have made significant progress in raising public awareness about AIDS. Some progress has been made in treating AIDS victims, but the high expense has left many victims without treatment.

3. How did the health care industry reach its present size and form?

Medicalization is the process of including personal or cosmetic problems in the realm of medicine. Examples include alcoholism, baldness, wrinkles, anxiety, and infertility. Medicalization has given doctors wide leeway to intervene in people's private lives. In addition, it has resulted in the use of medical arguments to help advance causes not immediately or directly connected with the treatment of illness. For example, loud rock music is cited as being damaging to hearing and bad for children's mental health. Medicalization also involves a redefinition of social issues and a reassignment of blame. For example, characterizing homeless people as mentally ill obscures the fact that much homelessness is related to unemployment and a lack of affordable housing. Opponents of medicalization have attempted to humanize some aspects of health care. For example, women's health groups have pressed for the demedicalization of the birth process.

The elevation of doctors' status also has contributed to the influence of the health care industry. Doctors began to acquire their current political and social power in the 1920s, when scientific advances and the rise of the American Medical Association increased their prestige. New laws established licensing requirements for physicians and made medicine a legally defined monopoly. Physicians also secured the right to set their own fees. Today only doctors have the authority to diagnose illness, to prescribe and evaluate treatment, and to share information with patients. They are at the top of the hierarchy in the health care system. Their power to control access to health care and their high social status have enabled them to demand some of the highest pay levels of any occupational group in the

United States.

Corporations have taken over much of the provision of medical services. The emphasis on profit may affect the quality and scope of the services provided.

4. What are three major problems of the U.S. health care system?

One major problem is unequal access to health care. Our health care system stresses intervention over prevention: the more people can pay, the higher the quality of the services. The health care system has three tiers: one for the well-off and well-insured, one for the poor who are eligible for government-funded Medicaid, and one for those with no insurance and not enough income to pay the bills for a serious illness. Because the United States does not have a national health care plan, the uninsured are at a serious disadvantage.

Second, the spiraling costs of health care make the problem of unequal access even worse. The emphasis on intervention has yielded many expensive high-tech treatments (such as coronary bypass surgery). These new medical technologies require highly trained workers, thereby adding to the cost of health care. The dramatic increase in the cost of malpractice insurance also raises the cost. In addition, the aging of the American population has created a greater need for medical services because older people use these services more than younger people. Finally, uninsured Americans place a financial burden on taxpayers, hospitals, and other patients.

As the cost of medical insurance rises, more Americans either do without insurance or buy reduced coverage. Employers pay a smaller proportion of the insurance bill, and insurance companies have become more selective and more punitive in their treatment of policyholders.

Third, the increasing cost of health care has caused doctors' traditionally absolute power to be questioned. For example, managed-care programs involve a review of a policyholder's hospital stay and treatment, both before it occurs and while it is under way. These programs also have begun to require second opinions and other such controls. The federal government has cut back on its two major health insurance programs, Medicare for the elderly and Medicaid for the poor. Eligibility requirements have been tightened, and changes have been implemented in the way hospitals are compensated for treating Medicare patients. Hospitals have responded by changing some of their procedures, such as reducing the number of days a patient stays in the hospital.

Cost concerns also have affected forms of health care delivery. *Health maintenance organizations* are organizations that provide medical services to subscribers for a fixed price each year. *Preferred provider organizations* are groups of doctors that offer specific services to specific groups of patients at discount prices. Most Americans want greater government intervention in controlling medical costs, but policy makers are still undecided about what actions to take. One reason is the political pressure from powerful elites and interest groups.

REVIEW OF CONCEPTS

Match the concept with the definition.

Concepts

a. AIDS
b. compression of morbidity
c. disease
d. health maintenance organization (HMO)
e. illness
f. medicalization
g. mortality rate
h. preferred provider organization (PPO)
i. sickness

Definitions

____ 1. An individual's subjective sense of not being well.

____ 2. The social recognition that one is ill.

____ 3. A situation in which illness would occupy only the last years of a person's life.

____ 4. The trend toward including personal problems in the realm of medicine.

____ 5. The relative frequency of deaths among members of a population segment.

____ 6. A health-care organization that provides all of its members' care for a fixed price per year.

____ 7. A group of doctors that offers specific services to groups of patients at discount prices.

____ 8. Medically diagnosed pathology.

Answers

1.	e	4.	f	7.	h
2.	i	5.	g	8.	c
3.	b	6.	d		

REVIEW QUESTIONS

After studying Chapter 15, answer the following questions. The correct answers are listed after the questions; each is followed by a short explanation. You are also referred to pages in the textbook for relevant discussion.

1. A small child reports that she feels "sick in her tummy." Her parents believe that she is not really sick and that she is trying to avoid going to school that day. They send her to school despite her insistence that she does not feel well. Which concept best describes the child's condition?
   a. profession
   b. disease
   c. sickness
   d. illness
   e. delusion

2. Which is a leading cause of death today but was ***not*** a leading cause of death in 1900:
   a. pneumonia
   b. lung disease
   c. heart disease
   d. tuberculosis
   e. influenza

3. The compression of morbidity would result in which one of the following?
   a. more centers devoted to treating disease among the elderly

b. more centers devoted to treating disease among the young

c. a decline in the number of medical centers since diseases overall would decline

d. a reduction in medical care costs as fewer people die

e. an increase in federal involvement in health care

4. Which is *not* an obstacle to the compression of morbidity?
   a. an interventionist health care system that is structured to treat illness once it appears
   b. exposure to risk factors such as smoking
   c. environmental pollutants such as toxic or carcinogenic fumes
   d. a health care system that emphasizes prevention and healthy lifestyles
   e. the outbreak of new acute diseases like AIDS

5. Which is a *true* statement about the social patterns of health and illness?
   a. Men outlive women.
   b. Women become ill more often than men.
   c. Whites have higher cancer rates than blacks.
   d. Male hormones protect men from heart disease.
   e. White men are more likely to have strokes than black men.

6. Which is *not* an aspect of poverty that causes ill health?
   a. less adequate nutrition
   b. less sanitary housing
   c. less stress
   d. fewer trips to the doctor
   e. more self-destructive behavior

7. Which is found in developed countries but not in underdeveloped countries with many people who live in poverty?
   a. higher rate of infant mortality
   b. unavailability of safe drinking water
   c. widespread diarrheal diseases spread by fecal contamination of food
   d. lower life expectancies
   e. infectious, parasitic, and respiratory diseases causing only 10 percent of the deaths

8. Unemployment has been linked to all but which one of the following?
   a. more visits to the doctor
   b. higher anxiety
   c. depression
   d. increased use of alcohol
   e. increased use of tranquilizers

9. Which two factors contributed to an increase in hunger?
   a. a decline in farm production and reduced federal social programs
   b. reduced federal social programs and a surge in unemployment
   c. a surge in unemployment and less public support for hunger programs
   d. less public support for hunger and an increase in AIDS victims
   e. an increase in AIDS victims and a decline in farm production

10. Which is *not* one of the groups who smoke and who are least likely to quit?
    a. women

b. members of the military
c. churchgoers
d. blacks
e. Hispanics

11. Which is **not** part of the tobacco industry's campaign to promote smoking?
    a. portraying smoking as fun, relaxing, sexy, and a matter of free choice
    b. portraying smoking as an addiction
    c. billions of dollars of advertisements per year for tobacco products
    d. vetoing the publication of antismoking articles in magazines that carry cigarette ads
    e. sponsorship of sporting events

12. What percentage of those who ever smoked have given up smoking?
    a. 10 percent
    b. 30 percent
    c. 50 percent
    d. 70 percent
    e. 90 percent

13. Which one of the following is *false?* Children of smoking mothers are more likely
    a. to be born prematurely.
    b. to develop unhealthy respiratory conditions from breathing ambient (surrounding) smoke.
    c. to refrain from smoking as adults.
    d. to be of low birth weight.
    e. to suffer from other problems such as stomachaches, ear discharges, and behavioral disorders.

14. Which is **not** a consequence of the AIDS epidemic?
    a. stigmatization, shunning, and attacks on those carrying the virus
    b. censorship of new stories featuring discussion of condoms and anal intercourse
    c. dampened enthusiasm for having sex with multiple partners
    d. calls for nationwide testing to determine who has AIDS
    e. calls for quarantine of AIDS victims

15. How many people in the United States test positive for the HIV virus?
    a. 25,000-50,000
    b. 100,000-150,000
    c. 500,000-600,000
    d. 1 million to 1.5 million
    e. 3 million to 3.5 million

16. Population segments with high incidence of AIDS are
    a. large and male
    b. urban and highly educated
    c. highly interconnected but not isolated
    d. highly interconnected but isolated
    e. loosely interconnected and isolated

17. The medicalization of society involves all but which one of the following?
    a. steep increase in medical malpractice suits

b. drug addiction and alcoholism now seen as medical problems rather than as sinful behavior
c. the labeling of mass murderers as sick
d. increased use of medical evidence and arguments in political settings
e. use of medical technology for cosmetic improvements rather than for curing disease or prolonging life.

18. Which is *not* a characteristic of medicine as a profession:
    a. Practitioners received advanced education and training.
    b. Doctors must be licensed by a government in order to practice.
    c. Doctors have a monopoly over the prescription of powerful drugs.
    d. Physicians are at the top of the hierarchy of health care workers.
    e. Patients, insurance companies, pharmacists, and physicians participate equally in discussions about the diagnosis and treatment of a disease.

19. Which is a *true* statement about the corporatization of health care?
    a. It is inconsistent with dominant American values of free enterprise, entrepreneurship, and profit making.
    b. It began in the late nineteenth century as part of the development of medical colleges in universities.
    c. It has reduced physicians' authority over the delivery of health care.
    d. For-profit hospitals generally are not profitable.
    e. For-profit hospitals are located in areas where most patients are poor or uninsured.

20. Which is a *true* statement about the American health care system?
    a. It is essentially a system of prevention rather than of intervention.
    b. It provides comprehensive care for all citizens.
    c. The health care one receives depends on one's financial and insurance status.
    d. Medical costs are falling.
    e. Almost every American lives close to skilled health care providers.

21. Health maintenance organizations and preferred provider organizations are designed primarily to
    a. provide better medical care.
    b. reduce medical care costs.
    c. elevate the status of doctors.
    d. reduce the need for more doctors.
    e. enhance federal responsibility for medical care.

22. Which is *not* a consequence of the rising costs of American health care?
    a. self-insurance systems, in which employers manage premiums rather than turning them over to insurance companies like Blue Cross.
    b. preferred provider organizations, in which the Medicare program pays a predetermined (discount) amount for the treatment of a patient's condition.
    c. easier access to needed health care by the poor and the uninsured.
    d. corporatization of health care.
    e. reduction of length of stay in hospitals.

Answers

1. *d.* The child reports a feeling that she is not well: this is defined as an illness. In this case,

however, her illness does not become a sickness because certain members of society (her parents) do not acknowledge that she is not well. See page 373.

2. *c.* Antibiotics now can often cure influenza and many lung diseases. Increases in deaths due to heart disease are due to sedentary lifestyles and diets rich in fats and salts. See page 374.

3. *a.* Since compression of morbidity refers to people remaining more free of disease until old age, we will need more medical centers to treat disease among the elderly. See page 374.

4. *d.* In compression of morbidity, illness would occupy only the last years of a person's life. It would be most likely to result if the American health care system refocused its attention on the maintenance of wellness and the elimination (or prevention) of conditions associated with ill health (such as smoking and environmental carcinogens). See page 375.

5. *b.* Women seem to experience more frequent cases of minor ailments, but on the average they outlive men by more than seven years. Social factors (less smoking and drinking than among men) and biological factors (a female hormone that deters heart disease) are both responsible for women's greater longevity. See pages 375-376.

6. *c.* People in poverty face greater levels of stress, which in turn leads them to engage in a variety of self-destructive behaviors such as excessive smoking, drinking, or drug use. See page 376.

7. *e.* Because of poor sanitary conditions, unavailability of uncontaminated food and water, and the lack of antibiotics, more than 40 percent of deaths in underdeveloped countries are caused by infectious, respiratory, and parasitic diseases. The causes of death are different for the rich and the poor. See page 376.

8. *a.* Even when unemployment does not lead to poverty, it causes increases in anxiety, depression, smoking, and drinking (all conditions associated with disease and ill health). For this reason, one study has suggested recently that the unemployment rate is a health policy as well as an economic policy. See page 377.

9. *b.* In 1981 the federal government withdrew funds for social programs. The surge in unemployment in 1982-84 resulted in tightened eligibility requirements for federal assistance programs. See page 378.

10. *c.* The tobacco industry targets its annual advertising budget at women, blue-collar workers, blacks, Hispanics, and members of the military. See page 378.

11. *b.* Description of smoking as a dirty, deadly addiction is more likely to be found in the campaign of antismoking movements than in ads from the tobacco industry. See page 378.

12. *c.* Antismoking movements have been successful in highlighting the health risks from smoking and from breathing the air polluted by nearby smokers. Per capita consumption of cigarettes has declined every year since 1973 and almost 50 percent of all those who ever smoked have given up smoking. See page 379.

13. *c.* A mother who smokes sets a powerful example to her children that smoking is acceptable and even enjoyable behavior. Children of smokers are more likely to become smokers themselves than children of nonsmokers. See page 380.

14. *b.* The AIDS epidemic has increased open discussion of sexual behavior. The previously taboo subjects of condoms and anal intercourse are now acceptable in the media. Homosexuality and bisexuality appear more in the public eye. See page 382.

15. *d.* In 1992, 1 million to 1.5 million people in the United States tested positive for the HIV virus. See page 380.

16. *c.* Population segments with high incidence of AIDS are highly interconnected, which allows the virus to spread quickly. They are also not isolated, which allows transmission to those not in the segment. See page 381.

17. *a.* The medicalization of society refers to the annexation to the medical sphere of many problems once considered nonmedical. In other words, physicians' authority and competence

have been expanded. An increase in medical malpractice suits is a symptom of the consumers' revolt *against* the medicalization of society. See page 385.

18.   *e.*   In the present health care system, doctors alone have the power to diagnose illness, to prescribe and evaluate treatments, and to convey information to patients about their condition. The corporatization of health care and the revolt by health care consumers, however, may begin to erode some of the physicians' monopolistic authority over medical matters. See pages 388-389.

19.   *c.*   Although some physicians are active in starting new for-profit hospitals and medical facilities, it is likely that concerns for corporate profit making will impinge on physicians' once-autonomous decisions regarding treatment strategies. For example, doctors at such hospitals may be asked to avoid expensive tests or procedures unless these are absolutely vital for the patient's well-being. See pages 389-390.

20.   *c.*   The health care system in America is the only modern system (except in South Africa) that does not provide comprehensive care for all citizens . In the three-tiered American system, those who have no health insurance policy and who are not poor enough to qualify for Medicaid often cannot afford to buy what they need to get well or to stay alive. See page 390.

21.   *b.*   Health maintenance organizations and preferred provider organizations are changes in how health care is delivered; both are designed to reduce costs. See page 393.

22.   *c.*   The poor are finding it increasingly difficult to qualify for Medicaid; even if they do qualify, they receive fewer benefits. The poor and the uninsured are often denied services by for-profit hospitals. The uninsured simply lack the money to cover the costs of a catastrophic illness or accident; this problem becomes greater as health care costs rise. See pages 391-392.

EXERCISES

Exercise 1

This exercise asks you to interpret the following statistics on infant mortality and to recommend possible solutions for the problem. The infant mortality rate is the number of babies per 1000 live births who are born alive but die before their first birthday. In 1985, 40,030 babies died in this country before reaching their first birthday; the infant mortality rate for that year was 10.6 per 1000 live births.

The following statistics were provided by the National Commission to Prevent Infant Mortality. For each example provide a sociological interpretation or explanation based on your understanding of the American system of health care. Then suggest policies or programs that might solve the problems identified in these statistics. In view of the structure of health care in this system, what is the likelihood that such solutions will be tried? To what extent is infant mortality a *public* problem or a *private* problem of individual families?

1.   The infant mortality rate in the black population in the United States is nearly twice that of the white population. In 1985 the rate for blacks was 18.2 per deaths per thousand, compared to 9.3 among whites.

2. The infant mortality rate in this country ranks the United States eighteenth among the industrialized countries of the world. Countries that have lower infant mortality rates include Japan, Canada, Ireland, Switzerland, and France.

3. The number of babies born without receiving adequate prenatal care has grown by nearly 10 percent since 1979.

Exercise 2

The American health care system is one of intervention rather than prevention. For each of the following health-related conditions, contrast an interventionist strategy with a preventionist strategy. In each case describe the social conditions that tend to favor one strategy or the other.

1. Lung cancer caused by smoking.

2. AIDS.

3. Injuries to professional athletes.

4. Malnutrition.

5. Job-related health risks.

6. Brain tumors.

7. Schizophrenia.

Exercise 3

Chiropractic is an alternative system of healing that traces disease to a failure of normal nerve function and that uses physical manipulation of certain body structures (such as the spinal column) as therapy. Physicians (organized through the American Medical Association) have long tried to restrict chiropractors' medical services and hospital privileges. Recently a federal court ruled that the AMA had conspired to prevent chiropractors from offering their professional services. The court ruled that the AMA may no longer impede the association of physicians with chiropractors; this ruling created the possibility that chiropractors may be able to admit their patients to hospitals.

1. How does the AMA's effort to restrict the practice of chiropractic illustrate the "professionalization of medicine" discussed in the text?

2. Is the court's decision consistent or inconsistent with the history of health care systems in the United States?

3. Is the court's decision consistent or inconsistent with the current "revolt" among health care consumers?

4. What are the implications of this decision for the increasingly high costs of medical care and for its anticipated "corporatization"?

Chapter 16

ECONOMICS AND WORK

OBJECTIVES

After reading Chapter 16, you should understand the following main points and be able to answer the objectives.

1. The economy is a social system. Capitalism and socialism are the basic economic systems.
   1.1 Define economic system.
   1.2 Show how the five key concepts help in understanding the economic system.
   1.3 Describe the four characteristics of capitalism
   1.4 Synopsize the origins of capitalism.
   1.5 Summarize the rule of government intervention in capitalist systems.
   1.6 Define socialism.
   1.7 Compare the history of socialism with the history of capitalism
   1.8 Outline Marx's views on socialism and capitalism.
   1.9 Compare socialism in Western Europe, the Soviet Union, and the Third World.

2. Modern corporate capitalism is no longer dominated by individual capitalists.
   2.1 Define corporation.
   2.2 Assess the amount of power held by corporations.
   2.3 Define interlocking directorates.
   2.4 Define oligopoly and assess the impact of oligopolies.
   2.5 Define multinational corporations and assess their impact.
   2.6 Describe the role of small businesses.

3. Work is an important social action.
   3.1 List the factors affecting job satisfaction.
   3.2 Describe how control in the workplace is related to size of an organization.
   3.3 Differentiate technical control from bureaucratic control.
   3.4 Describe changes in the patterns of work over the last few decades.
   3.5 Differentiate the primary labor market from the secondary labor market.
   3.6 Differentiate structural unemployment from cyclical unemployment.
   3.7 Explain why government statistics seldom reveal the true magnitude of unemployment.
   3.8 Define professions.
   3.9 Define productivity and automation.

CHAPTER SUMMARY

1. What role has capitalism played in the economic system?

The *economic system* is the social institution that fulfills our basic societal need for goods and services. The worldwide scale of the economic system has resulted in a global economy.

Capitalism is currently the predominant form of economic structure in the world. This is a way of organizing economic activity by emphasizing four things: 1) private ownership of the means of production; 2) self-interest and the profit motive as the major economic incentive; 3) free competition in the markets for labor, raw materials, and products; and 4) repeated investment for the purpose of accumulating capital. *Capital* is the wealth that is invested in generating more wealth by producing goods and services. Capitalism began in the late eighteenth and early nineteenth century when improved methods of production gave rise to the Industrial Revolution. Because agricultural production had increased dramatically, fewer people were needed to produce food; more could live in cities and work in manufacturing jobs. Manufacturing improved dramatically with specialization and division of labor. Capitalism transformed both the production and the distribution of goods.

The United States was the leader in the capitalist world from the late 1940s through the 1960s. Since then a new global economy has developed, in which the United States is no longer the clear leader and in which competition is intense.

Adam Smith believed that governments should not intervene in economic activities. He thought that competition would provide the rewards and punishments needed to make the system work. Others believed that governments are needed to intervene to head off some of the dysfunctional consequences of capitalism. According to this view, the government can play three roles: 1) enabler, providing the public with the goods and services that people in businesses need to carry out their economic transactions; 2) assister, offering help to various social groups; and 3) regulator, protecting businesses from unfair forms of competition, consumers from potentially harmful products, and minorities from unfair discrimination. Keynes believed that governmental intervention would help regulate the cyclical ups and downs of a capitalist economy. Galbraith argued that big government had become essential in the modern capitalist world because corporations needed a stable environment in which to plan new products and make large investments.

2. What role has socialism played in the modern economic system?

Socialism, which emerged in the nineteenth century, emphasizes putting social cooperation ahead of individual competition and placing the needs of society as a whole ahead of the benefits to a wealthy class. Marx argued that the exploitation of the working class by the capitalist class was an unavoidable structural consequence of capitalism. He believed that an emphasis on profits would result in overproduction and underconsumption, after which workers would unite to overthrow capitalism. (Such revolts never occurred.) Capitalism, said Marx, also produced other problems: an emphasis on competition at the expense of economic cooperation, exploitation and destruction of the environment, and a severely unequal distribution of wealth.

We can look to three examples of the implementation of socialism: western Europe, the Soviet Union, and Third World countries. The democratic socialist states of western Europe have not overthrown capitalism but have used government to limit its excesses and to protect the workers' welfare. The Soviet Union used a form of *communism,* a totally classless society in which all people contributed according to their abilities and all received according to their needs. Early efforts at central economic planning were not very successful for three reasons: 1) a lack of incentive to produce desirable, high-quality products in a cost-conscious way; 2) the difficulty of setting output quotas in ways that did not backfire on the central planner; and 3) the overwhelming job of coordinating producers and with suppliers. The economic system became intolerable for the Soviet people. In the mid-1980s,

Gorbachev attempted to address the problems through *perestroika*, a restructuring of the Soviet economy designed to introduce various economic reforms traditionally associated with a market system. However, the attempt was too little and too late. By 1988 the Soviet economy was in shambles and in 1991 the communist regime was overthrown.

At the heart of Third World socialism has been an attempt to combine all the producers of a country into a single force both to make them stronger in international capitalistic markets and to provide for guided growth. Implementation has involved central economic planning and state ownership of essential industries.

3. What role have business institutions played in the United States?

"Corporate America" refers to the large corporations such as GM and IBM. A *corporation* is an organization created by law to have an existence, powers, and liabilities of its own. Ownership and management are generally separated in a corporation. Large-scale capitalization and internal management have enabled corporations to grow enormously. Management has shifted from the founders of companies to professional managers with advanced degrees. Top managers control corporate America through a series of *interlocking directorships*, networks of people who serve as directors of two or more corporations. Corporate managers exert substantial collective power. Corporations also gain power by forming an *oligopoly*, a market structure in which a few large corporations dominate. Oligopolies inhibit competition. Finally, corporations exert power by becoming *multinational corporations*, firms with operations and subsidiaries in many countries. Many have become so large that national governments find it hard to regulate them. Multinational corporations also have a considerable impact on the political and social institutions of their host countries.

One-half of the American labor force is employed by small businesses, which have many different forms and functions. Most experience capitalization problems and vulnerability to marketplace fluctuations. Many small businesses are owned by ethnic minority members, particularly recent immigrants.

4. What meaning does work have for people?

Most Americans have favorable opinions about their work, especially those in white-collar, professional, and technical occupations for which substantial training is required. High pay and prestige generate job satisfaction, but so do factors such as the inherent interest of the work itself, a sense of doing something worthwhile, and the sense that one is supporting oneself and one's family. Alienation is particularly high among workers who do repetitive manual tasks.

The size of an organization determines the type of control. *Simple control* is direct and face-to-face, is usually exercised by the owner of the company and a few top managers, and is found in small firms. In large organizations two other forms of control exist. One is *technical control*, which arises from the technical organization of work (such as an assembly line). The other, more prevalent form is *bureaucratic control*, exerted by a hierarchical system that assigns rewards according to the level of a job.

The proportion of men age 16 and older who hold a paying job has remained steady at 80 percent for the past 100 years, while the proportion of women has increased from 15 percent to 63 percent. Several factors contributed to this dramatic increase: 1) an increase in the divorce rate, 2) the development of reliable contraception, 3) the revival of the feminist movement, and 4) the need for a second family income to counter the effects of inflation. A sharp rise in the number of service-oriented jobs paralleled the increase in the proportion of women in the labor force. Agricultural work and manufacturing jobs also declined.

Sociologists distinguish between two broad labor markets. In the *primary labor market*, workers are employed by stable, successful, usually relatively large firms. They have job security, sufficient benefits, and good incomes. The *secondary labor market* is smaller and much less stable. This sector includes domestic service, fast-food jobs, and small businesses. These jobs are often part-time or seasonal; wages are low and benefits are virtually nonexistent. Sociologists also distinguish between two types of unemployment. *Structural unemployment* is the result of changes in the patterns of jobs available and changes in the distribution of workers with various skills in various locations. It is tied to the structure of an economic system as it undergoes market changes. *Cyclical unemployment* occurs as part of the periodic downturns in capitalistic economies. Temporary joblessness is very common in our economy; it is estimated that two out of three Americans will lose a job at some time in their lives. Government statistics underrepresent the true magnitude of unemployment because the official unemployment rate is determined by counting only those who are actively seeking a full-time job. The poor are more likely to be unemployed, but the recent wave of corporate mergers has increased unemployment among middle-class and upper-class workers.

Professionalization has been an important trend in the primary labor market. *Professions* are categories of jobs in which entrance is restricted to those who possess specialized knowledge and skills that they have acquired from a long period of formal education. Law and medicine are the oldest and most highly respected professions. Professionals enjoy considerable autonomy and earn large incomes.

Productivity refers to the amount of labor, land, machinery, or other factors of production that are required to produce a given amount of output. Sociologists' main concern is the productivity of labor: how much human work is needed to produce a given amount of goods. Labor productivity has increased consistently over the last century. Productivity has been particularly enhanced by *automation*, the introduction of new labor-saving machinery and the reorganization of the workplace around it. Automation sometimes makes work less satisfying. Also, even highly educated and well-paid specialists are subject to forms of control such as special incentives and management of emotions.

REVIEW OF CONCEPTS

Match the concept with the definition.

Concepts

a. automation	g. interlocking directorships	k. productivity
b. capital		l. professions
c. capitalism	h. multinational corporations	m. secondary labor market
d. communism		n. socialism
e. corporation	i. oligopoly	
f. economic system	j. primary labor market	

Definitions

_____ 1. The social institution that accomplishes the production and distribution of goods and services within a society.

_____ 2. The use of machinery to replace human workers and the reorganization of the workplace around the machinery.

_____ 3. An industry dominated by only a few very large firms.

_____ 4. Categories of jobs in which entrance is restricted to those with specialized knowledge and skills acquired through a long period of formal education.

5. An economic system based on private ownership of the means of production, self-interest, and incentives; free competition; and repeated investment for the purpose of capital accumulation.

____ 6. Networks of people who serve on the boards of directors of two or more corporations.

____ 7. An organization created by law that has an ongoing existence, powers, and liabilities independent from those of its owners and managers.

____ 8. An attempt to replace the individualistic competition of capitalism by some form of social cooperation, placing the needs of society as a whole ahead of the benefits of a wealthy class.

____ 9. A giant, usually diversified corporation with operations and subsidiaries in many countries.

____ 10. The amount of output that a given input of labor or other resource can create.

____ 11. In Marx's theory, the state of a truly classless society in which totalitarian control by the state would no longer be needed.

Answers

1.	f	5.	c	9.	h
2.	a	6.	g	10.	k
3.	i	7.	e	11.	d
4.	1	8.	n		

REVIEW QUESTIONS

After studying Chapter 16, answer the following questions. The correct answers are listed after the questions; each is followed by a short explanation. You are also referred to pages in the textbook for relevant discussion.

1. K-Mart yearly plows back into the company at least 10 percent of its profits. This example reflects which feature of capitalism?
   a. creation of wealth
   b. competition
   c. private ownership of the means of production
   d. the profit motive
   e. capital accumulation

2. When did capitalism begin to dominate the economic landscape?
   a. in the late fifteenth and early sixteenth centuries
   b. in the late sixteenth and early seventeenth centuries
   c. in the late seventeenth and early eighteenth centuries
   d. in the eighteenth and early nineteenth centuries
   e. in the late nineteenth and early twentieth centuries

3. The United States is no longer the unquestioned leader of the capitalist world because

a. the global market has changed.
b. Japan has become the leader.
c. Western Europe has become the leader.
d. the high unemployment in the United States reduced its strength.
e. Americans have lost their work ethic.

4. The United States government imposes tariffs on imported clothing so that American garment workers have a better chance of keeping their jobs. Which of the roles played by governments in capitalist systems is illustrated in this example?
   a. defender
   b. enabler
   c. assister
   d. regulator
   e. transformer

5. Which one of the following does *not* characterize the state socialist economy in the Soviet Union?
   a. a deemphasis on basic human rights
   b. collective ownership of the means of production
   c. centralized planning for the collective good
   d. a vision of a truly classless society
   e. All characterize the socialist state economy.

6. Socialism attempted to remedy which two key problems in capitalism?
   a. inefficiency and redundancy
   b. redundancy and overproduction
   c. overproduction and underconsumption
   d. underconsumption and alienation
   e. alienation and inefficiency

7. The two distinguishing features of Western European socialism are
   a. a classless society and a lack of public ownership of the means of production.
   b. a lack of public ownership of the means of production and an absence of extensive central planning.
   c. an absence of extensive central planning and a classless society
   d. a decline in the importance of government and a lack of public ownership of the means of production.
   e. a decline in the importance of government and a classless society.

8. *Perestroika* was pursued in the Soviet Union to
   a. enhance peace.
   b. help the Soviet Union become more socialist.
   c. promote Gorbachev's popularity.
   d. promote democracy.
   e. introduce economic reforms associated with a market system.

9. The distinguishing feature of a corporation is
   a. its size.
   b. its ownership by shareholders.
   c. its management by professional managers.

211

d. its institutional structure.
e. its profit orientation.

10. Which large-scale business organization paved the way for the development of other such enterprises in the United States?
    a. pharmaceutical companies
    b. automobile companies
    c. insurance companies
    d. textile companies
    e. railroad companies

11. Which one of the following statements most accurately describes the production of goods in the United States?
    a. Most manufacturing is oligopolistic.
    b. Most manufacturing is democratic.
    c. Most manufacturing is pluralistic.
    d. Most manufacturing is competitive.
    e. Most manufacturing is segmented.

12. When lower-calorie "light" beers were introduced, a number of smaller breweries did not have enough money to buy the equipment needed to make this new product. Many went out of business. This example illustrates which of the following departures from the pure capitalistic market model?
    a. Government owns or regulates many of the means of production.
    b. Entrepreneurs are not always "free" to enter a competitive market.
    c. The goal of corporate growth has replaced the goal of maximizing profits.
    d. American consumers are not free to buy whatever products they desire.
    e. Advertising creates demand for a product.

13. Sam serves on the board of directors for the Mead corporation, Sears, and Bethlehem Steel. He meets other board members, shares interests with them, and uses these connections to exert control of these and other corporations. This example reflects
    a. interlocking directorships.
    b. conglomerates.
    c. conspicuous consumption.
    d. an oligopoly.
    e. a multinational corporation.

14. Which one of the following statements regarding multinationals is *false?*
    a. They often manipulate the economies of the nations in which they operate.
    b. They often avoid government regulations, high taxes, and labor unions.
    c. They often have a significant impact on the political and social institutions of the countries in which they operate.
    d. They often help bring about lower taxes and keep wages low to further their own growth.
    e. All are true.

15. At the Sears distribution center, there is an explicit and carefully specified manner of handling incoming and outgoing products. Computers are used extensively and products are moved in an assembly-line fashion. Which type of control is represented?
    a. simple control

b. technical control
c. bureaucratic control
d. personalistic control
e. mechanical control

16. Approximately what proportion of the paid labor force consists of women?
    a. 20 percent
    b. 35 percent
    c. 45 percent
    d. 53 percent
    e. 63 percent

17. What are the two major changes that have occurred in patterns of work?
    a. the increase in the proportion of women in the labor force and the decline of jobs in the industrial sector
    b. the changing cultural values regarding work and the decline of jobs in the industrial sector
    c. the increase in the proportion of women in the labor force and the increase in service occupations
    d. the changing cultural values regarding work and the increase in the proportion of women in the labor force
    e. the decline in farm employment and the changing cultural values regarding work

18. Sharon works at a floral shop and is employed according to the seasonal demand for flowers. Sharon is part of the
    a. primary labor market.
    b. secondary labor market.
    c. tertiary labor market.
    d. pink-collar labor market.
    e. restricted labor market.

19. Government statistics seldom reveal the true magnitude of unemployment because
    a. all government statistics are flawed.
    b. it is impossible to define "unemployed."
    c. it includes teenagers.
    d. it includes only those actively seeking a full-time job.
    e. so many unemployed people fail to report their status.

Answers

1. *e.* Returning a share of the profits to the business provides an enterprise with a growing supply of capital. This process is capital accumulation. See page 398.
2. *d.* Capitalism began to dominate the economic landscape in the late eighteenth and early nineteenth centuries. See page 399.
3. *a.* The global economy has mushroomed, especially with the rise in economic power of countries in Asia and western Europe. See page 401.
4. *c.* Government in modern capitalist systems play three rules: 1) enabler--providing the public with the goods and services necessary to carry out economic transactions; 2) assister--helping various social groups; and 3) regulator--protecting business and consumers. This example reflects the assister rule. See page 404.
5. *a.* The state socialist economy in the Soviet Union is based on collective (not private) owner-

ship of the means of production, centralized planning for the collective good (not decentralized planning by individual firms and consumers), and an ultimate vision of a truly classless society (not simply the equality of economic opportunity that we have). See page 407.

6. *c.* Socialism attempted to address two basic problems in capitalism: overproduction and under-consumption. See page 405.

7. *b.* Western European socialism differs from the socialist economic system that Marx envisioned in that it does not involve public ownership of the means of production and it does not involve extensive central planning. See page 407.

8. *e.* Gorbachev pursued *perestroika* to restructure the Soviet economy by gradually introducing economic reforms traditionally associated with a market system. See page 409.

9. *d.* The distinguishing feature of a corporation is its institutional structure. It is an organization created by law to have an existence, powers, and liabilities of its own. See page 410.

10. *e.* The railroad was both the model American corporation and the crucial innovation that made possible the development of other large-scale business enterprises. See page 411.

11. *a.* About 60 percent of manufacturing in this country is oligopolistic; industries are dominated by only a few very large firms. See page 413.

12. *b.* In the pure capitalist model, it is assumed that markets will be regulated by open competition. Some firms in the beer industry are so large, however, that they can control the market by introducing new products which smaller firms cannot afford to produce because start-up costs are too high. See pages 413-414.

13. *a.* Interlocking directorships are networks of people who serve as directors of two or more corporations. These people share similar backgrounds, have similar interests, and control corporate America. See page 413.

14. *e.* Multinationals are so big, so rich, and so powerful that all these outcomes can and do occur. See page 415.

15. *b.* Technical control is a structural type of control that is part of the work organization itself. The use of the computer and of highly specified procedures yields technical control. See page 418.

16. *e.* Women constitute 63 percent of the paid labor force. See page 419.

17. *c.* The two major changes that have occurred in patterns of work are the substantial increase in the proportion of women in the labor force and the dramatic increase in service occupations. See page 419.

18. *b.* The primary labor market is that in which workers are employed by stable, successful firms; the secondary labor market reflect the less stable niche in the economy, in which demand for products fluctuates. See page 420.

19. *d.* Government statistics seldom reveal the true magnitude of unemployment because the official unemployment rate is determined by counting only those who are actively seeking full-time employment. See page 421.

EXERCISES

Exercise 1

Listed in the table below are the percentages of people in each of five years who had a great deal of confidence in the people running the institutions noted. The data come from the General Social Surveys; each one includes about 1500 adults selected at random.

	1973	1977	1980	1983	1987	1991
Major Companies	29%	27%	27%	24%	30%	20%
Organized Religion	35%	40%	35%	28%	29%	25%
Education	37%	41%	30%	29%	35%	30%
Organized Labor	15%	15%	15%	8%	10%	11%
The Press	23%	25%	22%	13%	18%	16%
The Scientific Community	37%	41%	41%	41%	45%	40%
Congress	23%	19%	9%	10%	16%	18%
The Military	32%	36%	28%	29%	34%	59%

1. Describe the changes over time for the confidence people have in major companies. Explain any changes.

2. Compare the confidence level for major companies with the confidence levels for other institutions. Explain any differences.

3. Describe the changes over time for the confidence people have in organized labor. Explain any changes.

4. Compare the confidence levels for organized labor and major companies. Explain any differences.

5. Compare the confidence level for organized labor with the confidence levels for other institutions. Explain any differences.

Exercise 2

Look through the last several issues of *Forbes* or *Fortune*. Describe the image of capitalism portrayed in the magazine you selected. Give specific examples. Show how your observations link with the content of the chapter.

Exercise 3

Some people, like Christopher Jencks, have suggested that the American capitalist system should become more socialist. That is, there should be an income floor below which people are not allowed to fall. If they do, they would receive payment from the government. Similarly, those who make a great deal of money would be taxed at a substantially higher rate to pay for the "negative income tax." College would be free, like public education. Would such a system work? Would you personally favor it? Is it possible to merge features of the capitalist and socialist systems? How?

Chapter 17

POLITICS, THE STATE, AND WAR

OBJECTIVES

After reading Chapter 17, you should understand the following main points and be able to answer the objectives.

1. Politics and power are social processes.
   - 1.1 Define politics and power.
   - 1.2 Define legitimacy and describe its importance.
   - 1.3 Differentiate Weber's three forms of legitimate power: traditional authority, charismatic authority, and legal/rational authority.
   - 1.4 Summarize the Marxist view on power.
   - 1.5 Summarize the power-elite view on power.
   - 1.6 Define oligarchy and the iron law of oligarchy.
   - 1.7 Summarize the pluralist view on power.
   - 1.8 Show how the five key concepts help in understanding power and politics.

2. The state is formed by complex institutions and organizations that are specialized for exercising authority.
   - 2.1 Define state.
   - 2.2 Differentiate the state from the concept of government.
   - 2.3 Identify the social forces behind the rise of modern states.
   - 2.4 Define nation and nationalism.
   - 2.5 Describe the modern welfare state.

3. A democratic state is one based on political participation by the people.
   - 3.1 Define democratic state and representative democracies.
   - 3.2 Contrast totalitarian states with democratic states.
   - 3.3 Discuss the social foundations of democracy.

4. The three major channels for public participation in American representative democracy are voting, participation in political parties and campaigns, and interest groups and social protest movements.
   - 4.1 List three major channels for public participation in American representative democracy.
   - 4.2 Explain low voter turnout in American presidential elections.
   - 4.3 Define political party and note the functions served by political parties.
   - 4.4 Compare the simple plurality system to the proportional vote system.
   - 4.5 Describe how background factors affect voters' preferences.

4.6　Assess the decline in the importance of parties.
4.7　Define interest group and describe the role of the interest group in American politics.
4.8　Explain the rising importance of political action committees (PACs).

5. War is a major aspect of political power.
　5.1　Define war.
　5.2　Describe the history of war from early human societies to modern warfare.
　5.3　Explain how technological and political changes have affected the conduct of war.
　5.4　Discuss the uniqueness of nuclear war.

CHAPTER SUMMARY

1. What is politics and what is power?

Sociologists define *politics* as the process by which people gain, use, and lose power. *Power* is the ability to exert control over other people's behavior or experience, even when they resist. It is exercised in all domains of social life, but this chapter focuses on specialized institutions of political power, which constitute the state.

When power is legitimate, it is recognized as valid and is justified by those whom it controls. Sociologists use the term *authority* to describe power that is viewed as legitimate and is exercised with the approval of most individuals in a group or society. Weber identified three forms of legitimate power or authority. *Traditional authority* stems from beliefs and practices passed down from generation to generation, and usually consists of inherited positions based on kinship and decent, such as kingship. *Charismatic authority* derives from the belief that leaders have exceptional personal qualities which deserve respect and devotion. *Legal/rational authority* derives from a system of explicit laws that define legitimate uses of power. In this sense, power is vested in offices or positions, not in those who hold them.

2. How is political power distributed among members of a society?

Political power is not divided evenly among all members of a society. How extreme is this inequality? Three theoretical perspectives answer this question in three different ways. First, Marxist theories suggest that power is concentrated in the hands of the few who own the means of production. Powerful capitalists manipulate social and cultural arrangements to further increase their wealth and power, often at the expense of the powerless.

Second, the power elite view holds that power is concentrated in the hands of a few elite individuals including military leaders, government officials, and business executives, whom Mills called the *power elite*. This group consists of those who occupy the top positions in our organizational hierarchies; they have the same backgrounds and share the same interests and goals. Michels argued that any organization has a built-in tendency to become an *oligarchy*, a system ruled by a few people. His proposition that large-scale organization always leads to rule by a small minority has become known as the *iron law of oligarchy*.

Third, pluralist theories suggest that various groups and interests compete for political power. In contrast to Marxist and power elite theorists, pluralists view power as dispersed among many people and groups who do not necessarily agree on what should be done.

3. What is the state?

The *state* is an abstract entity composed of the public organizations in which autonomous power over a specified geographical region is concentrated. The modern state is distinguished by the existence of complex institutions and organizations that are specialized for exercising authority. The contrast between state and government points up the abstract nature of the former: government refers to the body of elected and nonelected officials who lead the state at any time, whereas the state itself transcends the terms in office of those who direct it.

In early human societies, personal power and official power often were combined in a single role, such as a chief. (States as we know them did not exist.) Gradually the separation of personal power from official power (that is, authority which resides in an office rather than in any particular office-holder) created the conditions for the emergence of the abstract state. Two major and interrelated factors led to the rise of the modern state: 1) expansion and consolidation of territories and 2) growth of international commerce. Both developments created the need for new governmental institutions. Those which proved effective were organized into bureaucracies: formal, rule-governed, hierarchical organizations of public servants.

The ideas of nation and nationalism were important for the formation of states and the rise of political bureaucracies. *Nation* refers to the cultural bonds that give a sense of shared identity to a group of people who occupy or aspire to occupy the same geographic territory. In the typical pattern today, people in a recognized nation share a common state, but this has not always been the case. When growing national identity is translated into a call for a distinctive autonomous state, the result is defined as *nationalism*. Nationalism has encouraged pressure for statehood among many dispossessed peoples.

The role of the state in social life has expanded greatly throughout the history of the United States and other Western nations. The *welfare state* provides for the welfare of ordinary citizens by taking over certain responsibilities once assigned to local communities and to families, such as unemployment compensation and health care. The modern welfare state provides many *collective goods and services*, things that cannot easily be bought and sold by individuals (such as education and public transportation). The welfare state began in the United States with President Roosevelt's New Deal. Both sociologists and politicians have debated the question: has the role of the state in managing society and the economy grown too large?

4. What is a democratic state?

In a *democratic state*, authority is rooted in the consent of the people. Most democratic countries are *representative democracies*, in which people elect public officials to represent their wishes and interests. In such democracies, clear and legally established limits are imposed on elected officials' actions. The opposite of democracy is *totalitarianism*, in which the government attempts to control every aspect of its citizens' lives and even their thoughts.

Several foundations are needed if democracy is to arise. First, a society must have universal education because literacy helps to keep people informed about public issues. Second, citizens must have the freedom of speech, not only in private but also in public discourse. Third, most (if not all) citizens must be treated as approximately equal. Fourth, certain cultural factors must be present, such as capitalism and a shared sense of basic values (for example personal freedom). Fifth, democracy depends on the people's willingness involve themselves in their political system by becoming informed about political issues and voting.

5. What are the three channels for participating in American representative democracy?

The three channels for participation are voting, political parties and campaigns, and interest groups and social protest movements. Citizens participate through voting and through political parties and campaigns; at least they are supposed to vote and to become politically aware. Voter turnout, however, has been declining steadily in the United States since 1960; only 55 percent of Americans eligible to vote did so in the 1992 presidential election. The main reason for such a low turnout is that many Americans feel their votes don't matter. Many Americans find political issues confusing; elections frequently make people apathetic towards politics; institutional barriers such as restrictions on voter registration inhibit voting. Also, because people seem to vote their resentments and fears, they are less likely to vote when these emotions do not exist. Those least likely to vote are the young, the less educated, the unemployed, and the poor.

A *political party* is an organization designed for gaining and holding legitimate political power. Parties perform several functions: 1) they link citizens with their government; 2) they link together the different branches and levels of government as well as various governmental and nongovernmental power structures; 3) they recruit candidates for elective office; 4) they help people to work out the connections between different issues and to produce compromises; and 5) they represent the range of public opinions, interests, and values. The two-party system has long been a part of American politics because of the simple plurality election process: if the winner takes all and the losers receive nothing, a vote for a minority (third) party, in effect, is wasted. This system is known as a *simple plurality system*. In *proportional vote systems*, a party places in office the same proportion of representatives as the proportion of votes it receives in the election.

The two major American political parties appeal to different kinds of voters. Republicans tend to be upper-income, professionals and managers, and white. Blacks remain Democratic, even as they move up the economic ladder. In recent years, young people have become more conservative and more likely to vote Republican. Women are more likely than men to be Democrats, perhaps because they are more likely to favor less militaristic candidates who are concerned with domestic welfare issues. Those with less education are more likely to vote Democratic; those with college educations are more likely to vote Republican. Graduates of elite colleges, however, are more likely to vote Democratic.

Parties seem to have become weaker and less important to American politics since the 1960s. More voters now label themselves independents. Even many members of Congress have departed from their party's official position. Technological advances in communications have contributed to this decline by enabling candidates to bring their message directly to the people.

Interest groups are organizations created to influence political decisions that concern their members. Many occupational, religious, environmental, and professional groups maintain lobbyists or *political action committees (PACs)* in Washington; the PACs work for the passage of legislation favorable to their members' interests. The increasing cost of getting candidates elected, as well as changes in campaign finance laws, have enlarged the roles played by PACs; they are the most rapidly growing source of campaign funds. They have a substantial effect on how politicians vote, and they have helped to weaken the ties of allegiance between politicians and their parties.

6. What is war? How has it changed?

War is the use of military means to resolve a dispute between societies or between factions within a society. The waging of war is connected closely to the rise and fall of legitimacy: civil wars and revolutions often are based on the belief that the current government no longer has legitimate claim to political power.

Wars in early human societies were small-scale events among kin groups. Few people were killed, and most wars were fought to settle disputes over debts and injuries. Three conditions were necessary for the emergence of modern war: governments to organize fighting forces, territorial boundaries, and sufficient wealth to tempt those outside one's political boundaries. Increasingly, people waged war to conquer other people's land and riches. Yet despite changes in the technology of warfare, war remained a man-to-man confrontation between large numbers of soldiers through the end of the Middle Ages. Then the emergence of nation-states profoundly altered the conduct of war: hostilities between states became large-scale conflicts involving a state's territorial boundaries, economic interests, and nationalistic goals. As nationalism fueled both war and revolution, mass citizen armies replaced mercenaries as the principal fighting force. Developments in military technology also changed the conduct of war. Increasingly efficient military technologies are achieved at high cost; the close coupling of military prowess with industrial and manufacturing productivity has given rise to a growing military-industrial complex.

No technology has altered the nature of war more profoundly than the invention of nuclear weapons. Nuclear war cannot be fought like conventional war: gains and losses have no meaning when each side has the capacity to annihilate the other. The United States and the former USSR pursued policies of *deterrence*: each country with nuclear power restrains (or deters) the other from nuclear attack because of its ability to retaliate and destroy the attacker. The United States and the former USSR have also negotiated several arms control treaties. With the downfall of communism in eastern Europe and the political reorganization of the former Soviet republics, the concept of mutual deterrence is rapidly becoming a thing of the past. Today's conflicts are less between communism and capitalism than between rival nationalist groups in the former communist countries or among Third World countries.

REVIEW OF CONCEPTS

Match the concept with the definition.

Concepts

a. authority	i. legitimacy	q. power
b. bureaucracy	j. nation	r. power elite
c. charismatic authority	k. nationalism	s. representative democracy
d. collective goods	l. oligarchy	t. state
e. democratic state	m. pluralism	u. totalitarianism
f. interest groups	n. political action committees	v. traditional authority
g. iron law of oligarchy	o. political party	w. war
h. legal/rational authority	p. politics	x. welfare state

Definitions

_____ 1. A democratic system in which the people aren't directly involved in making political choices, but rather elect public officials to represent their wishes and interests.

_____ 2. A type of authority identified by Weber that stems from traditional beliefs and practices passed down from generation to generation.

_____ 3. Power that is viewed as legitimate and is exercised with the social approval of most members of a group or society.

_____ 4. Either a) the ability to control people's behavior or experience even when they resist or b) the capacity to accomplish some end.

_____ 5. A coalition of military leaders, government officials, and business executives united by common interests and social background.

_____ 6. A group united by shared cultural bonds and usually sharing a state.

_____ 7. A type of authority identified by Weber that derives from a system of explicit rules defining the legitimate uses of power. It is vested in positions, not in specific individuals.

_____ 8. An abstract entity composed of the political institutions and other organizations that are specialized for exercising within a given territory.

_____ 9. An organization designed for gaining and holding legitimate political power.

_____ 10. The social process by which people gain, use, and lose power.

_____ 11. A state based on political participation by the people or their elected representatives.

_____ 12. Political system in which no opposing opinion or party is tolerated, and in which the government exerts great control over many aspects of citizens' lives.

_____ 13. The view that a political power structure is composed of a variety of competing elites and interest groups.

_____ 14. The belief that a people with a distinct culture (that is, a nation) should have its own state; pride in one's own nation goes hand in hand with this belief.

_____ 15. Formal, rule-governed, hierarchical organization of public servants.

_____ 16. A state that takes responsibility for the welfare of its people in such areas as education, health care, housing, social security, and working conditions.

_____ 17. Goods and services not easily bought and sold by individuals, and provided to citizens by the modern welfare state.

_____ 18. Rule by a few.

_____ 19. Michels's idea that a chain of events leads to the concentration of power in the hands of a few.

_____ 20. Organizations created to influence political decisions directly concerning members.

_____ 21. A type of authority identified by Weber, which derives from public recognition of exceptional personal qualities.

Answers

1.	s	8.	t	15.	b
2.	v	9.	o	16.	x
3.	a	10.	p	17.	d
4.	q	11.	e	18.	l
5.	r	12.	u	19.	g
6.	j	13.	m	20.	f
7.	h	14.	k	21.	c

REVIEW QUESTIONS

After studying Chapter 17, answer the following questions. The correct answers are listed after the questions; each is followed by a short explanation. You are also referred to pages in the textbook for relevant discussion.

1. Which of the following is a *false* statement about terrorism?
   a. Terrorism involves the use of violence.
   b. Terrorists' causes are sometimes good and principled, and terrorists occasionally are revered as heroes.
   c. Terrorists involve small groups of people.
   d. Terrorists have political aims.
   e. Terrorists have access to legitimate sources of political power.

2. Which is the best example of authority?
   a. A person robs a bank and uses a gun to take several hostages.
   b. The army of the Soviet Union seizes power against the will of the people of Poland.
   c. The Internal Revenue Service collects taxes every April 15.
   d. The Mafia threatens a casino operator to pay up or he will have an "accidental" fire.
   e. Idi Amin maintains control of Uganda by imprisoning, torturing, or murdering opponents of his regime.

3. The Reverend Jim Jones led a thousand people to the jungles of Guyana, where they hoped to establish a perfect society. Jones's followers believed that he was God and that he possessed extraordinary and even superhuman powers. Eventually he was able to command his followers to commit mass suicide. What was the source of Jim Jones's control over these people?
   a. politics
   b. religion
   c. legal/rational authority
   d. charismatic authority
   e. traditional authority

4. When Queen Elizabeth II gives up the throne of England, her eldest son, Charles, will become king. What is the basis for Charles's right to assume the monarchy?
   a. legal/rational authority
   b. traditional authority
   c. charismatic authority
   d. coercive power
   e. distributive power

5. When Charles assumes the throne, however, his political powers will be small compared to those vested in the elected Members of Parliament (a legislative body, which functions somewhat like our Congress). On what grounds does Parliament legitimately restrict the powers of the British monarch?
   a. Legal/rational authority
   b. traditional authority
   c. charismatic power
   d. nationalism
   e. civil rights

6. Which development did *not* accompany the rise of the modern state?
   a. separation of public and private spheres
   b. expansion and consolidation of territories
   c. growing bureaucracy of public servants
   d. unification of personal power and political power
   e. growth of international commerce

7. Only the _____ has a monopoly on the legitimate use of force within a given territory.
   a. nation
   b. bureaucracy
   c. interest group
   d. people
   e. state

8. French-speaking Canadians have tried periodically to make Quebec a separate state independent from Canada. They see themselves as possessing not only a language that separates them from English-speaking Canada, but also a distinctive history and culture. They are proud of themselves as Quebecois. This situation illustrates
   a. the iron law of oligarchy
   b. collective power
   c. collective goods
   d. nationalism
   e. human rights

9. Which is *not* a function of the modern welfare state?
   a. providing assistance to those who cannot help themselves, such as the aged and the poor
   b. suppressing minority opinion
   c. providing collective goods such as efficient public transportation
   d. regulating activities in the private sector (for example, enforcing air pollution standards at coal-burning factories)
   e. peacetime support of the military (including defense research)

10. The sophisticated, complicated, and expensive system of American education--from kindergarten to postdoctoral study--is an example of
    a. an oligarchy.
    b. traditional authority.
    c. a collective good.
    d. civil rights.
    e. deterrence.

11. Which statement is more likely to be true of a totalitarian state than a democratic state?
    a. Authority derives from the law and is rooted in the consent of the people.
    b. Government must follow the principle of due process.
    c. Government power should not be used in a capricious or arbitrary way.
    d. No opinion opposing the government is tolerated or recognized.
    e. Individuals and parties are granted only temporary authority.

12. What percentage of eligible persons voted in the 1992 presidential election?
    a. 25 percent
    b. 35 percent

c. 45 percent
d. 55 percent
e. 65 percent

13. Which statement was *not* offered as an explanation for the decreasing voter turnout in American elections?
   a. Many people believe that their votes do not matter.
   b. Many people find politics confusing.
   c. Many people believe that trying to influence politics is futile.
   d. Many people cannot identify personal interests at stake in elections.
   e. All of the above.

14. Who is most likely to vote Republican?
   a. a woman
   b. a black
   c. a middle-aged person
   d. a middle-school dropout
   e. a business executive

15. Billy makes $100 contribution to the National Rifle Association because he likes to use guns. He assumes that the NRA is working against legislation that would restrict the private ownership of firearms. The NRA is
   a. an oligarchy.
   b. a political action committee (PAC).
   c. in favor of disarmament.
   d. totalitarian.
   e. part of a welfare state.

16. Which statement supports the position of a sociologist who adopts a pluralist theory of the distribution of political power?
   a. A variety of groups with diverse interests competes for political power.
   b. Power is monopolized by a few people at the top of our organizational hierarchies.
   c. The ruling elite has similar backgrounds, values, interests, and goals.
   d. "Who says organization, says oligarchy."
   e. Power is held by the owners of the means of production, and they use it to further their economic interests.

17. Which statement does *not* describe warfare conducted in early human societies?
   a. War is a ritual activity, often following lines of kinship.
   b. Battles are episodic skirmishes in which few people are killed.
   c. Winning is of little consequence.
   d. The goal is expansion of territory or acquisition of goods.
   e. The civilian population is rarely involved.

Answers

   1. *e.* Terrorism is the use of violence by small groups of people to accomplish political aims that they feel unable to bring about by peaceful, legitimate means. See page 429.
   2. *c.* Authority is power that is viewed as legitimate and is exercised with the social approval of most individuals in a group or society. Though we may not like to pay taxes, we accept as

legitimate the state's right of taxation. See page 430.

3. *d.* Charismatic authority derives from public recognition of exceptional personal qualities. The key to charismatic authority lies in the followers' belief in the leader's gifts, not in objective evidence of those beliefs. See page 430.

4. *b.* Traditional authority stems from sacred traditions of loyalty to monarchs, chiefs, and priests. People in Britain accept this type of authority because this is the way in which the crown has always been transferred. See page 430.

5. *a.* Legal/rational authority derives from a system of rules--in this case, laws--defining legitimate uses of power. Unlike the traditional authority of King Charles II, legal/rational authority is vested in positions such as Member of Parliament, not in specific individuals who fill those positions. (MPs lose their parliamentary authority when they are voted out of office.) See page 430.

6. *d.* Emergence of the modern state was associated with separation of official political (or public) authority from private or personal authority. Heads of state are now officeholders, whose authority extends only for their elected or appointed term. We now consider it inappropriate for public officials to use their office (for example) for private financial gain. See pages 434-435.

7. *e.* A state is an abstract entity composed of the public organizations in which autonomous power over a specified geographical area is concentrated. States have a monopoly on the use of force within the territory under their control, although this monopoly depends on the acceptance of the state's legitimacy by its citizens. See pages 433-434.

8. *d.* Nationalism is the belief that a people with a distinct culture (that is, a nation) should have its own state. The case of Quebec is a reminder that even vigorous nationalism does not always succeed in creating a new nation-state. See page 435.

9. *b.* The welfare state is a broadly expanded state, which is found throughout the democratic, affluent, industrialized states of the West. It provides for the welfare of ordinary citizens by offering assistance to the needy, providing collective goods, and regulating the private economy. See page 436.

10. *c.* Collective goods (or services) are not bought and sold easily by individuals; they are provided to citizens by the modern welfare state. Though private schools have always been a part of American education, most of us are educated in state-supported institutions. See page 436.

11. *d.* A democratic state is based on political participation by the people. A totalitarian state is a political system in which no opposing opinion or party is tolerated, and in which the government exerts great control over many aspects of citizens' lives. See page 437.

12. *d.* Voter turnout has been declining since 1960 in the United States; in 1992 about 55 percent of eligible voters voted in the presidential election. In Western European democracies about 80 to 90 percent of eligible voters go to the polls. See page 438.

13. *e.* There is probably no single reason why such a low proportion of eligible voters goes to the polls; each of these factors is partly responsible. Several factors have been identified as increasing voter turnout: people participate in politics when they have personal interests at stake, and they vote to express their resentments or fears. See page 438.

14. *e.* These background factors are still somewhat influential in determining party preferences. Generally, support for the Republican party is strongest among those in managerial or professional occupations. Women and blacks tend to vote Democratic, as do those with little education. See pages 440-441.

15. *b.* PACs are a type of interest group: organizations created to influence political decisions that concern their members directly. PACs are particularly active in raising campaign funds for candidates likely to vote for legislation favorable to the group; Billy hopes that the NRA will use some of his money to help elect candidates who oppose gun-control legislation.

See page 444.

16. *a.* The pluralist view holds that a variety of groups and interest competes for power in American society; power is dispersed far more broadly than either Marxist or power elite theories would contend. See page 433.

17. *d.* In early human societies, there were few stable territorial boundaries or durable goods over which to fight. Modern warfare was precipitated by the formation of nation-states, the establishment of precise territorial boundaries, and the availability of sufficient wealth (money or other durable goods) to tempt others. See pages 445-446.

EXERCISES

Exercise 1

Max Weber identified three bases of legitimate authority (legal/rational authority, charismatic authority, and traditional authority), and contrasted these with the exercise of illegitimate power. This exercise requires you to read newspapers and newsmagazines daily for at least one week. Collect several examples of each of these four types of political leadership. Attach photocopies of the news articles; explain how each article illustrates a particular type of political power.

1. Legal-rational authority:

2. Charismatic authority:

3. Traditional authority:

4. Illegitimate power:

Exercise 2

This exercise asks you to interpret the following statistics. In 1967 women made up 1.0 percent of all people in the military; in 1973, when the United States adopted an all-volunteer force, women made up 2.5 percent of all people in the military; in 1976, when women were first admitted to the service academies, the percentage rose to 5.3 percent; today women make up about 15 percent of all people in the military.

1. How would you explain the steady increase in the proportion of women in the military?

2. What problems does this trend raise for the socialization of soldiers?

3. How have patterns of warfare changed--largely because of advancements in military technology-- in ways that might increase or alter the roles played by females in combat?

4. At present, laws and military regulations prevent women from engaging in direct armed combat that would bring them into face-to-face contact with the enemy. Give three reasons why these laws and regulations should be eliminated.

a.

b.

c.

Give three reasons why these laws should be retained and enforced.

a.

b.

c.

Exercise 3

The "state" is defined as an abstract entity composed of the public organizations in which autonomous power over a specified geographical area is concentrated. From nation to nation, the responsibilities assigned to the state vary dramatically. In the United States, for example, the central state is responsible for military defense and for maintaining certain standards of social welfare (as evidenced by the

Social Security program and by welfare programs such as Aid to Families with Dependent Children). The following activities are not now included among the responsibilities assigned to the central state in Washington. Decide whether it is likely that the American state will *ever* assume responsibility for each activity listed below. Decide whether you would personally be in favor of this change.

1. Broad regulation of the content of television programming.

2. Elimination of unemployment by creating enough government jobs to hire adults who cannot find employment in the private sector.

3. Creation of a nationwide curriculum for Grades 1 through 6 in all American schools.

4. Provision of free health care to all citizens.

Chapter 18
THE THIRD WORLD

OBJECTIVES

After reading Chapter 18, you should understand the following main points and be able to answer the objectives.

1. Third World countries share several basic characteristics.
    1.1   Define underdevelopment.
    1.2   Differentiate the First World, the Second World, and the Third World.
    1.3   List the countries included in the Third World.
    1.4   List the three characteristics Third World countries have in common.
    1.5   List the three distinguishing features of Western imperialism.
    1.6   Compare the two main groups of farmers in the Third World: peasants and landless laborers.
    1.7   List three problems experienced by Third world peasants.
    1.8   Describe how rapidly swelling cities are a problem in Third World countries.
    1.9   Define hyper-urbanization and consider its consequences.
    1.10 Summarize the consequences of the poverty and affluence in Third World cities.
    1.11 Describe the role of the informal sector of the economy.
    1.12 Show how the five key concepts help in understanding the Third World.

2. Several theories explain development in the Third World.
    2.1   Define modernization theory.
    2.2   Describe the five stages of economic growth.
    2.3   Assess modernization theory.
    2.4   Summarize the contributions of dependency theory.
    2.5   Assess dependency theory.
    2.6   Summarize the contradictions of world systems theory.
    2.7   Compare core nations with peripheral nations and semi-peripheral nations.
    2.8   Assess world systems theory.

CHAPTER SUMMARY

1.   What is the Third World? Which characteristics do Third World countries share?

The concept of a Third World suggests that the nations of the world can be divided into three groups. The *First World* includes the rich, industrialized nations of North America, Europe, and Japan, whose economies are based on private property, wage labor, and competition. The *Second World* refers to those countries which pulled out of the capitalist world system, and whose economies were based on collective or state ownership of the means of production and on centrally planned production and distribution of goods. The *Third World* includes the relatively poor, nonindustrialized nations of Latin America, Africa, and Asia, most of which were either colonies or clients of First World countries until they gained political independence. Third World countries are not homogeneous in politics, economics, history, culture, or other respects. Most, however, suffer from *underdevelopment*, the lack of modern economic growth. Underdevelopment is a global problem because its effects are felt worldwide. Third World countries also share several characteristics: a colonial heritage, an economy rooted in agriculture, and rapidly growing cities.

2. What characterizes Western colonialism?

Third World countries have experienced a long history of domination by Western powers and its corollary, underdevelopment. Western imperialism was unique in three ways. First, it usually was impelled by the profit motive and the individual pursuit of wealth. Earlier empires tended to be the product of political ambitions and desire for power. Second, earlier empires built on existing social and economic structures. In contrast, the rise of capitalism and the spread of industrialization in Europe were attended by demands for raw materials and food. As a result, they began to restructure the traditional economies of their colonies. Europeans altered the system of land ownership and destroyed traditional rulers and systems of authority.

The third unique feature of Western colonialism was cultural imperialism. European colonials imposed their own culture on their colonies. Many of the colonies gained independence after World War I, although such independence did not automatically generate economic independence. The U.S. policy toward nationalist movements and newly independent countries depended on whether these countries wanted to remain in the world capitalist system.

Neither did independence yield political stability. Few Third World countries are nations as defined in the previous chapter: one people with a common history and culture. This diversity is particularly evident in Africa.

3. What role does agriculture play in Third World status?

Farming is the most common occupation in most of the Third World, but agricultural development is limited. Poverty is rampant in rural areas.

The farmers of the Third World fall into two main groups, peasants and landless laborers. *Peasants* are small farmers who work with family labor and simple technology to grow crops and raise livestock primarily for their own consumption. Peasants are tied to the land economically, socially, and culturally. In some situations they own the land that they farm; in others, they do not. The family household is the center of peasant life. The peasant community is strongly traditional and conformist. Third World peasants experience several problems: 1) they usually have too little land, water, fertilizer, and other resources to produce even a minimum livelihood; 2) they often use relatively primitive farming techniques; 3) serious ecological damage exists.

Landless laborers are peasants who have lost the rights to land, children of landless peasants, or Indians who formerly lived by hunting and gathering. They usually work as hired hands on large farms. As a result, they lack autonomy. Their living standards vary considerably, depending on their treatment by the landowner. These laborers seldom leave the land.

Many landless laborers found it difficult to deal with commercialization, the shift from village-based food production to private property and the production of cash crops. Commercialization undermined self-sufficiency and increased vulnerability. Private property and commercialization heightened the gap between the rich and the poor. Some people think that land reform (giving peasants and landless laborers access to land of their own) is the solution to social and agricultural problems in the Third World. Land reform, however, may cause ecological problems because of the overpopulation in many of these countries.

4. What effects do large cities have in the Third World?

Third World cities have grown dramatically as people have moved there in response to population pressures and to shortages of land and opportunity in the countryside. Currently the rate of growth in Third World cities is more than twice the growth rate of First World cities at a comparable stage in their development.

One result of mass migration has been *hyper-urbanization*, a rate of urban growth that outstrips industrial and other forms of economic development, leading to widespread unemployment and over-burdened public services. Quite simply, no city can keep up with the demand this migration has generated. Abject poverty has been the result. These cities suffer from high crime rates and extensive homelessness.

Between one-fourth and two-thirds of Third World residents do not hold regular, salaried jobs. Most become part of the *informal sector* of the economy, the economic activity that takes place outside regular employer/employee relations and beyond government scrutiny and taxation. The informal sector generates a substantial *black market*, the illegal trade in stolen, untaxed, or other illegally distributed goods, drugs, other contraband, and foreign currency. A combination of government bureaucrats, wealthy businessmen, and middle-class consumers (all in the city) provides a major market for the informal sector.

As noted above, the countryside suffers from abject poverty. One reason why people continue to migrate to cities is that Third World governments subsidize the urban poor but not the rural poor. Governing elites fear the urban poor more than the rural poor.

5. Which theories explain development?

One theory that explains development is *modernization theory*, the belief that most of the poor countries of the Third World would eventually experience industrial revolutions like those which occurred in England and the United States. These theorists maintain that poor countries simply are missing crucial prerequisites for development, including such cultural traits as self-discipline and devotion to hard work. They also lack functional integration as evidenced in a complex division of labor. Most fundamentally, they have none of the technological and material means of production or the capitalist relations to which Karl Marx drew attention.

Modernization theorists outline five stages of economic growth. The traditional society constitutes Stage 1, in which production and technology are essentially prescientific. The preconditions for change emerge in Stage 2; most critical is the belief that economic progress is possible and necessary for some other purpose. In Stage 3, industries expand rapidly and generate a need for more factory workers and services to support them. Cities grow rapidly as well. In Stage 4 the drive toward maturity, growth is steady and the economy finds its niche in the international economy. There may be a shift from heavy industry to high-technology goods. Stage 5, the age of high mass consumption, is characterized by a shift to production of consumer goods. Because of improvements in income, people can afford more than the basics.

The major contribution of modernization theory lies in its emphasis on cultural values such as investment and economic innovation. It also emphasizes functional integration. Unfortunately, the expected modernization has not occurred as planned in most of the world's poor countries.

According to *dependency theory*, the main reason Third World why countries have failed to "take off" is that they are dependent on the already developed nations of the First World. Rich nations actually do more harm than good by supporting Third World governing elites. Not only do Third

World countries depend on First World countries; often they are dominated by one or more First World countries. The United States and other industrialized nations have a history of giving the most assistance to countries they consider friendly. Thus, First World business leaders have invested only in countries they perceive as hospitable. As a result, Third World governments have had to pay more attention to the foreigners who gave them aid than to the needs and wishes of their own people, and democracy often has been delayed. In addition, this practice has meant that the United States has supported a number of repressive dictators such as Ferdinand Marcos in the Philippines. Dependent development also has inhibited the growth of a strong, autonomous middle class, another condition essential for development and democracy. Foreign aid obviously has certain benefits, but it can slow development in the long run by making the local economy dependent on foreign supplies and expertise, and thus throwing it off balance.

Dependency theory highlights the close connection between political difficulties and the economic problems of underdevelopment. Dictatorship is the most prevalent form of government in the Third World.

A third theoretical approach is *world systems theory*, which emphasizes the social structure of global inequality. Wallerstein believes that the modern, capitalist world system is the web of production and consumption relations which have linked the First to the Third World since the rise of capitalism. Its main feature is that it is capitalist. In such a system, rich countries have all the advantages; a system of unequal trade has moved resources from the Third World to the First.

The world system develops a global division of labor that has three levels or parts: the core, the periphery, and the semiperiphery. *Core nations* include the world's powerful industrial economies: the United States, most western European nations, and Japan. The core nations provide the management and much of the essential equipment for the production of the world's goods. *Peripheral nations* are on the edges of the world system because they are the sellers of low-priced raw materials. Most are primarily agricultural, most depend on foreign aid, and most participate in the world system only on terms set by the core countries. *Semiperipheral nations* lie between the core and the periphery, and are moving up or down in the system. These nations are involved in the world system but are limited in their ability to influence it. Wallerstein believes that a country's opportunities for development depend largely on where it fits into the world system of capitalist trade. Semiperipheral countries can enhance their status by keeping wages low and their rate of investment very high.

REVIEW OF CONCEPTS

Match the concept with the definition.

Concepts

a. core nations
b. dependency theory
c. First World
d. hyper-urbanization
e. informal sector
f. landless laborers
g. modernization theory
h. peasants
i. peripheral nations
j. Second World
k. semiperipheral nations
l. Third World
m. underdevelopment
n. world systems theory

Definitions

____ 1. The advanced, industrial, capitalistic nations of the Northern Hemisphere (including Japan.)

____ 2. A rate of urban growth that outstrips industrial and other forms of economic growth, leading to widespread unemployment and overburdened public services.

____ 3. The absence of modern economic growth that characterizes Third World countries by comparison with the developed nations of the West.

____ 4. Wallerstein's theory that a nation's development is determined by its place in a world system that is defined by capitalist trade and divides the world into three categories: core, peripheral, and semiperipheral nations.

____ 5. The formerly communist nations of the old Soviet bloc, whose economies until recently were based on state ownership of the means of production and the centrally planned production and distribution of goods.

____ 6. Peasants who have lost the rights to land, children of landless peasants, or peoples who formerly lived by hunting and gathering but now must work as hired hands.

____ 7. The relatively poor, non-industrial nations of Latin America, Africa, and Asia (including China), most of which were either colonies or clients of the Western imperial powers in the past.

____ 8. Small farmers who, with family labor and simple technology, grow crops and raise livestock primarily for their own use.

____ 9. The view that the underdevelopment of Third World nations is due in large part to reliance on First World governments and corporations, which have a vested interest in maintaining a stable climate for investment, regardless of the local social and political costs.

____ 10. Economic activity that takes place outside of regular employer/employee relations and outside of regular government scrutiny and taxation.

____ 11. In world systems theory, countries on the fringes of the global capitalist economy, whose role is largely limited to providing raw materials and purchasing minor consumer goods.

____ 12. The view that economic development depends on cultural attitudes (and perhaps foreign aid) that promote investment in industrial enterprise and related support systems.

Answers

1.	c	5.	j	9.	b
2.	d	6.	f	10.	e
3.	m	7.	l	11.	i
4.	n	8.	h	12.	g

REVIEW QUESTIONS

After studying Chapter 18, answer the following questions. The correct answers are listed after the questions; each is followed by a short explanation. You are also referred to pages in the textbook for relevant discussion.

1. Mali lacks modern economic growth and is very poor. Sociologists would say that Mali is experiencing

a. underdevelopment.
b. overdevelopment.
c. discrimination.
d. disequilibrium.
e. dependency.

2. The Soviet Union is included in which world?
   a. The First World
   b. The Second World
   c. The Third World
   d. The Fourth World
   e. The Fifth World

3. Which one of the following is not included in the Third World?
   a. Taiwan
   b. Africa
   c. Peru
   d. Eastern European countries
   e. Iran

4. Which one of the following is *not* one of the unique features of Western imperialism?
   a. It was driven by the profit motive.
   b. It was driven by the pursuit of wealth.
   c. It altered the social and economic structures of colonies.
   d. It imposed European culture on the colonies.

5. The most common occupation in the Third World countries is
   a. factory worker.
   b. farming.
   c. managing organizations.
   d. skilled craftsperson.
   e. social service worker.

6. Peasants have all *except* which one of the following characteristics?
   a. They are farmers.
   b. They work with family labor.
   c. Their social structure emphasizes the family.
   d. They are traditional and conformist.
   e. They always own their own land.

7. Because landless laborers work as hired hands, the social structural constant in their lives is
   a. an emphasis on the family unit.
   b. a tight connection with the economic system.
   c. a lack of autonomy.
   d. the social life is provided by their employer.
   e. the government, which supplies social services.

8. How does the rate of city growth in Third World countries compare to that in First World countries?
   a. It is half as much.

b. It is about the same.
c. It is double.
d. It is triple.
e. It is five times as much.

9. Hyper-urbanization occurs when
   a. urbanization occurs faster than governments can control it.
   b. the birth rate exceeds the death rate.
   c. cities have no room to expand.
   d. the growth rate of a city outstrips industrial and other forms of economic growth.
   e. the service sector in a city grows faster than the manufacturing sector.

10. Which one of the following reflects the informal sector?
    a. Jose works for the local IBM operation.
    b. Georg works for the welfare department.
    c. Wen works for various people by exchanging his mechanical skills for services he needs.
    d. Lucinda is a school teacher.
    e. Olga is a veterinarian.

11. Which government action promotes migration to cities in the Third World?
    a. subsidizing the poor by keeping prices low
    b. providing free education
    c. providing free medical services
    d. providing free jobs training
    e. enhancing participation in the government by the poor

12. Which theory of development holds that poor countries go through stages?
    a. modernization theory
    b. Marxist theory
    c. dependency theory
    d. world systems theory
    e. stage theory

13. Which theory of development holds that poor countries become too closely connected to First World countries?
    a. modernization theory
    b. Marxist theory
    c. dependency theory
    d. world systems theory
    e. stage theory

14. Which theory of development explains why the United States supported several repressive dictatorships?
    a. modernization theory
    b. Marxist theory
    c. dependency theory
    d. world systems theory
    e. stage theory

15. Which theory of development takes a more social structural view?

a. modernization theory
b. Marxist theory
c. dependency theory
d. world systems theory
e. stage theory

16. Most of the world's population lives in
   a. core nations.
   b. peripheral nations.
   c. semiperipheral nations.
   d. semicore nations.
   e. The First World.

17. The main strategy for self-improvement by a semiperipheral country is to
   a. join the Marxist revolution.
   b. produce more goods such as sugar and rubber.
   c. implement democracy.
   d. reduce its dependence on First World countries.
   e. keep wages low and the rate of investment high.

18. Which country is the best example of the progression from peripheral to semiperipheral to core countries?
   a. The Soviet Union
   b. Turkey
   c. The United States
   d. Germany
   e. Japan

Answers

1. *a.* Underdevelopment is a lack of modern economic growth and is a global problem. See page 451.
2. *b.* The Second World refers to those countries that pulled out of the capitalist world system and whose economies were based on collective or state ownership of the means of production and on centrally planned production and distribution of goods. The Soviet Union fits this definition. See page 458.
3. *d.* The Third World countries are the poor, nonindustrialized nations of Latin America, Africa, and Asia. Eastern European countries are part of the Second World. See page 458.
4. *d.* Whereas earlier empires were the result of political ambitions and the desire for power, Western imperialism usually was driven by the profit motive and the individual pursuit of wealth. See pages 458-459.
5. *b.* Third World countries depend heavily on farming, even though agricultural development is stagnant. See page 462.
6. *e.* Peasants may or may not own the ground they farm. See page 462.
7. *c.* A lack of autonomy is the social structural constant that results from landless laborers loss of land and dependence on large farms as employers. See page 465.
8. *c.* The rate of city growth in Third World countries is about twice the growth rate of First World countries at a comparable stage in their development. See page 468.
9. *d.* Hyper-urbanization occurs when the rate of growth in a city outstrips the industrial and other forms of economic growth, leading to widespread unemployment and overburdened

public services. See page 470.

10. *c.* The informal sector of the economy refers to the economic activity that takes place outside of regular employer/employee relations and government scrutiny and taxation. See page 473.

11. *a.* Third World governments subsidize the urban poor by keeping prices low. The rural poor receive no such benefits. This practice encourages migration to the cities. See page 474.

12. *a.* Modernization theorists argue that poor countries undergo five stages of economic growth on the road to development. See page 475.

13. *c.* Dependency theorists argue that poor countries fail to develop because they become too dependent on the aid provided by First World countries.

14. *c.* Dependency theory holds that Third World governments had to pay so much attention to the foreigners who gave them aid that they became agents of the world economy whose main role was to keep their country's work force in line. As a result, democracy was put on hold and the United States supported repressive dictatorships. See page 477.

15. *d.* World systems theory emphasizes the social structure of global inequality, driven by capitalism. See page 479.

16. *b.* Most of the world's population lives in peripheral nations, countries on the edges of the world system because they are the sellers of low-priced raw materials. See page 479.

17. *e.* The main strategy for self-improvement by a semiperipheral country is to keep its wages very low and its rate of investment very high. See page 480.

18. *e.* Japan is the best example of the progression from peripheral to semiperipheral to core countries. See page 480.

EXERCISES

Exercise 1

Select an article in a newspaper or newsweekly about a Third World country.

1. Describe the focus of the story.

2. Show how three of the five key concepts are reflected in the story.

3. Describe any indicators that make this a Third World country, using the characteristics noted in the text.

4. Use the story to show any evidence for the three theories of development.

Exercise 2

You are a newly elected member of Congress. A bill in Congress proposes massive increases in foreign aid to Latin America.

1. Indicate the questions you would ask to help you decide how to vote.

2. Explain why you would or would not support the bill.

3. Show how the contributions of the three theories of development enter into your answers for #1 and #2.

Exercise 3

This exercise asks you to *apply* sociological theories to the solution of a practical problem. Hunger is a chronic problem in much of the Third World today. Although our planet continues to increase its annual output of food, not enough of it reaches those who need it most, leaving many people to die of malnutrition or starvation. Imagine that you were hired by the United Nations to provide expert advice on dealing with the problem of hunger in the Third World. Summarize the different advice you would give if you adopted the perspectives of each of these three viewpoints on social change in the Third World:

1. Modernization theory:

2. Dependency theory:

3. World systems theory:

Chapter 19

POPULATION AND ENVIRONMENT

OBJECTIVES

After reading Chapter 19, you should understand the following main points and be able to answer the objectives.

1. The numbers, characteristics, and distributions of a society's people help provide a sociological understanding of social trends.
   1.1 Define population structure.
   1.2 Define population distribution.
   1.3 Define demography.
   1.4 Show how the five key concepts help in understanding population issues.

2. Demographic analysis requires accurate and detailed information in order to assess population distributions and to project future trends.
   2.1 Define census and explain how the U.S. census works.
   2.2 Explain why censuses are often the subject of controversy.
   2.3 Assess the accuracy of the U.S. Census.

3. Demographers concentrate on three basic factors: fertility, mortality, and migration.
   3.1 Define the crude birth rate.
   3.2 Define fertility rate and replacement rate.
   3.3 Describe the pattern of changes in the birth and fertility rates in the United States, as well as the factors responsible.
   3.4 Define crude death rate.
   3.5 Define infant mortality rate.
   3.6 Differentiate life expectancy from life span.
   3.7 Explain how changes in mortality have had the strongest impact on the demographic history of the human population.
   3.8 Define migration rate.
   3.9 Differentiate emigration from internal migration.
   3.10 Differentiate immigration from internal migration.
   3.11 Define and illustrate age structure and show how the population pyramid is used to graphically represent a society's age structure.
   3.12 Define birth cohort.
   3.13 Show how population distribution by age is an example of a structural force at work.

4. Changes in the growth of the world's population have significant social consequences.
    4.1 List the years in which the world's population reached the second billion, the third billion, the fourth billion, and the fifth billion.
    4.2 State whether the world's population is growing more slowly or more rapidly than it was 20 to 30 years ago.
    4.3 State the proportion of the world's population that lives in the less developed countries.
    4.4 Describe and assess the thesis proposed by Thomas Malthus.
    4.5 Summarize Marx's reactions to the Malthusian doctrine.
    4.6 Outline the four stages of the demographic transition; describe the social consequences of each.
    4.7 State whether the demographic transition that occurred in industrialized countries also applies directly to currently developing nations.
    4.8 Describe how cultural factors affect the fertility rate.
    4.9 Trace the consequences of lower birth rates for the status of women.

5. The future of humanity and the future of the environment are closely connected.
    5.1 Define ecology.
    5.2 Describe how lifestyles in developed and underdeveloped countries affect the earth's ecology.
    5.3 Describe how population affects the earth's ecology.
    5.4 Define Green Revolution and consider its effects.
    5.5 List two reasons for the tip in the balance between the consumption and production of natural resources.
    5.6 Explain why dependence on fossil fuels is problematic.
    5.7 List two reasons why deforestation has occurred.
    5.8 Assess the effects of deforestation.
    5.9 Define pollution.
    5.10 Show how social factors convert pollution into a crisis.
    5.11 Define greenhouse effect and assess its impact.
    5.12 List three sources of water pollution.
    5.13 Describe conservation measures that will contribute to a sustainable world.

CHAPTER SUMMARY

1. Why are sociologists interested in demographic data?

Population data help us to understand social life. Sociologists are interested in relating these data to age, income, education, race, and other factors. Sociologists are particularly interested in the numbers of births, deaths, and migrations. Changes in these figures both reflect and cause changes in social institutions. Population data also are relevant when we assess the adequacy of a society's environmental resources and the impact of population numbers on an ecological setting. Although survey data are useful for establishing public opinion and attitudes, the conclusions of these surveys become more meaningful when placed in the context of changes in the demographic structure of a society.

Demography is the scientific study of how births, deaths, and migration affect the composition, size, and distribution of populations. Demographers study a society's *population structure*: the age, sex, education, income, occupation, marital status, race, and religion of its members. Demographic analysis addressed the five key concepts, particularly social structure and social action.

2. How do sociologists study populations?

Demographic analysis requires accurate and detailed information from a variety of sources so that population distributions can be assessed and future trends can be projected. The most important source of demographic data is the national *census*, which counts the total number of people as well as the numbers of people in various regions. Censuses often are the subject of political controversy because they may have implications for the distributions of power.

The U.S. Census may not be entirely accurate. For example, some argue that the 1990 census overlooked four to six million people; others dispute these estimates. About seven million people were overlooked in the 1980 census. Overall the poor, the young, immigrants, males, and minorities are more difficult to count than other people; these categories represent the more mobile groups in our society.

Demographers focus on the number of births, deaths, and migrations. The *crude birth rate* is the number of births per 1,000 people per year. This rate has varied dramatically over the last 50 years. Because the crude birth rate is unreliable for long-term analysis, demographers use the *fertility rate*: the average number of births a woman will have in her lifetime. Demographers refer to a fertility rate of 2.1 as the *replacement rate*: the rate at which a population will remain stable. The fertility rate was 2.1 in 1990. Birth and fertility rates in the United States have been declining steadily for many years. The rate of decline varies according to socioeconomic status. The U.S. birth rate is below its replacement level of 2.1 children per woman of childbearing age.

The *crude death rate* is the number of deaths per 1,000 people during a given year; it was 8.6 in 1991. This rate varies considerably by age and ethnicity. The *infant mortality rate* is the number of deaths among infants under one year of age per 1,000 live births in a given year. Although the infant mortality rate of 8.8 in 1991 is the lowest ever recorded in this country, it is still higher than in several other developed countries. *Life expectancy* is the average number of years of life remaining for an individual of a given age; *life span* is the maximum number of years a human being can live. Life expectancy has increased dramatically in the last century (74 in industrialized countries); life span has not. Changes in mortality have had the strongest impact on the demographic history of the human population.

The *net migration rate* is the difference between the number of people who leave a place and those who arrive each year, per 1,000 people. *Emigration* is migration from one's native land; *immigration* is migration to a new country. *Internal migration*--movement within a country--is also an important demographic phenomenon. People migrate for a variety of reasons including disasters, political and religious persecution, and the desire for adventure. The United States has only five percent of the world's population but takes in about 50 percent of the world's immigrants. Immigrants accounted for at least a third of this country's population growth in the 1980s.

The impact of the population dynamics outlined above can be summarized in the *age structure*: the pattern that emerges when people in a society are grouped by age. The *population pyramid* is a graphic representation of age structure. Population pyramids for different points in time show the changes in the age structure in a society. Also, they help examine *birth cohorts*: categories of people who were born in the same year or years. Clearly, population distributions reflect structural forces at work and help policymakers and social planners.

3. How has world population growth changed? What have been some of the consequences of these changes?

Several hundred thousand years were needed for the world's population to reach one billion. The second billion, however, was reached by 1930, the third by 1960, the fourth by 1975, and the fifth by 1987. Population experts predict a 6.4 billion world population by the year 2000. Even so, the world's population is growing more slowly now than in the 1960s and 1970s. The developed nations' share of world population has been dropping steadily since 1950.

In 1798, Thomas Malthus suggested that no population can continue to grow indefinitely because population increases geometrically, while food supplies increase only arithmetically. Hence while population doubles, the food supply increases by only one unit. Malthus believed that people simply would run out of food and that the only solution was to marry late and to have fewer children. The evidence, however, has not supported his thesis. Malthus failed to anticipate the full possibilities of the Industrial Revolution and did not foresee the technological revolution in agriculture. Marx saw the situation differently: whereas Malthus placed the blame for overpopulation and poverty on the individual members of society, Marx saw the issue in terms of underproduction. The unequal distribution of social wealth under capitalism made it seem that a "natural" limit on population was necessary. Marx suggested socialism as a solution to the problem of overpopulation.

Sociologists describe four stages in the development of the population structure; all four reflect the *demographic transition*, the shift from high birth and death rates to low birth and death rates. Both the birth rate and the death rate are high and stable in stage 1. Stage 2 is a transitional stage, with a continued high birth rate but a declining death rate. This stage has the potential for a high rate of population growth. In stage 3, the birth rate also drops as families realize they do not need so many children to provide for their old age and as new economic opportunities develop, especially for women. In stage 4 both the birth rate and the death rate are low and are in balance again. The significant increase in the chances for infant survival allows people to have fewer children. The demographic transition reflects past events in industrialized nations; it also is an indication of what might happen elsewhere.

As death rates in developing countries decline, the population should grow significantly because fertility rates remain high. In many countries, however, the falling death rate is not accompanied by a shift to an industrial economy. Hence such countries will continue to experience a need for many children. In short, the demographic transition that occurred in the industrialized countries of the West does not apply directly to many currently developing nations. People in these societies have not yet had the time to adjust the religious and cultural values that shape the birth rate.

Changes in the world population growth rate have implications for women's status. The status of women remains low in most traditional societies; whatever status women possess derives primarily from marriage and mothering. Reducing the birth rates in such societies clearly involves a dramatic change in women's roles; people will not change their patterns of childbearing until they have reasons to do so. Such reasons might include a reduction in infant mortality, the expansion of basic education, and participation in the labor force. Education and equal rights for women are two of the prerequisites for lowering fertility. The status of women also has been influenced significantly by the availability of contraceptives. Progress has been made. In 1965, Third World women averaged more than six children each; by 1991, this fertility rate had fallen to 3.9.

5. *How are the future of humanity and the future of the environment closely connected?*

Both population pressures and lifestyle differences place stress on the earth's *ecology*, the pattern of relationships between organisms (including humans) and between organisms and their environments. The effect of population pressures on the ecology can be seen most clearly in problems with the food supply. Nearly a billion people are chronically hungry, and as many as 400 million are so undernourished that their health is threatened or their growth is stunted. Severe hunger is concentrated in the Third World, particularly Latin America and Africa. One-third of the world's grain supply is fed to livestock to feed people in First World countries.

Between 1950 and 1984, worldwide grain production increased steadily because of the *green revolution*, the development of new strains of cereal crops such as corn, wheat, and rice that doubled or tripled the yield per acre. The green revolution yielded substantial short-term improvements, but at the price of long-term damage to the environment. Green revolution crops depend on intensive agriculture using high levels of irrigation, fertilizers, and pesticides, all of which take a substantial toll on the environment. Soil erosion is a major problem. Feeding the world in the future will be difficult because grain production will increase at only half the expected rate of population growth. As a result, the amount of food per person will decline.

Population pressures also cause depletion of resources and pollution. Until recently, humans consumed resources no faster than they were produced. This balance began to tip in recent decades, however, because humans began to use *nonrenewable resources*, natural resources that cannot be replaced. Substantial population growth also contributed to this imbalance. Industrialized nations consume more than half of the world's available energy, even though they have less than one-fourth of the world's population. The United States accounts for the largest share by far.

Dependence on fossil fuels is problematic for several reasons. One reason is location; two-thirds of the world's oil reserves and natural gas reserves are in the Middle East, a politically very unstable environment. Second, fossil fuels generate considerable pollution. Third, people around the world have rebelled against their governments' proposed solutions to energy problems. Between 1973 and 1986, energy efficiency in the United States increased by about 30 percent, oil imports declined dramatically, and the nation's annual fuel bill decreased by $150 billion. In 1985-1986, when world petroleum prices fell, oil imports and consumption began to increase again, and today have returned almost to their former peak.

In addition to overusing nonrenewable resources, people have been consuming renewable resources faster than they can be replenished. Deforestation, a major problem, has two major causes. The first is population pressure; many Third World nations use wood faster than it can be replaced. Second, because of commercial development for the global market, foreign investors or local entrepreneurs strip large areas of rain forest to obtain export lumber and minerals or to clear space for ranches and plantations.

Pollution is another major ecological problem. *Pollution* occurs when so much waste is produced that it overloads natural recycling processes, or when human beings produce materials that cannot be broken down naturally. Two social factors convert pollution into a crisis: 1) new technologies with new waste products and 2) levels of population density never reached before. Many modern practices and technologies contribute to a more general destruction of the earth's atmosphere. In recent years, pollution from human activities has threatened the two functions that atmosphere performs: 1) it acts as a blanket to trap warmth from the sun and keep rivers and oceans from freezing, and 2) it shields the earth from harmful ultraviolet rays. The *greenhouse effect* refers to the way atmospheric gases trap heat, like the roof of a greenhouse. The most common greenhouse gases are water vapor, carbon dioxide, methane, nitrous oxide and ozone. The concentration of these gases has been accelerating rapidly, primarily because of the burning of fossil fuels and the cutting and burning of forests. Global warming will result if this trend continues.

Water pollution is another major problem, which has three basic sources: 1) domestic waste, which has become a critical problem in Third World cities; 2) industrial waste, a problem in all cities; and 3) the effects of land use, particularly the erosion that results when land is cleared for agriculture.

In a sustainable world, economic growth and development are limited to levels that maintain the earth's ecology. Lester Brown recommends several conservation measures to promote sustainable growth: 1) stabilizing population size, 2) raising energy efficiency, 3) harnessing the sun's energy, 4) reusing and recycling materials, 5) reforesting, and 6) stabilizing the soil.

REVIEW OF CONCEPTS

Match the concept with the definition.

Concepts

a.	age structure	h.	fertility rate	o.	life span
b.	birth cohort	i.	Green Revolution	p.	migration rate
c.	census	j.	greenhouse effect	q.	pollution
d.	demographic transition	k.	immigration	r.	population distribution
e.	demography	l.	infant mortality rate	s.	population structure
f.	ecology	m.	internal migration	t.	replacement rate
g.	emigration	n.	life expectancy		

Definitions

____ 1. The maximum number of years of human life.

____ 2. The fertility rate at which a population will remain stable.

____ 3. The pattern that results from the age, sex, education, income, occupation, marital status, race, and religion of members of a population.

____ 4. Damage to the environment caused by waste levels that overload natural recycling systems, or by synthetic materials that cannot be broken down by natural processes.

____ 5. The average number of years of life remaining for a person of a given age.

____ 6. The movement of people into an area.

____ 7. The collection of gases in the earth's atmosphere that trap heat and may lead to global warming.

____ 8. A periodic counting of the population in which facts on age, sex, occupation, and so forth are also recorded.

____ 9. Movement of people from one place to another within a society.

____ 10. The difference between the number of people leaving a place and those arriving each year, per 1,000 people.

____ 11. The number of deaths among infants in their first year of life per 1,000 live births in a given year.

____ 12. The average number of births a woman will have in her lifetime.

____ 13. The movement of people out of an area.

____ 14. The scientific study of how births, deaths, and migration affect the composition, size, and distribution of populations.

____ 15. A four-stage process in which a population shifts from high birth and death rates to low birth and death rates.

____ 16. The pattern of relationships between organisms (including humans) and between organisms and their environments.

1.	o	7.	j	12.	h
2.	t	8.	c	13.	g
3.	s	9.	m	14.	e
4.	q	10.	p	15.	d
5.	n	11.	l	16.	f
6.	k				

REVIEW QUESTIONS

After studying Chapter 19, answer the following questions. The correct answers are listed after the questions; each is followed by a short explanation. You are also referred to pages in the textbook for relevant discussion.

1. Demography is the scientific study of how various elements affect the composition, size, and distribution of populations. Which of the following is *not* among the basic elements?
   a. marriages
   b. births
   c. deaths
   d. migration
   e. all are included

2. Which of the following questions would a demographer be most likely to investigate?
   a. What are the norms that govern behavior in a college classroom?
   b. What is the relationship between socioeconomic status and juvenile delinquency?
   c. What is the relationship between crime figures and racial distribution in cities?
   d. What will the increase in the number of people over the age of 65 mean for the Social Security system?
   e. How do the functions of religion change as a consequence of secularization?

3. Analysis of a society's population structure includes
   a. age.
   b. sex.
   c. education.
   d. income.
   e. all of these.

4. The census in America is taken every ___ year(s).
   a. One
   b. Five
   c. 10
   d. 15
   e. 20

5. The crude birth rate is the number of births per how many people per year?
   a. 100
   b. 1,000
   c. 10,000
   d. 100,000

e. 1,000,000

6. What is the fertility rate for the replacement rate?
   a. 1.0
   b. 1.5
   c. 2.1
   d. 3.3
   e. 4.8

7. The infant mortality rate is the number of deaths among infants under ___ of age per 1,000 live births in a given year.
   a. one year
   b. six months
   c. three months
   d. one month
   e. one week

8. Which one of the following is correct?
   a. Life span and life expectancy reflect basically the same thing.
   b. Life expectancy has declined over the last century, but life span has increased.
   c. Life expectancy has increased over the last century, but life span has remained stable.
   d. Both have increased over the last century.
   e. Both have declined over the last century.

9. Which demographic variable has had the strongest impact on the demographic history of the human population?
   a. births
   b. migrations
   c. marriages
   d. deaths
   e. life span

10. The migration rate is
    a. the number of people who leave a country per 1,000 people.
    b. the number of people who enter a country per 1,000 people.
    c. the sum of the absolute numbers who leave and who arrive each year per 1,000 people.
    d. the difference between the number of people who leave and those who arrive each year per 1,000 people.
    e. the difference between the sum of those who leave and arrive and the birth rate for a year, per 1,000 people.

11. Although it has five percent of the world's population, the United States takes in about ____ percent of the world's immigrants.
    a. 10
    b. 20
    c. 30
    d. 40
    e. 50

12. With a high birth rate, the population pyramid will

248

a. be square.
b. be wider near the bottom.
c. be narrower near the bottom.
d. resemble an inverted triangle.
e. be rectangular.

13. Malthus's dire predictions were based on his belief that which two variables would increase at different rates?
    a. population size and food supply
    b. food supply and medical advances
    c. medical advances and death rates
    d. death rates and technological developments
    e. technological developments and population size

14. A small European country has the following demographic characteristics: declining birth rate, stable death rate, stable immigration, and increasing emigration. This country is experiencing
    a. the first stage of the demographic transition.
    b. high fecundity.
    c. the first signs of Malthus's population predictions.
    d. a decrease in population size.
    e. a high dependency ratio.

15. What is the greatest stumbling block to lowering the birth rate in developing countries?
    a. availability of birth control devices
    b. education of people in the use of birth control devices
    c. social values that support the ideal of a large family
    d. limited food and energy resources
    e. poor nutrition and medical care

16. A key factor in the reduced birth rate, and hence in the enhanced status of women, is
    a. better medical care.
    b. a lessening division of labor between the sexes.
    c. expansion of education.
    d. a lower crude death rate.
    e. increased availability of abortions.

17. The Green Revolution refers to
    a. substantial increases in the amount of money the U.S. gives to foreign countries.
    b. the reduction in the death rate.
    c. the collection of gases in the earth's atmosphere that trap heat and may lead to global warming.
    d. the creation of new strains of grains that greatly increased the yield per acre.
    e. the rapidly increasing economies of Third World countries.

18. Resource depletion and pollution have
    a. accelerated the division between First World and Third World countries.
    b. been more of a problem in Third World than in First World countries.
    c. been largely alleviated in First World but not in Third World countries.
    d. been largely alleviated in Third World but not in First World countries.
    e. become problems we simply cannot solve.

19. The two main reasons for deforestation are
    a. pollution and population pressures.
    b. population pressures and commercial development.
    c. commercial development and inadequate reforestation.
    d. inadequate reforestation and lack of education.
    e. lack of education and pollution.

20. A sustainable world is one in which
    a. we produce enough food for everyone.
    b. we reduce the death rate in Third World nations.
    c. ecological issues become a government priority.
    d. unemployment is low so production can be high.
    e. economic growth and development are limited to levels that maintain the earth's ecology.

Answers

1. *a.* Demography is the scientific study of how births, deaths, and migration affect the composition, size, and distribution of populations. Although the number of marriages may be studied, it is not one of the basic elements. See page 489.
2. *d.* Demographers study how changes in the distribution of a population influence social, economic, and political developments. See pages 489-491.
3. *e.* A society's age structure includes the age, sex, education, income, occupation, marital status, race, and religion of its members. See page 489.
4. *c.* The United States conducts an elaborate census every decade. See page 491.
5. *b.* The crude birth rate reflects the number of births per 1,000 people during a given year. See page 492.
6. *c.* A fertility rate of 2.1 is the replacement rate, the rate at which a population will remain stable (in the absence of immigration). See page 492.
7. *a.* The infant mortality rate is the number of deaths among infants under one year of age per 1,000 live births in a given year. See page 493.
8. *c.* Life span reflects the maximum number of years a person can live; this figure has not changed much over the last century. Life expectancy reflects the average number of years of life remaining for an individual of a given age; it has increased dramatically over the last century. See page 494.
9. *d.* Of all demographic variables, changes in mortality have had the strongest impact on the demographic history of the human population. See page 494.
10. *d.* The migration rate is the difference between the number of people who leave and those who arrive each year, per 1,000 people. See pages 494-495.
11. *e.* Even with only five percent of the world's population, the United States still takes in about 50 percent of the world's immigrants. See page 495.
12. *b.* With a high birth rate, the population pyramid will be wider near the bottom, reflecting more people in the lower age groups. See page 496.
13. *a.* Malthus believed that population increases geometrically, while food supplies increase arithmetically. This imbalance would cause people to run out of food. See page 499.
14. *d.* With fewer births, the same number of deaths, and a higher number of people leaving the country, this country will experience a decrease in population. See page 500.
15. *c.* Although the other factors are important, the major stumbling block continues to be social values that support the ideal of a large family. Until people in developing countries lose their reasons for having large families, these other developments are not likely to result in a lower birth rate. See page 502.

16. *c.* The expansion of education, especially for females, has contributed significantly to reduced birth rates. School attendance causes later marriages and creates better employment opportunities. Education also presents the idea of a better future and reduces suspicion of such modern inventions as birth control methods. See page 503.

17. *d.* The Green Revolution refers to the invention of new strains of cereal crops such as corn, wheat, and rice that doubled or tripled the yield per acre. See page 504.

18. *a.* Resource depletion and pollution problems, as well as attempts to alleviate them, have accelerated the division between First World and Third World nations. See page 506.

19. *b.* The two main reasons for deforestation are population pressures and commercial development. Many Third World countries use wood for many purposes; an increase in the population increases the demand for wood. With commercial development for the global market, companies strip large areas of rain forest to obtain export lumber and minerals or to make way for ranches and plantations. See page 508.

20. *e.* A sustainable world is one in which economic growth and development are limited to levels that maintain the earth's ecology. See page 513.

EXERCISES

Exercise 1

Study the table on the next page. Pay particular attention to how the population pyramid changes at different points in time. Also examine the proportions of males to females.

1. Examine each of the population pyramids and develop a profile of the age distributions at each point in time.

2. Describe how the pyramids change over time and explain why the shapes of the pyramids are different.

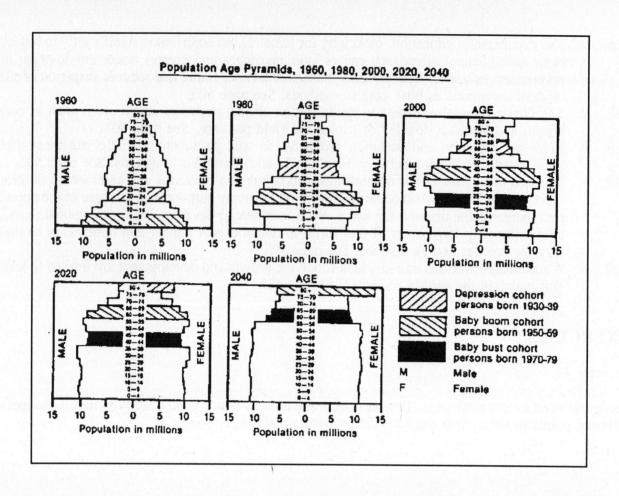

Population Age Pyramids, 1960, 1980, 2000, 2020, 2040

3. Trace the depression cohort, the baby-boom cohort, and the baby-bust cohort over time.

4. Outline the implications of the changes in age structures and population over time for such issues as the following: the Social Security system, the need for schools and teachers, the draft, labor-force participation, economic trends, and social trends.

Exercise 2

Explain how your socialization experiences would have been different had your first decade been in the 1980s.

Exercise 3

Outline the pro and con sides to this issue: zero population growth should be declared official policy by the United States government.

Chapter 20

COMMUNITIES AND URBANIZATION

OBJECTIVES

After reading Chapter 20, you should understand the following main points and be able to answer the objectives.

1. Community is a relatively large group of people who have common values and interests, relatively enduring ties, frequent face-to-face interaction, and a sense of being close to one another.
   - 1.1 Contrast social life in Diagonal and on Manhattan's Upper West Side; discuss implications for the concept of community.
   - 1.2 Define community.
   - 1.3 Define urbanization; discuss several of its positive and negative consequences.
   - 1.4 Show how the five key concepts help in understanding community.

2. Sociologists disagree about the effects of urbanization on community.
   - 2.1 List the three sociological perspectives on the effects of urbanization on community.
   - 2.2 Contrast *Gemeinschaft* and *Gesellschaft*.
   - 2.3 Evaluate the theory (of Tonnies, Simmel, and Wirth) that urbanization has caused the disintegration of community.
   - 2.4 Discuss evidence (from Gans and Suttles) for the persistence of community in large urban centers.
   - 2.5 Describe Fischer's view that urbanization has transformed community, and the idea that cities enable new forms of community to emerge.

3. A city is a relatively large, densely populated, permanent settlement of people who are socially diverse and who do not produce their own food directly.
   - 3.1 Define city.
   - 3.2 List the factors that enabled people to begin to live in cities.
   - 3.3 Use the case of Venice to describe the preindustrial city.
   - 3.4 Use the case of nineteenth-century Boston to consider the effects of industrialization on urbanization.
   - 3.5 Define metropolis; illustrate its principal features with the case of contemporary Los Angeles.
   - 3.6 Define Consolidated Metropolitan Statistical Area and megalopolis.

4. Two sociological orientations have been developed to explain patterns of urban land use: urban ecology theory and the political-economy perspective.

4.1 Define urban ecology.
4.2 Compare the three urban ecological models of land use: concentric zone, sector, and multiple nuclei.
4.3 Use the example of Harlem to illustrate the invasion/succession model and the neighborhood life-cycle model.
4.4 Contrast the political-economy perspective and urban ecology theory.
4.5 Discuss the rise of the corporate city and the city as growth machine.

5. Several current trends affect the American community.
5.1 Characterize the change in the proportion of Americans that live in small towns and rural areas.
5.2 Describe the change in the quality of life in rural America.
5.3 Define gentrification.
5.4 Describe the functional change in American cities.
5.5 Give examples of how American cities are becoming global cities.
5.6 Define suburbs.
5.7 Summarize the effects of suburban cities.

CHAPTER SUMMARY

1. What is community?

Community is defined as a relatively large group of people who have common values and interests, relatively enduring ties, frequent face-to-face interaction, and a sense of being close to one another. The small Iowa town of Diagonal accurately displays social life in a community: everybody knows everybody, residents participate in many community activities, neighbors watch each other's every move, and people share a routine rhythm of everyday life.

Most Americans today do not live in places like Diagonal. Many more of us live in places like the Upper West Side of Manhattan in New York City. The contrasts to Diagonal are striking: on the Upper West Side people do not orient their lives to community activities, they remain aloof from neighbors and cultivate anonymity, they worry about crime but leave social control to the police, and they like to shop in trendy boutiques and eat in restaurants serving the latest ethnic fad food. The differences between Diagonal and the Upper West Side are those of place: social life in a small town differs dramatically from life in an urban neighborhood.

Urbanization is the process whereby large numbers of people leave the countryside and small towns in order to settle in cities and surrounding metropolitan areas. It is urbanization that leaves fewer people in places like Diagonal, while many more people flock to the metropolitan areas of New York and Los Angeles. In 1900, 13.6 percent of the world's population lived in cities; today 45 percent live in cities. Urbanization has unquestionably contributed many positive things to modern life: cities facilitate artistic and scientific innovations, they provide a place where people from diverse backgrounds can mingle, and they allow for highly specialized jobs and avocations. City life, however, is also marked by pollution, high rates of crime, and a stressful pace.

2. What are the effects of urbanization on community?

Sociologists disagree on the effects of urbanization on community. One perspective suggests that community disintegrates as people come to live in large, densely populated urban centers. This view has roots in Tonnies's distinction between *Gemeinschaft* and *Gesellschaft*. The word *Gemeinschaft* can be translated as "community," and is used to describe a setting where everyone knows everyone else;

people remain at their place of birth; residents share common ancestry, values, aspirations, and traditions; and people create strong emotional bonds through frequent face-to-face interaction. *Gesellschaft* can be translated as "society." This word describes a completely different setting where people live in a large, densely settled population; they are strangers to one another and interact in impersonal ways; they have diverse values, roles, ancestries, and traditions; and there is much more social and geographical mobility. Although Tonnies coined these concepts in 1887, he would have described Diagonal as *Gemeinschaft* and the Upper West Side of Manhattan as *Gesellschaft*.

Tonnies believed that social life in the Western world has shifted from *Gemeinschaft* to *Gesellschaft*, much to his regret. He felt, as did Simmel and Wirth, that urbanization destroyed the possibility of the kind of community life that was found in small towns and rural villages. In Simmel's view, residents of cities are overstimulated by constantly changing and extraordinarily varied stimuli. The response is often a high degree of stress; many urban residents "tune out" (that is, they become indifferent to what goes on around them in public places) in order to avoid being overwhelmed by the bombardment of social and sensory stimuli.

Wirth noted that urban populations have three characteristics--large size, high density (crowding), and great heterogeneity (different kinds of people)--and that each of these traits prevents the kind of personal interactions and relationships that characterize community. It is impossible to know more than a tiny fraction of the population in a large city; crowded living conditions encourage friction and irritations among residents; heterogeneity or differentiation precludes relationships based on shared values and norms. The impersonal nature of urban life, says Wirth, leads to increased rates of mental illness and crime among city dwellers. More recent research shows that urban population density itself does not always cause these negative consequences; instead, increasing rates of mental illness and crime occur in cities with *particular* characteristics (for example, high unemployment and widespread poverty).

A second perspective suggests that urbanization does not destroy community; rather, community can persist within large cities. Empirical support for the "persistence of community" idea comes from ethnographic studies by Gans in Boston and Suttles in Chicago. In Boston's largely Italian West End, Gans found close and enduring ties and reliance upon networks of mutual support. Community life was extremely important for residents of the West End: a resident would feel lost if separated from his or her peer group. Suttles's study of Chicago's multi-ethnic Near West Side neighborhood revealed the same patterns: residents gathered at a corner grocery store or restaurant to gossip and to catch up on news in the same way as those living in a small village congregated at the general store on Main Street. The close ties and mutual cooperation persist *despite* urbanization.

A third perspective suggests that urbanization transforms community: cities neither destroy community nor allow it to persist but give rise to entirely new and different kinds of community. For example, because of the diversity of interests and tastes in large cities, residents who do not necessarily live in the same neighborhood and who are not from the same ethnic group might form community-like relations (called an urban subculture) on the basis of some common activity. Violin playing, organic foods, or feminist theory might generate close personal relations among a group of people scattered widely in an urban region: residential propinquity (living near someone else) and common ethnicity are no longer seen as essential for the development of community. Fischer found that urbanism did not destroy community but simply changed the composition of people's networks of friends. Moreover, Fischer found that the uncaring appearance assumed by city dwellers in public (perhaps as a way of protecting themselves from potentially dangerous interactions with strangers) contrasts sharply with the close and caring relationships in their private lives.

3.   What conditions led to the emergence of the first cities?

A *city* is a relatively large, densely populated, permanent settlement of people who are socially diverse and who do not produce their own food directly. This definition highlights two features of all cities:

their dependence upon agricultural products from outlying areas and their social heterogeneity (wide differences in occupations, social class, values, and lifestyles).

Several factors were important in the invention of the first true cities: domestication of plants and animals, along with improved technologies for irrigation and fertilization, increased the availability of food. No longer did human groups need to be nomadic, moving about the countryside in search of new fruits and vegetables to harvest or game to hunt. Reliable quantities of food produced by continuously maintained fields and pastures enabled people to live in semipermanent villages.

Increased agricultural yields meant that fewer people needed to work directly in food production, and a more diversified division of labor emerged. As workers became more specialized (proportionately fewer were self-sufficient farmers), they needed to live near those who performed other jobs, on which they depended. Centralized power structures provided order for these increasingly diverse social and economic activities, and cities became centers of kingdoms and empires.

4. How did industrialization affect urbanization?

The effects of industrialization on urbanization can be discerned from a "before-and-after" comparison: the sociological contrasts between preindustrial fifteenth-century Venice and the newly industrialized Boston of the late nineteenth century are striking. In Venice's Golden Age, about 190,000 residents were packed into a very small space. The simple but slow means of transportation--foot, boat, or horse-drawn wagon--limited the range in which people and goods could move. Venice's population did not rise much above this number because of technological limitations on moving food from the countryside to the city, and on preventing spoilage once it arrived. Furthermore, Venice was dirty and plagued by disease; periodic epidemics took the lives of many people. Crime was also a persistent threat. The population was divided sharply by differences in wealth, although even the poor in Venice were better off than their economic counterparts in the country. Class conflict never erupted in Venice, in part because of the absolute power of the ruling class. The cultural achievements of Venice in its Golden Age--in architecture, art, handicrafts, and science--were profound.

Boston in the late nineteenth century was a city built during the early years of the industrial revolution in America. Interestingly, industrialization of *agriculture* was a key factor in the urban explosion of places like Boston. New farm implements (such as tractors and harvesters), mass-produced and increasingly efficient pesticides, herbicides, fertilizers, and feeds, and improved means for transporting and storing food all led to dramatic increases in the number of city dwellers each farmer could feed. Fewer workers were needed on the farms; at the same time, more hands were needed in the new mills and factories of the early industrial city.

Industrialization also had direct effects on the growth of Boston. Improvements in the metropolitan railroad system meant that people and goods could move over longer distances and still be part of "the city." New engineering technologies enabled the construction of taller buildings and increased the population density of core neighborhoods. Deadly epidemics were virtually eliminated by improvements in public hygiene; indoor plumbing and municipal sewer systems became common at this time.

Boston covered a larger geographical territory than fifteenth-century Venice. Residential suburbs expanded along trolley lines, a sign that people now could live at considerable distances from where they worked. Manufacturing plants also began to move out from the hub along the railroad spokes. These developments contributed to a residential segregation of aristocrats and wealthy people from factory workers and the poor (in pre-industrial Venice, the poor and the rich lived on the same street). Still, in 1900 it was only six miles from the Boston City Hall to the most distant suburb, a tiny distance when compared with the sprawl of Los Angeles or Calcutta today.

5. What happens as cities grow very large?

A *metropolis* is a major city with surrounding municipalities caught up in its economic and social orbit; there is no better example than Los Angeles today. The Los Angeles metropolitan area is forty times larger than Boston at the turn of the twentieth century; its 14 million residents are distributed relatively sparsely in low-density neighborhoods of single-family units. According to the Census Bureau, Los Angeles constitutes a *Consolidated Metropolitan Statistical Area (CMSA)*, which is an interlinked cluster of one or more cities and their surrounding suburbs that together have a population of over one million people. The open land that once separated Los Angeles from San Diego has all but disappeared in urban sprawl. Sociologists use the term *megalopolis* to refer to two or more neighboring metropolises whose geographical areas have sprawled so far that their outermost edges merge with one another.

Increased use of private automobiles is partly responsible for the sprawl of Los Angeles: houses, factories, and offices no longer need to be built along public transportation lines (land between the spokes was built up rapidly). From the air, Los Angeles appears as a grid of freeways. The availability of this extensive network of freeways means that residents of Los Angeles sometimes must commute 50 or even 100 miles to and from work (nineteenth-century Bostonians would not have been able to commute more than 10 miles round trip). Most automobile trips do not go to or from "downtown"; offices, factories, shopping malls, and recreational facilities are scattered throughout the metropolitan region, often at the intersections of major freeways.

6. How do urban ecologists explain patterns of urban land use?

Sociologists have developed two perspectives to explain why cities take certain "shapes," that is, why the use of urban land (for residences, offices, or industry) follows recognizable patterns. One perspective is called *urban ecology*, which examines how the social uses of land are the result of an interaction between various groups of people and their physical/geographical environment. Urban ecologists have produced three models describing the development of urban spaces.

First, the *concentric zone model* suggests that the center of cities is a business of offices and shops; it is surrounded by a transition area characterized by residential instability, low rents, and high crime rates. Beyond this transitional ring are residential neighborhoods, with the poorest groups living closer to the city center than wealthier groups. Second, the *sector model* also suggests that the business district is located at the center of a city, but different land-use development tends to occur in specialized sectors along major transportation routes that radiate out from the center. Heavy industry may settle along railroads; residential neighborhoods may grow along freeways. Third, the *multiple nuclei model* suggests that a city has not one center (or nucleus) but a series of nuclei, each with a specialized function.

Urban ecologists have also studied processes of change in urban land use. The *invasion/succession model* describes changes in urban neighborhoods in terms of invasions by a new kind of resident, followed by competition for available land and ultimately by the emergence of a new use for the area. The history of Harlem illustrates the invasion/succession model.

The *neighborhood life cycle model* is an extension of the invasion/succession model, in which neighborhood change is seen as an extended series of invasion/succession episodes. Neighborhoods move through the following cycle of stages: development (new apartment buildings were built in Harlem), transition (overbuilding took place in Harlem and property values fell), downgrading (developers allowed buildings to deteriorate and many eventually abandoned them), thinning out (white residents of Harlem moved out), and renewal (housing in parts of Harlem has been upgraded). Contemporary urban ecologists see cities as integrated wholes, in which each part contributes some specialized function to the integration of the whole. As change occurs in one area (e.g., blacks moving into Harlem), other areas respond and adapt (perhaps new luxury housing was built in the Bronx to house affluent whites fleeing Harlem). Cities adapt in ways that improve their chances of survival in ever-changing physical and social environments. In the view of urban ecologists, the shape of cities arises from the process of functional adaptation to changing environments.

7. *How does the political-economy model explain patterns of urban land use?*

The *political-economy view* examines the political economy of urban space; the shape of cities is the result of powerful groups who promote urban growth in ways that advance their economic and political interests. Those who control important institutions such as banks, corporations, and real estate use their power to shape the growth and development of cities to their advantage. Sociologists who work in the political-economy tradition have given special attention to two aspects of urban development.

First, Gordon describes the rise of the modern corporate city. The typical large American city, with its downtown cluster of skyscrapers housing corporate headquarters and its widely dispersed manufacturing facilities on the outskirts, is not merely the result of developing transportation systems, as urban ecologists would suggest. Rather, the corporate city was built in this way by and for those who control the largest corporations; its spatial pattern reflects the economic and political interests of this group. The corporate towers in the center city are physical embodiments of the centralized power of modern corporations and represent its complete separation of administrative from production functions.

Second, Molotch uses the political-economy perspective to interpret the *growth* of American cities. Molotch suggests that in a capitalist society, the expansion of cities becomes a source of increasing wealth and power for those who control urban land. The *growing* city, in effect, is a machine that increases the value of property and thus enhances the wealth of those who own it. Land-owning elites encourage the growth and development of cities. Local government often fuels the growth machine, for example, by providing tax breaks to developers who build new offices or factories in the city.

8. *What are the current trends in American communities?*

Change has occurred in all three segments of communities: rural America, big cities, and the suburbs. In the forty years between 1950 and 1990, the percentage of Americans living in small towns and rural areas declined from 36 percent to 25 percent. Technological developments and market changes hastened the decline. Young people are the most likely to move away. The quality of rural life is declining. Small town economies are fragile. The poverty and unemployment rates are high. Health care and education have suffered.

Cities have undergone restructuring. Many have experienced *gentrification*: the conversion of working-class, often run-down areas of a city into middle- and upper-middle-class neighborhoods. The most profound change has been in the occupational structure, from centers for the production and distribution of goods to centers of administration, finance, and information processing. The rapidly changing ethnic composition of many cities has made them global cities.

Suburbs are spinoffs of metropolitan centers, to which most (but not all) remain economically tied. Suburban attractions include home ownership, relative freedom from big-city problems, more control over local institutions, and similarity in social class, race, and religion. The last decade has seen an increase of 29 communities passing the 100,000 mark, the unofficial dividing line between a town and a city. Most are on the edges of a metropolis. Suburbs today are increasingly being knit together to create a new form of community: the suburban city. One effect of the growth in suburbs is that the socioeconomic gap is widening between center cities and suburbs and between whites and minorities.

REVIEW OF CONCEPTS

Match the concept with the definition.

Concepts

259

a. city
b. community
c. concentric zones
d. Consolidated Metropolitan Statistical Area (CMSA)
e. *gemeinschaft*

f. gentrification
g. *gesellschaft*
h. invasion/succession model
i. megalopolis
j. metropolis
k. multiple-nuclei model

l. neighborhood life-cycle model
m. political-economy view
n. sector model
o. urban ecology
p. urbanization

Definitions

_____ 1. An interlinked cluster of one or more cities and their surrounding suburbs that together have a population of over one million people.

_____ 2. Tonnies's term for a society characterized by social and geographic mobility and by a large, densely settled population in which most people are strangers to one another and interact in impersonal ways.

_____ 3. A sociological approach to studying cities that examines how the social uses of urban and are the result of an interaction between various groups of people and their physical/geographical environment.

_____ 4. A relatively large, densely populated, and permanent settlement of people who are socially diverse and who do not produce their own food.

_____ 5. Tonnies's term for a small traditional community in which everyone knows everyone else and people tend to remain where they were born, both socially and geographically. People share common ancestry, values, aspirations, traditions, and many common roles. These factors together, plus daily face-to-face interaction, tend to create strong social and emotional bonds.

_____ 6. Two or more neighboring metropolises that have sprawled so far in geographical area that their outermost edges merge with one another.

_____ 7. A sociological perspective on cities that sees them as the product of decisions made by powerful groups on their own behalf.

_____ 8. A relatively large group of people who have common values and interests, relatively enduring ties, frequent face-to-face interaction, and a sense of being close to one another.

_____ 9. Harris and Ullman's model of urban land use in which cities develop as a series of separate centers called nuclei, each with its own specialized function.

_____ 10. A model of neighborhood change that sees this process as part of a larger series of invasion/succession episodes. The complete process includes the following stages: development, transition, downgrading, thinning out, and renewal.

_____ 11. Burgess's model of urban land use in which cities develop a central business district that is surrounded by several concentric rings, each devoted to a different set of economic and social activities.

_____ 12. A model of neighborhood change that focuses on invasion by a new kind of resident, followed by competition for available land and ultimately by the emergence of a new use for the area.

____ 13. The process whereby large numbers of people leave the countryside and small towns in order to settle in cities and surrounding metropolitan areas.

____ 14. The conversion of working-class, often rundown areas of a city into middle- and upper-middle-class urban neighborhoods.

____ 15. A major city with surrounding municipalities caught up in its economic and social orbit.

Answers

1.	d	6.	i	11.	c
2.	g	7.	m	12.	h
3.	o	8.	b	13.	p
4.	a	9.	k	14.	f
5.	e	10.	l	15.	j

REVIEW QUESTIONS

After studying Chapter 9, answer the following questions. The correct answers are listed at the end of the questions; each is followed by a short explanation. You are also referred to pages in the textbook for relevant discussion.

1. Which would be *less* likely in the small-town of Diagonal than in the urban neighborhood of Manhattan's Upper West Side?
   a. a continual round of community-centered activities
   b. everybody knowing everybody
   c. anonymity
   d. close scrutiny of neighbors' behavior
   e. very low rates of serious crime

2. In 1900, 13.6 percent of the world's population lived in cities; now 45 percent live in cities. This change resulted from processes of
   a. urbanization.
   b. gentrification.
   c. invasion.
   d. succession.
   e. community.

3. Which is *not* a positive or beneficial result of urbanization?
   a. opportunity for people from diverse backgrounds to mingle
   b. innovations in the arts and sciences
   c. specialization of products and services
   d. innovations in business
   e. high rates of stress

4. Which is *not* part of the definition of community?
   a. residents sharing common values
   b. relatively enduring ties among residents
   c. frequent face-to-face interactions
   d. small size
   e. a sense of "we-ness"

5. Which is a characteristic of *Gemeinschaft*, as identified by Tonnies?
   a. diverse ancestry
   b. different, specialized work roles
   c. low rates of social and geographical mobility
   d. fragmented ties among people
   e. impersonality

6. According to Louis Wirth, which three factors of urban living led to social relations that are depersonalized and fragmented?
   a. industrialization, increased literacy, and the decline of religion
   b. crime rates, pollution, and poor schools
   c. large population, high density, and social heterogeneity
   d. fewer police, fewer firefighters, and fewer social workers
   e. unemployment, poverty, and substandard housing

7. Which pattern of social life was *not* found by Gans in his study of Boston's West End?
   a. residents interacting regularly with each other
   b. friendship not based on residential proximity or ethnicity but on a common interest in some hobby or other activity
   c. frequent exchanges of gossip
   d. people feeling connected through peer groups to hundreds of other residents
   e. networks of mutual support

8. Which is *not* part of the definition of a city?
   a. permanent settlement
   b. relatively large population
   c. democratic government
   d. social diversity
   e. residents not producing their own food directly

9. Which factor was most important in preventing the world's first true cities?
   a. insufficient population
   b. lack of written language
   c. inadequate network of roads
   d. absence of institutionalized religion
   e. lack of innovations in agriculture and transportation

10. Which is more likely to be found in preindustrial cities (like fifteenth-century Venice) than in cities during the early period of industrialization (like Boston at the end of the nineteenth century)?
    a. larger population
    b. city spread out over larger territory
    c. rich and poor living in close proximity

d. improved public hygiene and lower rates of disease

e. more efficient transportation of food from farm to city

11. In late nineteenth-century Boston, which is *not* an effect of industrialization on urbanization?

    a. increased agricultural yield
    b. decreased need for agricultural laborers
    c. increased need for factory workers
    d. decreased population density
    e. improved speed and efficiency in the transportation of goods and people

12. Which pattern could be found in the modern metropolis of Los Angeles but *not* in late nineteenth-century Boston?

    a. residential segregation of rich and poor
    b. residential development between rather than along major transportation lines
    c. residential areas separated from manufacturing areas
    d. efficient systems for transporting food from country to city
    e. outbreaks of virulent epidemics relatively rare

13. One can now drive from Kittery, Maine to Quantico, Virginia and (almost) never leave an urbanized space: the edge of one city overlaps the edge of the next. Sociologists call this pattern

    a. preindustrial city.
    b. megalopolis.
    c. metropolis.
    d. rural boom towns.
    e. gentrification.

14. The urban ecology approach to urban land use would be most interested in

    a. the city as a growth machine.
    b. how changes in the world economy affect urban growth.
    c. how the completion of a new freeway results in relocation of stores to suburban shopping malls.
    d. the effects of federal government cutbacks on the provision of city services.
    e. how the relocation of factories to the periphery of cities helped to control labor unrest.

15. The center of Indianapolis is made up of large stores, government buildings, and high-rise office buildings. This core is surrounded by an area of transition with substandard housing, high turnover of residents, and high crime rates. This pattern is consistent with which urban ecological model?

    a. city as growth machine
    b. multiple nuclei
    c. sector
    d. invasion-succession
    e. concentric zone

16. In New York City, Wall Street is a financial center, Times Square is an entertainment center, and Madison Avenue is an advertising center. This case best illustrates

    a. the suburbanization model.
    b. the concentric zone model.
    c. gentrification.
    d. the sector model.

e. the multiple nuclei model.

17. Real estate developers in Harlem find that they have overbuilt luxury apartments houses. Demand dwindles, rents plummet, and blacks begin to move in. This situation illustrates which stage in the neighborhood life cycle model?
    a. development
    b. transition
    c. downgrading
    d. thinning out
    e. renewal

18. The rise of the corporate city has meant that corporations often control the major economic and political institutions in the city. Which perspective does this development reflect?
    a. the political-economy view
    b. the concentric zone model
    c. the multiple nuclei model
    d. gentrification
    e. invasion-succession

19. Which one of the following is *false* regarding rural American life?
    a. The proportion of the population that is rural is declining.
    b. Young people are increasingly likely to stay in rural areas.
    c. A very small proportion of rural Americans farm.
    d. Poverty and unemployment are high in rural America.
    e. Health care and education have been declining in rural America.

20. What population is the unofficial dividing line between a town and a city?
    a. 10,000
    b. 50,000
    c. 100,000
    d. 500,000
    e. 1,000,000

Answers

1. *c.* Anonymity means that people know almost nothing about those who live around them. This condition is much more likely to be found on the Upper West Side than in Diagonal. See page 518.
2. *a.* Urbanization is the process whereby large numbers of people leave the countryside and small towns in order to settle in cities and surrounding metropolitan areas. See page 519.
3. *e.* Along with encouraging high rates of stress, urbanization has other negative consequences: pollution and high rates of crime and of mental illness. See page 520.
4. *d.* Communities are the same as primary groups except for one characteristic: primary groups are generally small, while communities involve larger numbers of people. According to sociologists, community describes a particular quality of social relationships rather than a particular physical place inhabited by people. See page 520.
5. *c.* In a *Gemeinschaft* (which translates loosely as "community"), there is little geographic and social mobility. People continue to live where they were born, and there is very little movement up or down the stratification ladder. See page 520.
6. *c.* According to Wirth, the large population of cities, the crowding (high density), and the so-

264

cial heterogeneity (many sociologically important differences among residents) cause high rates of mental breakdown, depression, suicide, crime, delinquency, corruption, anonymity, and indifference to others. See page 521.

7. *b.* Gans found the persistence of traditional community in the midst of an urban Boston neighborhood. Common ethnicity and residential proximity (being friends with one's nearest neighbors) were important in building close, enduring ties. The formation of community ties among those with common tastes or hobbies is part of Fischer's theory of transformation of community in urban settings. See page 522.

8. *c.* A city is defined as a relatively large, densely populated, permanent settlement of people who are socially diverse and who do not produce their own food directly. The government of a city need not be democratic; some cities have flourished in totalitarian states. See pages 523-524.

9. *e.* The first true cities emerged because innovations in agriculture and transportation enabled people to take advantage of fertile soils. See page 523.

10. *c.* In Boston during the era of early industrialization, residential segregation of social classes became a prevalent pattern. Trolley lines to new residential suburbs enabled the wealthy to move away from the poor while still being able to commute to work downtown. In relatively tiny and densely populated Venice, rich and poor often lived on the same street. See page 526.

11. *d.* Industrialization resulted in the development of cheap steel and the invention of the elevator. These innovations enabled engineers and architects to build higher residential buildings, which in turn increased population density (defined as the number of people living in a circumscribed area). Density, however, was not uniform throughout industrializing Boston: residential density was much lower, for example, in the newer, distant suburbs than in neighborhoods closer to the city. See page 525.

12. *b.* In Boston, residential construction closely followed trolley or streetcar lines so that people could commute to and from work. When private automobiles replaced streetcars, people could use their cars to drive to homes that were not necessarily built along major transportation lines (freeways). See page 527.

13. *b.* Megalopolis (literally, "great city") is defined as two or more neighboring metropolises that have sprawled so far in geographical area that their outermost edges merge with one another. See page 528.

14. *c.* Urban ecologists are most interested in the interaction between the physical/geographical environments in cities (the building of a new freeway, for example) and city residents' land-use patterns (such as creation of new suburban shopping malls). See page 529.

15. *e.* The concentric zone model suggests that the central city is occupied by stores and offices. It is surrounded by an area of transition, marked by residential instability and high crime rates. This area, in turn, is surrounded by rings of residential neighborhoods. See page 529.

16. *e.* The multiple nuclei model suggests that cities develop a series of separate centers, each with its own specialized functions. See page 530.

17. *b.* The neighborhood life cycle model describes urban change in terms of a sequence of invasions and successions. Invasion begins during the transition stage, when different forms of land use or different populations move into an already-developed area. See pages 531-532.

18. *a.* The political-economy view sees the changing shapes of cities as reflecting deliberate decisions that have been made by powerful groups and coalitions in order to direct urban growth to their own advantage. Powerful groups such as corporations often control the major economic and political institutions. See page 532.

19. *b.* When the demand for U.S. farm products on the world market and commodity prices in the United States fell in the 1980s, many farmers looked elsewhere for work. Young people are the most likely to move away. See pages 534-535.

20. *c.* The unofficial dividing line between a town and a city is 100,000. In the last decade, 29 communities passed this mark. See page 539.

EXERCISES

Exercise 1

1. Imagine yourself as a city planner who has been asked to design a new town, one that would be built "from scratch" and would maximize the virtues of "community." What would this new town look like in terms of the following characteristics? It might help you to draw a rough map of this planned city.

    a. Population size:

    b. Racial or ethnic composition:

    c. Socioeconomic or social class composition:

    d. Housing (residential density):

    e. Spatial locations of major activities (residences, factories, offices, shops, etc.):

    f. Transportation system (public and/or private):

    g. Other distinctive or unique features:

2. How do the characteristics you have described above increase the sense of community among residents of your planned city?

3. How is your planned new town different from the typical American city of comparable size? Which sociological orientation explains these differences best--urban ecology theory or one of the various political-economy perspectives?

Exercise 2

The physical structure of buildings and streets in a city greatly affects patterns of interaction among its residents. For example, every city (and every college campus) has its public spaces where people congregate informally and where it is always possible to find people gathered for no particular reason. Thinking first about the *city* in which you now live and then about the *campus* of the college you now attend, identify one such place where people "hang out." Visit these two places and answer the following questions:

1. What are the physical or geographic features that make these spots attractive for hanging out?

2. Compare the two spots in terms of the kinds of people who hang out there (for example, are they young or old, black or white, male or female)? Explain the differences.

3. Do you note any variation in the number and kind of people who hang out at these spots, depending on the time of day? Why?

4. Do your observations of social life at these gathering places lend support to any one of the three sociological perspectives on the effects of urbanization on community (disintegration, persistence, or transformation)?

Exercise 3

Buy a street map of the city in which you now live; make sure it has an alphabetical index of street names. These maps are usually available at bookstores, magazine stands, drugstores, or gas stations. Then find a copy of the local Yellow Pages, which almost always can be found in your university or city library. Choose several categories of businesses and services (for example, doctors' offices, gas stations, clothing stores, grocery stores, shoe stores, restaurants, bookstores, boutiques). Look up each category in the Yellow Pages and note the street address for each business or office (if the list is very long, take a random sample). Then mark the location of each on your street map, using a different-colored marker for each category.

1. Are businesses and offices scattered randomly throughout the city, or is there some pattern in their locations? Do different categories of businesses (for example, restaurants as opposed to gas stations) distribute themselves differently around the city?

2. Do you find examples of certain shops or offices *clustering* together in close proximity? Why might a shop or an office choose to locate close to its competitors? What kinds of shops or offices are scattered widely throughout the city (that is, with no "clumping")? Why?

3. Evaluate these land-use patterns in terms of the three models proposed by urban ecologists (concentric zone, sector, multiple nuclei). Do either of the political-economy perspectives (corporate city, growth machine) help you to understand the spatial locations of businesses and offices?

4. Imagine how your map would differ if you had done this exercise 30 years ago, before the rise of freeways and shopping malls. How have these two developments reshaped life dramatically in American cities?

Chapter 21

SOCIAL MOVEMENTS AND COLLECTIVE ACTION

OBJECTIVES

After reading Chapter 21, you should be able understand the following main points and be able to answer the objectives.

1. A crowd is a type of collective action.
   - 1.1 Distinguish between collective action and social movements; give examples for each.
   - 1.2 Define crowd.
   - 1.3 Distinguish among Blumer's four types of crowds.
   - 1.4 Define mob.
   - 1.5 Summarize the social psychological view of crowds.
   - 1.6 Describe the role of rumors in collective action.
   - 1.7 Indicate the contributions of emergent norm theory.
   - 1.8 Describe the contributions of rational-choice theory.
   - 1.9 Define precipitating event.
   - 1.10 Use the Los Angeles riot to show how the five key concepts help in understanding collective action.

2. Social movements are special cases of collective action.
   - 2.1 Show how social and economic deprivation gives rise to social movements.
   - 2.2 Define relative deprivation.
   - 2.3 Indicate the role of resource mobilization in social movements.
   - 2.4 Define social revolutions and summarize Skocpol's explanation for revolutions.
   - 2.5 Use the civil rights movement, the women's movement, and the environmental movement to show the effects of social movements.
   - 2.6 Use the five key concepts to understand the civil rights movement, the women's movement, and the environmental movement.

CHAPTER SUMMARY

1. What are crowds? How can they be explained?

Sociologists distinguish between collective action and social movements. *Collective action* is a socially shared but relatively nonroutine response to events, things, or ideas. It involves large numbers of people who may not even know each other. A *social movement* is a conscious, collective, organized attempt to cause or resist large-scale change in the social order by noninstitutionalized means.

A *crowd*, an expression of collective action, is a temporary collection of people who gather around some person or event and who are conscious of and influenced by one another. Crowds are short-lived and loosely structured; they use conventional spaces or buildings for unconventional purposes. Herbert Blumer identified four kinds of crowds. A *casual crowd* forms spontaneously when something attracts the attention of passersby, such as a street musician. A *conventional crowd* gathers for a specific purpose and behaves according to established norms--for example, a concert audience. In an *expressive crowd*, the emotionally charged members are carried away by their enthusiasm and intense feelings, and behave in ways they would consider unacceptable in other settings. Expressing feelings is their primary goal. The crowd at The Woodstock Music and Art Fair is an example. An *acting crowd* is an excited, volatile collection of people who focus on a controversial event that provokes their indignation, anger, and desire to act. An example might be the spectators at a soccer match when the referee makes a questionable call. When a large acting crowd engages in violence or threatens to do so, it is known as a *mob*.

Crowd action has a long history and has figured prominently in American life. Several approaches help to explain crowd behavior. According to the psychological view, crowd behavior is the result of regression to primitive levels of psychology. Psychologists believe that a collective mind develops, which makes individuals think, feel, and act differently than they would if each person were alone; this process is known as *deindividuation*. Herbert Blumer modified these early ideas, offered by Le Bon, by tracing the social contagion to an "exciting event" that creates unrest in a group of people.

A second approach focuses on the role of *rumor*, an unverified story that circulates from person to person and is accepted as fact, although its source may be vague or unknown. Rumors serve as a means by which the crowd members communicate their fears or frenzy to one another. They proliferate intense and ambiguous situations. Rumors also affect people's desire to find meaning in events. Most rumors are short-lived. The mass media play an increasingly important role in crowd action today, as in the Los Angeles riots.

A third approach is *emergent norm theory,* which maintains that people develop new social norms as they interact in situations that lack firm guidelines for coping. These newly developed norms then exert a powerful influence on behavior. New norms do not emerge instantly but evolve through gradual social exploration and testing.

Finally, rational choice theorists have shown that people do not always lose their heads (their rationality) simply because they are part of a crowd. They continue to assess the costs and benefits of alternative courses of action.

The Los Angeles riots are perhaps the most notable example of crowd action in recent history. On the surface, they were caused by the Rodney King verdict. Sociologists call this verdict a *precipitating event*: an incident that confirms people's suspicions and fears. In the Los Angeles riots, the Rodney King verdict confirmed people's beliefs that the criminal justice system is biased against African-Americans. In reality, however, the origins of those riots are much more complex. The five key concepts help to explain the riots in greater depth.

2. *What are social movements? How can they be explained?*

A social movement was defined above; its main features are that it is collective, promotes or resists large-scale change, and employs noninstitutionalized means. Social movements are more sustained than crowd action, and include formal organizations with hierarchical structures. In their willingness to use unconventional tactics, they differ from more institutionalized efforts to influence social patterns.

Sociologists have offered two theories to explain the emergence of social movements. First, deprivation theory suggests that social movements arise when people feel that they are socially and economically deprived. Inadequate food, clothing, and shelter are the kinds of deprivation that sometimes lead to revolutionary social movements. Marx believed that the economic boom and bust cycle of a capitalist society would aggravate the misery of the working class to such a point that eventually the workers would organize to overthrow their oppressors. The French sociologist de Tocqueville made deprivation theory more sophisticated by pointing out that revolutionary movements do not occur when economic and social deprivation are at their worst, but when conditions have begun to improve. People revolt because they realize that a better life is possible; their optimism for the future is encouraged by the slight improvement in conditions. They will even take violent steps to bring about the improvement. Other sociologists have suggested that relative deprivation, not absolute deprivation, is the cause of revolution. *Relative deprivation* occurs when a large gap exists between what people expect from life and what they receive.

A second theory begins with the assumption that perceived deprivation is not enough to cause a revolution. *Resource mobilization theory* suggests that deprived people must mobilize themselves and the necessary resources in order to pursue the desired changes. A social movement will promote its cause successfully if it can mobilize human resources (organizational talent and leadership, for example) and material resources (such as money and channels of communication). In some cases the resources are mobilized from outside the group, from people or organizations with little or nothing to gain from the movement's success.

According to resource mobilization theory, four factors contribute to the success of a social movement. First, social movements with effective organization (which enables and facilitates communication, planning, and mobilization of resources) are more likely to be successful than those without. Second, social movements thrive when the external social environment provides certain favorable opportunities. Third, McAdam suggests that the success of social movements is facilitated by "cognitive (or mental) liberation." This concept refers to the collective perception by members of a disadvantaged group that they suffer from an unjust situation which could be changed for the better. Finally, the success of a social movement hinges on effective leadership. Many modern social movements thrive because outside leaders fill some or all of the leadership roles; grass-roots support for a social movement often emerges only after organizers from outside the local community or group have started the process.

Deprivation theory and the resource mobilization model are complementary; that is, each identifies a distinctive set of factors associated with the success of social movements. Skocpol makes a further, important contribution to this effort. She defines *social revolution* as the rapid, basic transformation of a society's state and class structure, accompanied by and partially carried out by class-based revolts from below. She explains social revolution by combining aspects of Marxist and resource mobilization theories.

3. What are the differences and similarities between contemporary social movements?

Three social movements in American society have had basic, long-term effects: the civil rights movement, the women's movement, and the environmental movement.

The civil rights movement began in the south in the 1950s as a grass-roots protest against laws that enforced racial segregation and excused racial terrorism. Until then, African-Americans had seldom confronted the existing power structure directly. Several factors account for the emergence of this movement in the 1950s. First, blacks and whites had common experiences in World War II, but their experiences were very different when they returned to the United States; this phenomenon was an example of relative deprivation. Rising expectations were a second factor. In 1954 the U.S. Supreme Court rejected the "separate but equal" doctrine and declared segregated schools inherently unequal; by implication, any form of segregation was unconstitutional. However, attempts at integration encountered violent opposition by whites. A third factor was structural opportunity. Black communities achieved the critical mass necessary for effective collective action when the mechanization of agriculture pushed former sharecroppers off farms and into southern towns and cities.

Black churches played a dominant role in mobilizing local people. The civil rights movement also had outside support, particularly from the mass media. The movement seemed to be losing momentum by the late 1960s, although the riots in Watts and in many other cities reversed that trend. Subsequently, the United States government began to increase efforts to overcome racial inequality.

The women's movement originated in the early part of the century with demands by women for the right to vote. Feminist protests then declined until the early 1960s. The 1963 publication of Betty Friedan's *The Feminine Mystique* is often described as the birth of the modern women's movement. Friedan identified the discontents of women growing up in a world where they did not have the same opportunities as men. Increasing numbers of women came to see that their dissatisfactions were shared. Many more women were brought into political activism through the black civil rights movement. Also important were the commissions to investigate the status of women, which were established in each of the 50 states in 1963.

The women's movement sought official equality of rights between men and women, as well as changes in the way women fit into society. The organizational structure included both large formal organizations and small, more informal groups. The most important organization was the National Organization for Women (NOW), founded in 1966. By the 1970s the women's movement had made substantial progress in expanding female career opportunities but a movement opposing the passage of the Equal Rights Amendment presented a major obstacle. Such a movement, a *countermovement*, forms to resist a movement already under way. This and other kinds of collection action damaged the women's movement because they gave legitimacy to antifeminist men by allowing them to point out that many women were antifeminist.

An agenda for the environmental movement was provided in 1962 by Rachel Carson's *Silent Spring*. Her descriptions of the consequences of widespread use of pesticides sparked a widespread movement concerned with human destruction of the physical environment. The environmental movement differs from those discussed above in several ways. First, it presents itself as universal rather than as operating on behalf of only one segment of the population. Second, it is global. Third, the concern for the environment is not a single, unified drive but is embodied in many movements, each with its own focus and strategies. The *politicos* include established organizations such as the Sierra Club; these groups, which maintain lobbies in Washington, concentrate on getting pro-environment laws passed and influencing government agencies. The *greens* include environmental activists who are suspicious of government and big business, and of groups (such as the politicos) that seek change through these channels. They believe that the environment can be saved only through drastic changes in people's attitudes, values, and lifestyles. The *grass-roots activists* are people who fight to keep their local communities from being polluted or destroyed by developers. Finally, the *globals* are individuals and groups that focus on the big picture and worry about the future of the planet as a whole.

REVIEW OF CONCEPTS

Match the concept with the definition.

Concepts

a. acting crowd	g. emergent-norm theory	l. rumor
b. casual crowd	h. expressive crowd	m. social contagion
c. collective action	i. mob	n. social movement
d. conventional crowd	j. precipitating event	o. social revolution
e. countermovement	k. relative deprivation	p. structural conduciveness
f. crowd		

Definitions

____ 1. Blumer's term for a spontaneous gathering whose members give temporary attention to an object or event and then go their separate ways.

____ 2. Blumer's term for a crowd whose members express feelings and behave in ways they would not consider appropriate in other settings.

____ 3. A rapid and basic transformation of society and social class structure.

____ 4. Smelser's term to describe aspects of social structure that facilitate collective action.

____ 5. An incident that sparks collective action by confirming people's suspicions and fears.

____ 6. Blumer's term for an excited, volatile collection of people who are focused on a controversial event that provokes their indignation, anger, and desire to act.

____ 7. The principle that crowds develop new norms in order to define ambiguous situations.

____ 8. A deliberate, organized effort to bring about or resist large-scale social change through noninstitutionalized means.

____ 9. Blumer's term for people who gather for a specific purpose and behave according to established norms.

____ 10. An unverified story that circulates from person to person and is accepted as fact, although its original source may be vague or unknown.

____ 11. Socially shared but relatively nonroutine responses to events, things, or ideas.

____ 12. A temporary collection of people, gathered around some person or event, who are conscious of and influenced by one another.

____ 13. The relatively rapid and unintentional spread of a mood or behavior from one individual to another.

____ 14. A social movement that forms to resist a movement already under way.

____ 15. A large crowd whose members are emotionally aroused and who are engaged in, or threaten to engage in, violent action.

Answers

1.	b	6.	a	11.	c
2.	h	7.	g	12.	f
3.	o	8.	n	13.	m
4.	p	9.	d	14.	e
5.	j	10.	l	15.	i

REVIEW QUESTIONS

After studying Chapter 21, answer the following questions. The correct answers are listed after the questions; each is followed by a short explanation. You are also referred to pages in the textbook for relevant discussion.

1. Which is **not** an example of collective action?
   a. an air traffic controllers' strike
   b. workers on an assembly line
   c. a revolutionary movement
   d. the hula hoop fad of the 1950s
   e. the stock market panic of 1929

2. Which is **not** a typical feature of collective action?
   a. socially shared responses to events, things, or ideas
   b. often striking departures from habitual patterns of everyday life
   c. small numbers of people involved
   d. people involved who do not know each other
   e. nonroutine responses to events, things, or ideas

3. On a dark and stormy night, a resident of a small Michigan town phoned the local radio station to report an unidentified flying object. The radio station repeated the story on the air, and soon the police were flooded by reports of UFO sightings. This example of collective action best illustrates which of Smelser's concepts?
   a. social strain
   b. structural conduciveness
   c. breakdown of social control
   d. generalized belief
   e. mobilization of participants

4. In 1968 activists protesting the Vietnam War received considerable television exposure when they staged mass rallies and demonstrations in Chicago during the week of the Democratic National Convention. This situation illustrates which factor identified by Tilly's resource mobilization theory of collective action?
   a. social strain
   b. organization
   c. opportunity
   d. mobilization of resources
   e. shared interests

5. At a local manufacturing plant, a man is fired for not reporting to work on time. Tension is high at the plant because the employees have just returned to work after a long, bitter strike. A rumor begins to circulate among the workers: not one but 50 workers will be fired--and then 70. This story suggests that
   a. rumors are less common in tense situations.
   b. rumors are not accepted as facts.
   c. some details are exaggerated as the rumor circulates.
   d. people faithfully repeat the details of a rumor.
   e. rumors typically deal with personal affairs.

6. Which is a *false* statement about rumors?
   a. Rumors proliferate in tense and ambiguous situations.
   b. Information passed in rumors is often unproven and suspect.
   c. Rumors reflect people's desires to find meaning in events, and represents a form of group problem solving.
   d. The mass media fuel rumors.
   e. Most rumors are born, live, and die in a relatively short time.

7. Crowds differ from other social groups in that crowds
   a. involve many more participants.
   b. involve fewer participants.
   c. depend on outside agitators.
   d. are short-lived and loosely structured.
   e. are generally inspired by political beliefs.

8. Which is the best example of Blumer's acting crowd?
   a. an audience in a theater
   b. people attending a street art festival
   c. a crowd weeping at the site of a train wreck
   d. people at a rock music festival
   e. protesters at a weapons manufacturing plant who overturn two cars.

9. A new show of impressionist painting arrives at the Metropolitan Museum. The throng of people who attend are
   a. an expressive crowd.
   b. a social movement.
   c. a conventional crowd.
   d. a casual crowd.
   e. an acting crowd.

10. Which statement is part of the emergent norm theory of mob behavior?
    a. Only hoodlums, drifters, and criminals participate in riots.
    b. Participants in riots weigh carefully the individual costs and benefits of their participation in a mob or a riot.
    c. People are caught up in the emotion of crowds and lose their normal reasoning capacities.
    d. People in crowds follow a new set of rules that define their perceptions of the situation.
    e. Crowd behavior is impulsive, unpredictable, and totally out of control.

11. In a newspaper account of the Detroit riots, the reporter writes: "The rioters and looters picked their victims carefully. They would break into stores only when they knew the police were not in the immediate area. Most of the looting took place in stores that had reputations for ripping off ghetto residents by charging high prices for shoddy goods. Stores that sold items that were easy to carry and worth a lot of money were among the most often looted." This account is most consistent with which explanation of mob behavior?
    a. emergent norm theory
    b. psychological theory (Le Bon)
    c. relative deprivation theory
    d. rational decision making theory
    e. riffraff theory

12. Which is the most important factor in causing social movements, according to deprivation theory?
    a. The economy and the standard of living are getting worse.
    b. The economy and the standard of living are getting better.
    c. The poor live in inadequate housing and do not have much to eat.
    d. People are frustrated because they perceive themselves as worse off than others.
    e. Outside agitators whip up support for a revolution.

13. Which factor is *not* identified by resource mobilization theory as important for the development of a successful social movement?
    a. feelings of frustration resulting from people's perceptions that long-awaited improvements in living conditions are arriving too slowly
    b. resources coming from those outside the movement
    c. organization (which facilitates communication and planning)
    d. favorable opportunities in the external environment
    e. cognitive liberation

14. According to the resource mobilization view, the popularity of Betty Friedan's *The Feminine Mystique* illustrates which factor identified as important for the success of a social movement?
    a. resources provided by those outside the group
    b. organization
    c. favorable opportunities in the external environment
    d. cognitive liberation
    e. effective leadership

15. Which of the following was *not* identified by Skocpol as important for the development of a social revolution?
    a. Revolutions are started intentionally.
    b. Revolutions emerge from crisis situations.
    c. Revolutions result from international developments (such as military defeat).
    d. Revolutions are not affected only by developments within the country in which the revolution occurs.
    e. States (political organizations) develop their own interests independent of the interests and structures of the dominant class.

16. According to the textbook, why has the women's movement failed to secure passage of the Equal Rights Movement?
    a. Few women felt that they were victims of gender discrimination.
    b. Conservative countermovements have been successful.
    c. Effective communication networks within the women's movement were never developed.
    d. An effective organizational hierarchy was not developed.
    e. Too many women were entering the labor force in full-time jobs.

17. The environmental movement differs from the civil rights movement and the women's movement in that it
    a. is more universal and global.
    b. has a longer history.
    c. has had greater impact.
    d. incorporates more about all the theories explaining social movements.
    e. incorporates both social and cultural factors.

18. In which decade did the civil rights movement emerge?
    a. 1940s
    b. 1950s
    c. 1960s
    d. 1970s
    e. 1980s

Answers

1. *b.* Collective action refers to socially shared but relatively nonroutine responses to events, things, or ideas. Workers on an assembly line are not engaged in collective behavior because they are organized into a highly structured and routinized division of labor and because their actions do not depart from conventional norms. See page 546.

2. *c.* Collective behavior typically involves large numbers of people in fads, fashions, crazes, rumors, mass hysteria, panics, or riots. See page 546.

3. *b.* Structural conduciveness refers to general conditions of society that must be present if collective behavior is to occur. In this example, the existence of the radio station and its ability to spread the UFO message quickly to hundreds of listeners facilitated mass hysteria. See page 551.

4. *c.* According to Tilly, collective behavior is often encouraged when developments in the external environment provide an opportunity for a group to act on its interests. The TV cameras allowed protesters to air their views before a major political party and millions of voters. See page 556.

5. *c.* Leveling is the process through which a rumor becomes shorter and more easily grasped. Sharpening is the process through which certain details become exaggerated. As this rumor circulated, the fact of the worker's tardiness was lost and the number of supposedly fired workers increased from one to 50 to 70. See page 549.

6. *d.* Although the media play an important role in crowd action, the media generally play a minimal role in fueling rumors. See page 549.

7. *d.* A crowd is a temporary collection of people who are gathered around some person or event and are conscious of and influenced by one another. Compared to other kinds of social groups, crowds have a short life span and are not well organized. See page 547.

8. *e.* An acting crowd is an excited, volatile collection of people who are focused on a controversial event that provokes their indignation, anger, and desire to act. See page 547.

9. *c.* The museum-goers are a conventional crowd because they gather for a specific purpose and because they behave according to established norms. Their interactions are highly routinized and impersonal. See page 547.

10. *d.* In their emergent norm theory, Turner and Killian suggest that people in crowds develop new social norms (and new social relationships) that guide their behavior. Crowd behavior is not always irrational and impulsive; rather, people follow emerging rules that define the situation in a way (for example) that makes violence acceptable. See page 549.

11. *d.* According to rational decision making theory, people in mobs or riots weigh the costs and the rewards of their participation. In this case, rioters minimized the risks of arrest and jail while maximizing the cash value of the looted goods. See page 550.

12. *d.* Common to deprivation theories is the view that certain psychological processes are essential in the formation of social movements. People *perceive* themselves to be unfairly deprived relative to others, and as a result they are frustrated; these frustrations lead to movements, often violent, for change. See page 555.

13. *a.* Feelings of frustrations are regarded as important for social movements by relative deprivation theory, not by resource mobilization theory. The resource mobilization view emphasiz-

es factors that convert psychological dissatisfactions into collective action. See pages 555-556.

14. *d.* McAdam's concept of "cognitive liberation" is similar to Tilly's concept of "a sense of shared interests." It is a shared perception by members of an aggrieved group that they suffer an unjust situation which collective action could change. See page 556.

15. *a.* Skocpol defines a social revolution as a rapid and basic transformation of society and social class structures. Revolutions are not started intentionally, according to Skocpol, but emerge from crisis situations. See page 577.

16. *b.* A countermovement is a social movement that seeks to resist changes sought by existing social movements. Several antifeminist groups were instrumental in preventing passage of the ERA. See page 562.

17. *a.* The environmental movement differs from other social movements in that it is universal (affecting all of a population instead of just one segment) and global. See page 564.

18. *b.* The civil rights movement began in the South in the 1950s, as a grass-roots protest against laws that enforced racial segregation and excused racial terrorism. See pages 557-558.

EXERCISES

Exercise 1

We all participate in various kinds of collective action, but we rarely think about this activity in sociological terms. This exercise asks you to evaluate an episode from your own life in terms of sociological theories of collective action.

1. Describe your participation in some form of crowd or collective action. Pick one specific example.

2. Describe how each of the following apply to your experience, as relevant.

   a. Blumer's four types of crowds:

   b. The role of rumor:

   c. Emergent norm theory:

   d. Rational decision making:

e. Structural conduciveness:

f. Functional disintegration:

g. Cultural clashes:

h. Social contagion:

i. The role of power:

Exercise 2

Although the United States was a nation born in revolution, a social revolution has not taken place in this country since 1776. Use each of the following three theoretical perspectives to produce different explanations for why there has been no successful social revolution in the 200-year history of the United States.

1. Relative deprivation theory:

2. Resource mobilization theory:

3. Skocpol's theory of social revolutions:

Exercise 3

This exercise asks you to plan a program of propaganda aimed at solving one of the most important problems facing American society. Propaganda is defined as information that appeals to people's emotions and prejudices and is used to inspire certain kinds of collective behavior. All successful revolutions and social movements depend to some extent on propaganda. One of the best sociological studies of propaganda is *Mass Persuasion* by Robert K. Merton, with the assistance of Marjorie Fiske and Alberta Curtis (Harper and Row, 1946). Merton describes the case at hand:

> September 21, 1943 was War Bond Day for the Columbia Broadcasting System (CBS). During a span of eighteen hours--from eight o'clock that morning until two the next morning--a radio star named Kate Smith spoke for a minute or two at repeated intervals. On 65 distinct occasions in the course of the day, she begged, cajoled, demanded that her listeners buy war bonds. [The result was]: 39 million dollars of bond pledges in the course of one day. Here apparently, was an extraordinary instance of mass persuasion (pp. 2-3).

1. Now imagine that today's federal government decides that the only solution to current economic problems is to sell "Budget Bonds" in order to balance the federal budget. Policymakers decide to hold an all-day marathon appeal on television--a "telethon"--similar to the appeal used to sell war bonds in 1943. In your opinion, what single celebrity should take the place of Kate Smith? Why? What qualities would you look for in selecting someone to make the appeal? Why?

2. In the 1943 war bond drive, Kate Smith emphasized the following themes or values as part of her pitch. For each theme, decide whether it would be useful in selling Budget Bonds today.

Sacrifice (all Americans need to give up something in order to solve the problem):

Participation (those who pledge to buy bonds are pulling together in a common effort):

Family (buying the bonds will give your children a better America):

Competition (New York has pledged more so far than Los Angeles):

Facilitation (all you have do is call in your pledge at this local number):

3. What new themes or values would you propose in order to sell Budget Bonds today?

4. Speculate on the possibilities of *success* for a present-day bond drive to balance the federal budget. What does your thinking tell you about the limits of propaganda in shaping collective behavior?

Chapter 22
SOCIAL CHANGE

OBJECTIVES

After reading Chapter 22, you should understand the following main points and be able to answer the objectives.

1. Social change refers to basic alterations, over time, in the behavior patterns, culture, and structure of society.
   1.1   Define social change.
   1.2   Explain why socialization of a child is not social change.
   1.3   Show how the five key concepts help in understanding social change.

2. Several theoretical approaches are used to study social change.
   2.1   List the four basic questions sociologists ask about social change.
   2.2   Describe Marx's view of social change as a process of struggle.
   2.3   Discuss Weber's emphasis on rationalization as a key to social change.
   2.4   Explain the importance of social solidarity for Durkheim's theory of social change.
   2.5   Compare evolutionary and cyclical models of social change.

3. Social change has several causes.
   3.1   Show how the natural environment is a cause of social change.
   3.2   Show how population trends are a cause of social change.
   3.3   Show how innovation is a cause of social change.
   3.4   Distinguish innovation from discoveries and inventions.
   3.5   Show how diffusion is a cause of social change.

4. Science and technology play major roles in social change.
   4.1   Define science.
   4.2   Show how science is a source of social change.
   4.3   Show how technology is a source of social change.
   4.4   Describe how science and technology have contributed to global change.
   4.5   Give three reasons for the gap in social change between modernized nations and developing nations.

CHAPTER SUMMARY

1. What is social change?

Social change refers to basic alterations, over time, in the behavior patterns, culture, and structure of society. Sociologists are interested in the large-scale and enduring changes that affect patterns of daily life or the structure of social institutions. Not all instances of change will be examined in this chapter: although socialization changes a maturing child profoundly, in itself it does not represent a historical alteration of child-rearing patterns or of the structure of the family. Thus it is not included here as social change.

Sociologists ask several questions about social change: 1) What is the fundamental "engine" of social change? 2) Is there a direction to social change? 3) Are the causes and direction of social change identical everywhere and at all times? and 4) What are the consequences of social change?

2. What are the basic theoretical approaches to social change?

Karl Marx viewed social change as a process of struggle. All people must struggle to overcome the limits of nature and existing technology: members of a hunting and gathering society can "invent" agriculture in order to increase food supply. These advances in production caused changes in social organization: as human societies became more productive, control over productive processes became concentrated in the hands of the few. A second struggle was the result: the struggle between social classes for control of the production process and of social life itself. This struggle pits one social group against another. For example, Marx anticipated that capitalism would yield to a classless socialism when workers revolted against the owners of productive property (factories).

According to Max Weber, both the material means of production and cultural values and beliefs were important for social change. Weber identified *rationalization*--the tendency to base action on a logical assessment of effects--as one important cumulative pattern in historical change. Only in modern Western societies did Weber see a decline in the importance of tradition for individual decisions. The ethos or values of Protestantism encouraged a rational outlook on life, and many changes were based on rational assessments of the efficiency of various means for reaching desired ends: governments were bureaucratized, jobs were specialized, rules and regulations proliferated. Even private decisions, such as whether to get married or have a child, are evaluated rationally in terms of their relative costs and benefits.

Emile Durkheim's theory of social change centers on the shift from the mechanical solidarity of simple societies (in which people are held together by the similarity of their values and activities) to the organic solidarity of modern, complex societies. In modern societies, increases in size, differentiation in the workplace, and new technologies of communication and transportation together increased *dynamic density*: the frequency of interactions among members of a society. Increases in dynamic density as well as increasingly dysfunctional competition among similar people all trying to play the same social roles brought on the shift from mechanical to organic solidarity.

Evolutionary and cyclical theories also explain social change. Evolutionary theories originated in Darwin's biological theory of evolution. Spencer drew parallels between the evolutionary development of biological species and that of human societies. Adaptation to the environment was seen as a general mechanism of social change; only the "fittest" social forms survived. Spencer believed that human societies have the capacity to learn about themselves and their environment, and can adjust intentionally to changing environments in ways that increase their chances of survival. He also thought that societies changed from simple, homogeneous forms to complex, differentiated forms. Lenski also saw parallels between biological and social evolution, but recognized that every human society has a cultural as well as a genetic heritage. He believed that to grow in size, complexity, wealth, or power, a society must create and use new information that can lead in turn to the new sources of energy needed to sustain its enlarged activities. Societies that do not make technological advances will not grow and probably will not survive.

According to the *cyclical perspective,* social change is neither cumulative nor progressive; it simply goes in cycles. Spengler argued that a society in its youth is creative, idealistic, and flexible; as it matures, it becomes rigid, materialistic, and prone to social disintegration. Kennedy identified three factors that cause the cycles: productive economic resources, revenue-raising capacity, and military strength.

3. What are the causes of social change?

Social change has four basic causes. First, the physical environment provides the opportunity for social change, but also constrains or limits the kinds of change that humans pursue. Availability of natural resources has had a significant effect on social change. Natural disasters or catastrophe also have had a major impact, bringing some civilizations to an end. The geographic location of a human society also shapes its development. Our present complex interaction with the physical environment brings about new environmental changes such as global warming.

Second, population trends cause social change. Changes in the size or structure of a population can have profound effects on social behavior and social organization. The rapid increase and the uneven distribution of population size will cause major social changes, particularly in developing countries.

Third, social change is affected by *innovation*: the social creation and institutionalization of new ideas, products, processes, or structures. Three types of innovation bring about social change. One is *discovery:* new knowledge about the external world, such as resulted from Columbus's voyage. By themselves, discoveries do not directly cause social change, but social change occurs when people begin to make choices on the basis of the new knowledge generated by discoveries. Second, *new ideas* bring about social change. The "progress period" is an example. The idea of progress has a long history in most Western cultural traditions. However, Lasch said that our belief in progress is not supported by the historical changes of the past, and will be suicidal if continued into the future. He believes that progress has created a "culture of consumption" which we will not be able to maintain because of current levels of resource exhaustion and environmental degradation. In Lasch's view, we need a new age of limits that would be dominated by small-town values of family, community, and tradition. The third category of innovation is *invention*: the making of a new product or process. Material inventions have affected social change since the beginning of time. Some important inventions, such as the public opinion poll, reflect new social processes or techniques rather than new materials.

In addition to the natural environment, population trends, and innovation, *diffusion* is a fourth cause of social change. Diffusion is the spread of innovations from one social setting to another, occurs both within and across cultures. Cross-cultural diffusion has contributed to the development of a global society. Rates and patterns of diffusion vary considerably.

4. How have science and technology brought about social change?

Science is a method for establishing reliable and useful knowledge about natural and social phenomena. Science contributes to the growth of knowledge, but also may cause a shift in the basis of authority in modern societies. Scientific knowledge is being employed increasingly in the rationalization of public and private choices. Many people believe that science should play a major role in debates about public policy, but such an emphasis may cause a loss of democratic control in policy decisions. Also, scientific evidence is often used to support competing views on a particular public policy.

Technology, the application of knowledge to the solution of practical problems, includes both new ~es or tools and new social and cultural arrangements. These altered institutional structures are both consequences and causes of inventions, that is, the relationship between technology and society is interactive. Technological changes affect different people differently, a fact that complicates its role in progress. Also, the rate and direction of change in technology are not determined by the technology itself, but by social and cultural factors.

Changes in science and technology have helped to develop a global society. They have also accentuated the difference between the rich and the poor countries. Four factors have contributed to this increasing gap. First, modernized rich nations developed over centuries, without outside interference. In contrast, most of the developing nations were colonies subject to the manipulation of trade conditions to serve the colonial powers. Second, developing nations have experienced rising expectations as a result of constant exposure to Western-style affluence. Third, population pressures have created enormous resource problems for poor nations. Finally, the poor in the world also are often neglected or exploited by their own corrupt government leaders and administrators.

REVIEW OF CONCEPTS

Match the concept with the definition.

Concepts

a. cyclical perspective
b. diffusion
c. discovery
d. dynamic density

e. evolutionary models
f. innovation
g. invention
h. rationalization

i. science
j. social change
k. technology

Definitions

____ 1. The making of a new product or process.

____ 2. A method for establishing reliable and useful knowledge about natural and social phenomena.

____ 3. New knowledge about the external world.

____ 4. The social creation and institutionalization of new ideas, products, processes, or structures.

____ 5. The tendency to base action on a logical assessment of anticipated effects.

____ 6. Theories that explain processes and patterns of changes that lead to diversity--the idea that survival is dependent on adaptation to changing environments

____ 7. The belief that history moves in cycles that are neither cumulative nor progressive.

____ 8. The application of knowledge to the solution of practical problems.

____ 9. Basic alterations, over time, in the behavior patterns, culture, and structure of society.

____ 10. The spread of innovative patterns from one social setting to another.

____ 11. The frequency of interactions among members of a population; a cause of social change postulated by Emile Durkheim.

REVIEW QUESTIONS

After studying Chapter 22, answer the following questions. The correct answers are listed after the questions; each is followed by a short explanation. You are also referred to pages in the textbook for relevant discussion.

1. Sociologists interested in social change would be *least* likely to investigate
   a. the impact of the U.S. Constitution on American social life.
   b. growth of commercial child care centers.
   c. the decline of manufacturing jobs due to robotics.
   d. changes experienced by a child in the process of socialization.
   e. the invention of the computer.

2. Which one of the following is *not* one of the basic questions sociologists ask about social change?
   a. What is the fundamental "engine" of social change?
   b. Is there a direction to social change?
   c. Are the causes and direction of social change identical in human societies everywhere and at all times?
   d. What are the consequences of social change?
   e. How much does social change affect people's personalities?

3. Social change is a process of struggle between social classes over control of the forces of production. This view is found in
   a. Weber.
   b. Marx.
   c. dependency theory.
   d. Durkheim.
   e. modernization theories.

4. Mary and Bob are deciding whether they want to have a child. They weigh the costs and the benefits. Mary says, "Wouldn't it be fun to have a baby around?" but Bob wonders if they have enough money to convert the attic into a nursery. Mary remembers that her grandmother had 12 children and that she "never gave a thought to whether she should or shouldn't have another one--people just had babies until they couldn't." The change in attitude from Mary's grandmother to Mary and Bob illustrates which theory of social change?
   a. Weber's emphasis on rationalization
   b. dependency theory
   c. Durkheim's emphasis on social solidarity
   d. cyclical perspective

e. Marx's theory of social change as struggle

5. Societies once were held together by common values and activities shared by everybody. Now societies are held together by our mutual dependence: we rely on others to do important things that we cannot do ourselves. This idea is part of whose theory of social change?
   a. Bell
   b. Marx
   c. Durkheim
   d. Weber
   e. Wallerstein

6. Those who argue that social change is an evolutionary process
   a. suggest that there is no cumulative, progressive direction to historical change.
   b. identify the direction of historical change but do not identify the mechanism driving social change.
   c. adopt a cyclical perspective.
   d. suggest that historical change does have a cumulative direction, and identify the mechanisms driving social change.
   e. all died before World War I.

7. A recent best-seller by Paul Kennedy, *The Rise and Fall of the Great Powers*, suggests that nations pass through a lifetime of changes, from birth through adolescence and maturity to death. This idea is consistent with
   a. the power perspective.
   b. the cyclical perspective.
   c. Lenski's evolutionary theory.
   d. Weber's emphasis on rationalization.
   e. Wallerstein's world systems theory.

8. The effect of the natural environment on social change is different today than it was 100 years ago in that
   a. we have far more natural disasters and catastrophes today.
   b. its effects are less prominent today.
   c. the environment is an external force operating independently from people today.
   d. people interact with the environment in a complex manner today.
   e. it was much better understood 100 years ago.

9. McDonald's hamburgers now can be purchased in many of the largest cities in Europe and Asia. This phenomenon illustrates
   a. cultural innovation.
   b. modernization.
   c. diffusion.
   d. technological innovation.
   e. dynamic intensity.

10. The United States Constitution's unprecedented emphasis on the rights of individual citizens illustrates
   a. cultural innovation.
   b. diffusion.
   c. dynamic intensity.

d. rationalization.
e. invention.

11. Watson and Crick's work on the structure of DNA is an example of
   a. a discovery.
   b. a new idea.
   c. diffusion.
   d. an invention.
   e. a cyclical theory.

12. Lasch believes that
   a. progress has created a desire for goods and services that cannot be maintained.
   b. progress follows in cycles.
   c. progress is creating informational overload.
   d. many things not before identified as progress now are coming to be defined as progress.
   e. progress is an overused term.

13. Which is *not* a consequence of increased use of personal automobiles in the United States?
   a. increased geographic mobility for work and recreation
   b. changed patterns of dating and courtship
   c. creation of new industries connected to automobile production
   d. sprawling suburbs and shopping malls along freeways
   e. improved air quality

14. The fluoridation controversy illustrates what about science?
   a. Science can provide definitive answers to social policy questions.
   b. Science is part of social progress.
   c. Science is unable to answer social policy questions.
   d. Science is subject to human error.
   e. The authority of science is never absolute.

15. The "death by dieselization" example reflects what about technology?
   a. Technology does solve many social problems.
   b. The relationship between technology and society is interactive.
   c. Technology cannot solve our most basic problems.
   d. Technology has its effects in a cyclical but unpredictable fashion.
   e. Technology ultimately does result in a revolution and subsequent classless society.

16. Which is *not* part of the explanation for the growing gap between the rich and the poor nations of the world?
   a. Modernized nations developed without the interference of more advanced countries, but this opportunity is not available to poor countries today.
   b. Religious fundamentalism and civil wars prevail.
   c. Overpopulation exists.
   d. Expectations are rising because of glimpses of Western-style affluence.
   e. Governments are corrupt.

Answers

d. Social change refers to basic alterations, over time, in the behavior patterns, culture, and

288

structure of society. Sociologists usually are interested in changes that have a widespread and enduring effect on patterns of daily life or institutional arrangements. The development of a child through socialization does not cause basic structural changes. See page 571.

2. *e.* Sociologists are not concerned with the effect of social change on people's personalities; psychologists might ask this question. But sociologists do ask the other questions. See page 571.

3. *b.* Marx believed that social change was a process of struggle; one struggle united all people in an effort to conquer nature by expanding productive capabilities. With the expansion of productive powers, however, and with the accompanying concentration of power in the hands of the few, a new struggle pitted the powerless classes against those who controlled the means of production. In such a struggle, capitalism soon would give way to socialism. See pages 572-573.

4. *a.* Mary and Bob have rationalized the process of child bearing by weighing logically the costs and the benefits of having a baby. In Weber's view, the replacement of "traditional" thinking (like that of Mary's grandmother) by rational thinking is an important cumulative pattern in historical change. See page 573.

5. *c.* Durkheim was interested in the changed basis of social solidarity or integration, which he described as the transition from mechanical solidarity in simple societies (based on homogeneity or sameness) to organic solidarity in complex societies (based on specialization and differentiation, leading to interdependence). See pages 574-575.

6. *d.* Those who adopt an evolutionary perspective on social change (both classical and contemporary) see a direction in historical change from simple to complex social organization, and identify adaptation and selection as the mechanisms of change. See pages 575-576.

7. *b.* The cyclical perspective suggests that history moves in cycles which are neither cumulative nor progressive. Nations rise and fall successively. See pages 576-577.

8. *d.* In the past the environment was an external force operating independently from the people who had to deal with it. Today we find ourselves in a complex interaction with the physical environment. See page 577.

9. *c.* Diffusion is the spread of innovative patterns from one social setting to another. See page 583.

10. *a.* The novelty of this strong emphasis on individual liberties makes it a cultural innovation: a new idea or value that alters behavior patterns or social structures significantly and enduringly. Cultural innovations stand in contrast to technological innovations, knowledge applied in new practical ways to the material aspects of life. See page 579.

11. *a.* Watson and Crick discovered the structure of DNA, the hereditary molecule containing genetic information. It is a discovery because it reflects new knowledge about the external world. See page 579.

12. *a.* Lasch believes that a belief in progress has created a "culture of consumption" that cannot endure in the face of now-obvious signals of resource exhaustion and environmental degradation. See page 580.

13. *e.* This question is a reminder that most technological innovations have mixed consequences, some good and some bad. As with the computer revolution that followed, there is scarcely an area of social life that has not been altered by the invention and institutionalization of the private automobile. See page 582.

14. *e.* Science has become a source of authority. However, as the fluoridation controversy illustrates, the authority of science is never absolute. It is often contested in controversies that raise difficult questions about our current reliance on scientists and their knowledge. See page 584.

15. *b.* Cottrell's case study of Caliente showed how dieselization of locomotives affected the community and how the community enabled steam locomotives at an earlier time. The relation-

ship between technology and society is interactive. See page 586.

16. *b.* Religious fundamentalism, civil war, international terrorism, and revolution are *consequences*, not causes, of the gap in wealth between the rich and the poor nations of the world. See pages 589-590.

EXERCISES

Exercise 1

The department of sociology on your campus will move soon into a new building designed to house four of the social sciences: sociology, anthropology, economics, and political science. In accordance with an old tradition, it was decided to put a time capsule into the cornerstone of the new building; the capsule will not be opened for 100 years. Because the building is named the Max Weber Center for Social Sciences, it seems appropriate to include items that reflect the social and cultural life on your campus today. The time capsule must fit into a box measuring four feet on each side.

1. Make a list of the items you would include in the time capsule.

2. Why did you include these items?

3. What aspects of life on your campus do you feel would be most important to convey to students one century in the future?

4. Which items in the time capsule do you think will be considered most unusual or most antiquated by students in the 2090s?

Exercise 2

The chapter outlined four causes of social change: the natural environment, population trends, innovation (discoveries, new ideas, and inventions), and diffusion. Give examples of each of these regarding how each has brought about social change that has affected you personally.

The natural environment:

2. Population trends:

3. Innovation.
   a. Discoveries:

   b. New ideas:

   c. Inventions:

4. Diffusion:

Exercise 3

How would human society change if the following improbable events occurred during the next year?

1. A limited nuclear war, causing the deaths of millions and the destruction of countless cities and towns:

2. Discovery of life on another planet in our solar system:

3. Discovery of a male contraceptive that is 100 percent effective, with no undesirable side effects:

4. Formation of a third political party in the United States that attracts supporters equal in number to those supporting the Republican and the Democratic parties:

5. Invention of a computer that is capable of independent and creative thought:

6. Advances in genetic engineering that would allow couples to determine the gender (and other physiological features) of their children:

7. Beginning of a prolonged worldwide drought that reduces agricultural yield drastically:

NOTES

NOTES

NOTES

NOTES

NOTES

NOTES